Who's Got Dibs on Your Kids?

How the Pied Pipers of our society are leading your kids on a path away from you, your beliefs, your faith, and ultimately AWAY FROM GOD!

BETTY PFEIFFER

Xulon ELITE

Who's Got Dibs on Your Kids?
How the Pied Pipers of our society are leading your kids on a path away from you, your beliefs, your faith, and ultimately AWAY FROM GOD!
by Betty Pfeiffer

Printed in the United States of America.

ISBN 9781498462549

Hyperlinks were active at time of printing.

Definitions are from the Merriam-Webster Dictionary online.

www.xulonpress.com

Table of Contents

Introduction

Dibs. That's a funny word. But kids know what it means. When they open the door after school, and the warm air and fragrance of your baking hits them, they shout, "Dibs on the cookies!" Or after a long ride, "Dibs on the bathroom!" When someone says, "dibs", it means *me first*.

So, as the title of this book asks, who's got dibs on your kids? If that starts your teeth grinding a bit, thinking that anyone but God and you has first claim—or *any* claim—to your kids, you are in for a surprise.

In the past I trusted those in a position of authority. I had no reason to think that anyone would *want* to harm me or my family. Teachers went into the profession because they loved kids, and wanted to not only teach them the ABCs and 123s, but expand their minds to be in awe of the wonders of this world. The goal of doctors and nurses was to keep us healthy, and cure us when we weren't. The people we elected to govern us wanted a community, state, or nation of successful people leading lives of self-determination with liberty and justice for all.

Yes, I admit it—I was an idealist and an optimist. Perhaps it was because that is an easier position to hold than to constantly be on guard; perhaps I was naïve; perhaps I was a fool. The passing of years and confrontations with reality have changed my views.

If you are now as I was then, be prepared to have your eyes opened. Even after countless hours of research, I shudder at the schemes to take our kids' minds and hearts and spirits away from their families and God.

You'll discover it's a bit like the Wizard of Oz—the man behind the curtain. (Oh, no. Don't look behind the curtain! Look over here. Look over there. Just don't look behind the curtain!) The schemes will be hidden behind smokescreens, diversions, and outright lies.

On the other hand, sometimes you'll realize that control of your kids is blatant, more like the "Pied Piper of Hamelin." You may be told that others know better than you, the parent. They can take your kids away from you, and there is nothing you can do about it—all in the name of "the child's best interest."

Robert Browning's morality poem recounts the tale of how in 1284 a piper led all the children of Hamelin, Germany, away into a cave in a mountain because the city fathers would not pay him for ridding the town of rats.[1,2] They were more interested in their worldly goods than watching out for the safety of their children. The story, reputed to be true, has been told in many forms, but the image of the Pied Piper resonates through them all—a still-familiar figure almost 800 years later. This brief excerpt from Browning's poem "The Pied Piper of Hamelin: A Child's Story" may help you realize the significance of the Pied Pipers in the lives of your kids today.

. . . Once more he stept into the street;
And to his lips again
Laid his long pipe of smooth straight cane;

And ere he blew three notes (such sweet
Soft notes as yet musician's cunning
Never gave the enraptured air)
There was a rustling that seemed like a bustling
Of merry crowds justling at pitching and hustling,
Small feet were pattering, wooden shoes clattering,
Little hands clapping, and little tongues chattering,
And, like fowls in a farm-yard when barley is scattering,
Out came the children running.
All the little boys and girls,
With rosy cheeks and flaxen curls,
And sparkling eyes and teeth like pearls,
Tripping and skipping, ran merrily after
The wonderful music with shouting and laughter.

. . . And to Koppelberg Hill his steps addressed,
And after him the children pressed;
Great was the joy in every breast.
"He never can cross that mighty top!
He's forced to let the piping drop,
And we shall see our children stop!"
When, lo! as they reached the mountain-side,
A wondrous portal opened wide,
As if a cavern was suddenly hollowed;
And the Piper advanced and the children followed,
And when all were in to the very last,
The door in the mountain-side shut fast.

✞

"Such is the destiny of all who forget God; so perishes the hope of the godless. What they trust in is fragile; what they rely on is a spider's web" (Job 8:13–14).

✝

As you read through this book, you'll learn there are many forces pulling strings behind curtains, and Pied Pipers who want to lure your kids onto their paths. They hope you won't notice, won't care, and won't warn your kids about the mesmerizing sound of the piper's tunes.

You may take what you read here and act on it, or you may begin your own path of research as I did. Whichever course you choose, daily thank God for His protection of you and your children, and pray for His direction in your life as you raise your kids in the training and instruction of the Lord. He has given you the task. He knows all things, so He knows it will be difficult. In spite of all your work and prayers, some kids will still be led astray.

The many faces and paths of the Pied Pipers appear to be good, pleasurable, and certainly safe. Are they? *Who's Got Dibs on Your Kids?* will provide insight into the multitude of enticements your kids face every day without even realizing the danger in "just trying it"—"just looking once"—"everyone else is doing it." However, the knowledge they acquire comes from almost endless sources. How can you and your kids know whom and what to trust? The answer to that question is where it all begins. If you aren't sure, you soon will be.

✝

"But I am afraid that just as Eve was deceived by the serpent's cunning, your minds may somehow be led astray from your sincere and pure devotion to Christ" (2 Corinthians 11:3).

Who's Got Dibs on Your Kids' TRUST?

Establishing the Foundation

"Trust in the Lord with all your heart and lean not on your own understanding; in all your ways submit to him, and he will make your paths straight" (Proverbs 3:5–6).

I still remember tossing our kids up into the air and enjoying their squeals of delight. And when we grabbed their wrists and spun them around and around, they shouted "*More, More,*" when we stopped. They had absolute trust in us, that we would make the catch, that we would hold tight and not let go during the spin.

Not one of our boys knew it was possible we might let him drop, crashing to the floor, or spin out across the yard. Up to that point we had never dropped him, nor let him spin into oblivion. We had earned his trust.

Before we consider who has dibs on your kids, you must first determine who *you* believe your kids should—no, *must*—trust. Until you establish in *your heart and mind* whom or what your kids must trust, the rest of the chapters on who has dibs on your kids' minds, bodies, emotions, and morality, are all pointless. A firm foundation of where your kids' trust belongs is fundamental.

Who is trustworthy? Start with God!

Trust must first be placed in God, and in His Word as revealed in the Bible. He has proved Himself trustworthy.

In the Garden of Eden He promised to send a Savior. *He did.*

He promised childless Abraham, in his old age, that he would be the father of many nations. *He was.*

He promised to give His people a land flowing with milk and honey. *He did.*

Jesus told His disciples that three days after He was killed, He would be raised again to life. *He was.*

You can probably make a much longer list of when God was true to His word. That would be a good exercise for you. When you finish this chapter you'll see space for you to do that. Spend some thoughtful time with it. If you are not already convinced that God is worthy of your trust, you will be.

Parents worthy of children's trust

Just as God has earned the trust we have in Him, we must earn the trust of our children. Can your kids trust you? Have you earned that trust? Trust must never be taken for granted. It must be earned, day after day. You want your kids to trust you. If you break that trust, even once, your kids may not fully trust you again.

God gave you the gift of your children. In the Bible He also gives you guidelines and evidences of the trust He has in you to carry out your role as Christian parents. We'll look at those as we go along.

At the close of this chapter, after you finish the list of how God has proven himself trustworthy, repeat the exercise. This time the list will be those instances where you have demonstrated that your kids can trust you. Don't worry if the list is shorter than God's. He has proven His trust over millennia, and you've only been at it a few years. Besides, you are, and always will be in this life, imperfect. You will make mistakes. You will go back on your word. Don't give up. Admit to your children when you violate their trust, and start to earn it back. God knows it won't all go smoothly. David recognized his shortcomings in Psalm 94:18–19: "When I said, 'My foot is slipping, your unfailing love, LORD, supported me. When anxiety was great within me, your consolation brought me joy.'"

The Bible tells of the confidence God has in you as parents. You can find His support all the way from the Old Testament through the New Testament. In Proverbs 22:6, Solomon tells us, "Start children off on the way they should go, and even when they are old they will not turn from it."

In Luke we find Jesus is fully confident that fathers want only good things for their children: "Which of you fathers, if your son asks for a fish, will give him a snake instead? Or if he asks for an egg, will give him a scorpion?" (Luke 11:11-12).

God truly believes you are capable of doing a good job raising your children. He *trusts* you. However, He never claims it will be easy. No matter how difficult the task may be, and you *will* face many difficult times as a parent, God will always be there to help.

Are others with authority trustworthy?

When you turn your kids over to anyone—babysitter, day care, teacher, pastor, scout leader, sports coach—you are giving them authority for that period of time. How confident are you that the person who will be caring for and influencing your kids is trustworthy? How much checking have you done? How long did you speak with the person one-on-one to know how they talk, or what they believe? If not, why did you feel perfectly confident that your kids would be in good hands?

Perhaps, "My friend recommended . . ." Find out what background knowledge your friend has of this person. Even more to the point, does your friend agree with you that Christian principles should be the bedrock of your kids' lives?

Sports teams are popular. At tryouts don't judge the prospective coach by the fact that his teams are always winners. How they won is more important than how many times they won. And what did the coach say when they lost?

It's hard to imagine that your kids haven't wanted to join a group because their best friends belong. Do you remember your mom saying something to you about "If they jumped off the Brooklyn Bridge, would you jump too?"

Teachers can be a big influence on your kids. Perhaps you don't have a choice—their teachers are their teachers. The school doesn't let you pick and choose. Does that relieve you of all responsibility about what will be taught in class? You may honestly think so. We'll discuss this more later.

The list of reasons is endless. The one making decisions about who is trustworthy for even a short time must be you. You cannot, however, protect your kids from all the bad influences and false information that life will present to them. They have to be able to recognize when they are being led astray.

Making the case for knowledge

My husband and I recently visited some Civil War battlefields.

Wilson's Creek Battlefield in Missouri has a path going back a mile through woods to the site of the battle at Gibson's Mill. The day was cloudy and cool after a light rain. We strolled, stepping over an almost-immobile turtle, breathing in the scents of damp earth and wet fallen leaves.

A shrub captured our attention. About shoulder high, it had bright red, arching branches and stems. Fingers of berries hung in various stages of ripeness, ranging from green to hot pink to purplish-black. We had never seen a plant like this before and wondered what it was. When we returned to the Visitor Center, we asked the ranger if she could identify it. She couldn't but offered to call a man who knew "everything about the Wilson's Creek site." She described it just as we had to her, listened, thanked him, and hung up.

"He says it's sumac," she said.

Looking at each other, we shook our heads. While some varieties of sumac do have red stems and branches, we knew this was not sumac. I told her, "It's not sumac. The leaves of sumac along the path have already turned red. This plant's leaves are green, not shaped like sumac leaves, and the branches and stems are very red."

The ranger didn't even try to hide her outrage. "He says it's sumac, and he knows everything there is to know about this place." She turned and went back to her desk.

Back home, a quick Internet search told us the plant we had seen was pokeberry. Not sumac.

If we had not known what sumac looked like, we might have gone through the rest of our lives believing the plant was—must be—sumac. We had to have some basic knowledge of plants to know we were being given bad information.

Are you equipping your children with enough information that they will be able to recognize falsehoods, and what is not in accord with God's Word? Will they be able to know if the source is trustworthy?

The importance of trusting God and yourself

When children leave home for the first time . . . oh wait, are you thinking when they go to college, or get married? That's not the first time. I'm talking about going to a friend's house to play, or to pre-school or kindergarten or even day care. *That* first time. When they go, are they prepared to hear words, (curse words, vulgar words) or ideas (evolution, homosexuality) contradictory to what they hear and learn at home? Are *you* prepared for that? Have you explained that they might hear something different? Have you told them if they do, they should feel free to come home and tell you so you can talk about it with them? Or do you think they're too young at three or four or five years of age to go into all that?

You can't just think you'll sit down and cover all the bases in twenty minutes. But a few seconds on a shopping expedition when someone utters a foul word, saying "What you just heard is a bad word. We don't use that word." Or "What you just heard uses God's name in a wrong way. It makes God unhappy to hear His name used like that. We don't want to do things that made God unhappy, do we?" It's not something that takes a college degree in "Explanations to a Child." Just be alert, and aware of opportunities to teach and reinforce.

It's important to let your kids know they can trust you for good advice, and to trust in God above all things, because they will be learning that not everyone believes what you believe. There will be many differences, and without a firm foundation your kids are first going to be confused, then skeptical of you and your knowledge and advice, and then probably going over to the other side. It is very hard to bring them back!

Part of parenting is to teach your children to be aware. You do this already: you teach them about hot and cold water faucets, how to cross streets safely, what the sky looks like when they should take an umbrella. They must have enough knowledge about a variety of things to make their lives safer. The same need-to-know is true for informational dangers they will come upon.

Some are not aware that God firmly puts the responsibility of teaching the will and the love of God on the parents. First in line is the father: "Fathers, do not exasperate your children; instead, bring them up in the training and instruction of the Lord" (Ephesians 6:4). If Dad isn't around, or for some reason can't do the job, it falls to Mom. Note that Dad and Mom come before your pastor, Sunday school, and VeggieTales.

Unfortunately, many Christian fathers do not take this proactive charge seriously enough. Prepare your children with the truth. Teach them what threatens truth and why. As they grow older, teach them what it means to passively resist, and why such resistance is necessary. Let them know that at some point active resistance may be necessary. Teach them that the truth from Jesus, kept active in their hearts and minds, will inoculate them from any attempt to mold their brain into someone else's idea of "knowledge" and "truth."

First, and most important, teach your children—what do they say in court?—the truth, the whole truth, and nothing but the truth: the truth about who to trust and why, the truth about science matters, the truth about morality—you get the picture. Then teach them how to have an alarm go off in their head when something seems contrary to the truth. Teach them to courteously disagree. Encourage them to tell you about things that seem wrong.

Outside influences

So, who and what are going to influence your kids? Here is a list that may overwhelm you when you look at it. The influences will vary depending on your kid's age. I'll go into detail about some of the factors in later chapters. Some are so obvious you don't need me to elaborate on them. Some, I think, will surprise you.

- School
    * Teachers

    * Boards of Education
    * School Districts
    * State Departments of Education
    * Federal Department of Education
    * Textbooks
    * Outside speakers
    * Other students
- Printed material
    * Books
    * Magazines
    * Newspapers
    * Pamphlets and other such material
- Libraries
- Television
- Video games
- Social Media
- Texting
- Friends
- Movies
- Boy Scouts
- Girl Scouts
- The President of the United States

Yes, I realize that is a formidable list. And it probably isn't even complete. You're likely thinking about this time, "This writer is a kook! She doesn't want my kids to do or read anything!" Not so.

Jesus says in John 17:15, "My prayer is not that you take them out of the world but that you protect them from the evil one." You probably know the expression that we "live in the world, but not of the world." God has put us all, even your kids, in this sin-filled world, and that is where He expects us to live and work to His glory. But if we are not aware of the many traps the "evil one" (the Pied Piper) sets for our kids, they are certain to be caught in them.

In March 2015 it was announced that Google was about to implement a new way to bring up relevant pages when you do a search. Previously, one of the methods was to see what links, and how many, go to and from a page. That system apparently will be scrapped, and the new algorithm—it may have already been implemented—will bring up those pages first that it considers most "trustworthy." Isn't that wonderful? You and your kids will no longer have to sift through different opinions. Google will put the ones that carry "the truth" on any subject right up front for you. Isn't there a danger that Google's idea of truth may be different from yours, and the results may be biased? No, that couldn't happen, could it?

Until now Google has had a system, the Knowledge Graph, that stored information based on input from users, somewhat like Wikipedia, but on a much larger scale. Over time, less and less information was being gathered. They needed to step up the input. Thus was born the Knowledge Vault. It stores information in forms that both machines and people can read. The algorithm will constantly and automatically gather information from the web, analyze it, and ascribe a "truth" value to it. Of course, the "establisher of truth" will not be some mindless machine; it will be those who program the rules that the machine will follow. Will Google's idea of truth be evolution or creation? How will it view the justification of abortion? Will the truth of God's statements regarding homosexuality be regarded the same as those who promote gay marriage? How much trust will you put in that first page or two of results when you or your kids do a search?

Not surprising is the report that Microsoft, Facebook, Amazon, and IBM are charging ahead to build similar Knowledge Vaults. The claim is that soon the Internet will contain all of human knowledge—disseminated by those who are certain they can recognize the truth better than anyone else.

The 1.6 billion facts Google is said to have will be exponentially expanded with this new method. Some claim it will pull information from Gmail, Google+, and YouTube. Google denies that it will search any personal information.

Almost two-thirds of the searches around the world are done through Google. The Washington Post calls it "a shaper of online reality, helping determine what we see and how." Research claims that search engines can and do have a significant impact on voters and, ultimately, who wins elections. And the ones searching the Internet for information don't even know they are being led—possibly led astray.

Matt Stempeck, director of civic media at Microsoft New York, said that when you try to "correct people's misconceptions" (read that, "their opinion differs from mine") they become rather "defensive." So he figures that if they go to Google for the answer they will be more likely to accept information they otherwise would have questioned or disagreed with. Do I hear the Pied Piper's notes in the air?

None of the tasks of raising your kids is easy, but keeping them on the right track regarding their morals, philosophy of life, science, history, and other fundamentals of learning will be especially demanding. Your kids are at risk. There are people, and organizations, and governments who want to take your kids from you and all that you believe in. Does that sound like an overstatement? Even Diogenes said, "The foundation of every state is the education of its youth."

Who has dibs on your kids? Christ? You? Someone else? Know who you and your kids can trust.

✝

"Those who know your name trust in you, for you, Lord, have never forsaken those who seek you" (Psalm 9:10).

Chapter Challenge

Ways God has earned my trust:

_______________ _______________

_______________ _______________

_______________ _______________

_______________ _______________

_______________ _______________

Ways I have earned my kids' trust:

_______________ _______________

_______________ _______________

_______________ _______________

_______________ _______________

_______________ _______________

Who's Got Dibs on Your Kids' ORIGINS?

The Battle of the Big Bang and Evolution vs. Creationism

"Where were you when I laid the earth's foundation? Tell me, if you understand" (Job 38:4).

The first and foremost issue in science—where the followers of the God of the Bible face off against unbelievers—is how the world and everything in it came to be: The Big Bang and Evolution versus Creationism.

Most of us can agree on two things: we weren't there when it happened, and we can't reproduce the "beginning" in a laboratory.

Therefore, no matter how we believe the universe, our world, and all living things began, all we have to hang on to is faith in our belief. For both sides, it is a "theory" because neither belief system has a scientific means to prove it.

The Big Bang theory

Many scientists will rebel if you try to tell them evolution and the "Big Bang" versions of how the universe began are just theories. However, from their standpoint, *our* belief in God's creation of the universe, our world, and everything in it including man is a theory. We believe it because God told us He did it, and we trust the Word of God. We didn't see it happen, and God doesn't give lab classes.

The Big Bang theory of the origins of the universe was initiated early in the twentieth century when Einstein came up with his General Theory of Relativity[1] that said the "fabric" of space could expand and contract. Several astronomers, mathematicians, and cosmologists toyed with the idea. In 1929 Edwin Hubble observed and confirmed that the universe was continuously expanding. That drove him to the conclusion there must have been a point in time when all matter, the entire universe, was contained in a single blob in space.

Something triggered a massive explosion, Hubble decided, sending out particles, planets, stars, galaxies into that "space." More than eighty years later NASA still ponders what triggered that explosion, or in their words "this incredible burst of expansion called 'inflation'."[2]

The Big Bang theory has a lot of merit. NASA says they are looking to gravitational waves as carriers of information, the "*only known form of information* that can reach us undistorted from the instant of the Big Bang." (Emphasis mine.) I wish they would open the Bible. The Big Bang theory sounds to me like God saying, in a voice I sometimes try to imagine with its thundering command, "Let there be . . ." and there *was*! Just like that. BANG!

I would like to learn more about our universe, and I believe science will continue to furnish us with more amazing data. The photographs taken of outer space are jaw-dropping. If you haven't seen them, go to the Hubble website at http://hubblesite.org/gallery/ and prepare to be in awe. I thought my favorite was the Pillars of Creation, but as I thumbed through them I kept changing my mind.

Evolution vs. creationism

The question of how it all began has troubled mankind for a very long time. Believers in the God of the Bible have a huge advantage over those who do not believe God created the world. We don't fight the concept.

Science has advanced enough that many scientists who previously held strongly to Darwin's theory of macro-evolution now support what Michael Behe, professor of biochemistry at Lehigh University, calls "irreducible complexity."[3] In Behe's words, "Irreducible complexity is just a fancy phrase I use to mean a single system which is composed of several interacting parts, and where the removal of any one of the parts causes the system to cease functioning."

Behe's famous example of irreducible complexity is the ordinary mousetrap. It consists of five parts: hammer, spring, catch, platform, and holding bar. Without any one of those parts the mousetrap cannot work. Behe's book, *Darwin's Black Box*, explains this beautifully in detail.

There are many examples in nature that reinforce this idea of irreducible complexity—creatures that cannot have evolved because until all the parts were there none of the parts would have worked. They would not have been able to continue to exist. Understanding the basics of irreducible complexity leads one to the conviction that efficient living organisms don't just happen—there must be an intelligent design for everything, and thus, an Intelligent Designer.

One of Behe's critics, PZ Myers, while reviewing another of Behe's books, *The Edge of Evolution*, said:

> [A] radical anti-evolutionist extremist. . . the amazingly incompetent mish-mash . . . rank incompetence . . . That Designer sure has been busy! He's been working hard to sculpt life on earth towards generating human beings and chimpanzees and malaria parasites, right down to specifying the amino acid sequences of active sites in their proteins. Most of the arguments are gussied up versions of the kind of hand waving, ignorant rationalizations you'd get from some pomaded fundagelical Baptist minister who got all his biology from the Bible, not at all what you'd expect from a tenured professor of biochemistry at a good university."[4]

The sardonic tone referencing the Designer cannot be overlooked. Myers failed to note that Michael Behe was a confirmed evolutionist until his work revealed the truth to him—there had to be an intelligent designer behind it all.

Atheist scientists will not go so far as to admit the Intelligent Designer is God, but some make a step in the right direction. They admit there is too much in the theory of evolution that cannot be scientifically accounted for.

Still the majority of the scientific world views with loathing anyone holding to a belief other than evolution. So that's what your kids are taught.

Common Core State Standards (not truly "state" but *federal* standards) were accepted by forty-six states. Details about Common Core are covered later, but for now just be aware that it requires teaching evolution.

When your kids are in their science class, do they know the gaps not only in the fossil record but in the theory of evolution itself? Do they know the chart of embryos used by biologist Ernst Haeckel in

1868 to substantiate the premise of common descent, is a fake—and scientists have known it is a fake for over a hundred years—but it is still often found in textbooks?[5]

What your kids will learn in school

Lucy Long Ago: Uncovering the Mystery of Where We Came From is a highly illustrated book for ages 9–12. It is sometimes used as additional reading in public schools, and is available in libraries. *Lucy Long Ago* is a beautiful book. Like much material based on the theory of evolution, it quotes highly regarded scientists. Let's take a brief look at Lucy.

At the time of the writing of *Lucy Long Ago* scientists believed the fossil (named Lucy) was 3.2 million years old. This was proclaimed the "missing link" between what we know as *Homo sapiens* and the split from apes some 7–10 million years ago. Scientists concluded that Lucy had been three feet six inches tall, which would be about the size of a bonobo chimpanzee. She had a brain the size of a chimp, long curved fingers and toes useful for climbing trees, a protruding face or jaw line (most *H. sapiens* have flatter faces) and big teeth.

Lucy was the size and shape of a chimpanzee, and could climb trees like a chimpanzee. Do you think she may have been a chimpanzee? Those who believe Lucy was on the way to becoming a human say she may have walked a little more upright than a chimpanzee, but chimpanzees can and do walk upright at times.

Dr. Donald Johanson, the man who discovered Lucy in 1974, answered some questions at a lecture at the University of Missouri in Kansas City in 1986. Let's look at a couple of them.[6]

Q: How far away from Lucy did you find the knee? (The knee bones were discovered about a year earlier than the rest of Lucy.)

A: About 200 feet lower and two to three kilometers away (about 1.5 miles).

Q: Then why are you sure it belonged to Lucy?

A: Anatomical similarity

After more discussion where Dr. Johanson's commitment to his belief in homology became clear, he made this rather revealing statement: "[I]f you don't believe homology, then you don't believe evolution, and evolution is a fact!" (Homology is a similarity of structure between parts of different organisms e.g. the wing of a bat is like a human arm.)

The March 22, 2001 issue of *Nature* told of a fossil that had been dated at 3.5 million years[7]. It had a flatter face than most chimps, and the molars were a bit smaller. This one, seemingly more like humans in some ways, served to kick Lucy into the scientific gutter. *USA Today* proclaimed that "Lucy has been losing favor over the past 10 years," and Rick Potts of the Smithsonian Institute stated, "I and many others believe Lucy needs to be replaced." I didn't read about that in my local paper. And it's a pretty good guess your kids haven't heard that in their science classes either.

The March 6, 2015 issue of *Science* had an article about evolution. It references the rising concern that teachers are "wishy-washy" about teaching evolution.[8] A survey showed that a lot of teachers prefer to avoid, and try to avoid, teaching evolution. Some teachers explained: "I'm, you know, pretty ignorant on this topic . . . is there enough of scientific evidence to say for sure?" and "Evolution is one of those subjects that I'm still a bit shaky about."

A 2007 study of 926 high school biology teachers found that 13% of the teachers acknowledged they believed in creationism. (How many believed but were afraid to acknowledge it we will never know.) Only 28% stated they provided students with a thorough understanding of evolution. Researchers called the remaining "the cautious 60%" who admitted they spent as little time as possible teaching evolution, which the research labeled "the most fundamental concept in modern biology."

Eric Plutzer of Penn State said that the schools' faculties need to understand that "Getting them to understand evolution is not simply a matter of having them take more science courses." If studying science more diligently will not help teachers (or their students) understand evolution, what will? Indoctrinating, conditioning, programming—those are all synonyms for brainwashing, not education.

It became apparent that high school kids had what the educators saw as "wrong" ideas about evolution—the theory just didn't make sense to them. Those considering the problem decided the whole topic is just "too complex" for high school age kids.[9]

The evidence that makes it all too complex for your kids

Following is a list of some of the "empirical evidence" on which your kids may be taught to rely.

- Haeckel's drawings of embryos – Faked.
- Archaeopteryx (reptile) identified as first known bird – Disproved. (Now "a very important fossil" but not direct ancestor of modern birds.)
- Peppered moths – Claimed to demonstrate natural selection. Moths were pinned or glued to trees to demonstrate change. Moth experts knew the photos were bogus because live moths perched on a tree trunk would not have their wings spread. – Faked.
- Darwin's finches – Although studied by Darwin when he was in Galapagos Islands, he did not immediately associate the varied beaks with evolution. Another man made that connection later. In fact, the beaks of the finches became larger in times of drought, (which some used as evidence for natural selection) but became smaller again when rainfall was abundant. – Oscillation not evolution.
- Four-winged fruit fly – Said to have evolved from the two-winged fruit fly. It is a mutation; however, it did not occur in

nature but in the laboratory. Additionally, the second set of wings lacks flight muscles and has no benefit to the fruit fly. – Misrepresented.
- Drawing of ape-like creature evolving into erect-walking man based on philosophical belief. There is no evidence to substantiate the evolution as shown. – Misrepresented.
- The Piltdown man – called the "missing link" was exposed as a fraud in 1953. – Fraud.

Many reasons justify continuing the fight against the teaching of evolution, but the first and foremost is that it fundamentally calls God a liar. God starts his Holy Word by declaring that he was around before everything, he made everything, and at the time he made it, "it was very good." If we permit that very basic, foundational truth to be denied, how can we support anything in Scripture that follows?

Cosmos – The origin of the universe and more

Do your kids watch television? You may be among the few parents who won't let that happen, but most kids watch TV. In fact, a 2014 survey by the Nielsen Company reported that kids ages eight to eighteen watch between twenty and twenty-four hours of television every week.[10] If your kids are spending time that way it is likely that they have seen the series *Cosmos*.

The most recent, the second generation of *Cosmos*, titled *Cosmos: A Spacetime Odyssey*, came out in 2014. Put together by Fox and National Geographic, and narrated by Neil deGrasse Tyson, it has an undeniable WOW! factor. Teachers across the United States are looking forward to using it in their science classes in school. There's probably not a kid around who is going to object to that. Not only is this series beautiful to behold, but it makes science interesting—just not altogether factual. But who's going to notice with all the cool special effects?

A look at the problems in *Cosmos*

Cosmos has some problems that you may not have paid attention to because of the "bling," but you can bet impressed themselves on the minds of your kids. Before, during, or after your kids are exposed to *Cosmos*, talk with them about it. Raise their awareness of the subtleties that a casual viewing may not notice. What are they? Here are just a few:

- In the first episode the Roman Catholic Church burned Giordano Bruno, a defrocked Italian Dominican friar, at the stake in the sixteenth century. That really happened, but right from the beginning of *Cosmos*, the implication is that religion is anti-science. Bruno was not a scientist nor did he make any scientific discoveries. (*Cosmos* does state that Bruno was not a scientist.) He did express what the church at that time considered heretical ideas, one of which was that the earth revolves around the sun. But he was not burned at the stake for that—he also denied the doctrine of the Trinity, the Virgin Birth, claimed that everyone would be saved, and loudly proclaimed those and other doctrinal deviations. The Catholic Church at that time would have had some rather serious problems with a man with such doctrinal differences, aside from his scientific statements.
- The Big Bang is demonstrated as the origin of the universe. Not as a theory. Over and over again we are told that the universe is more than 13 billion years old.
- The laws that govern the universe were initiated by, or at the same time as, the Big Bang. Think about that. If the laws of physics did not exist at the time of the Big Bang there would have been nothing but chaos.
- The words evolution, and evolved, are also used as facts. There is a casual reference to our ancestors living in trees and having long tails.

- Weaving fact with allegation, Tyson dismisses the Judeo-Christian belief that the world is thousands, not billions, of years old. He states that light travels at a known speed (fact) and that if the earth were only thousands of years old we would not be able to see many of the cosmological bodies because their light would not have reached us yet. God said, "Let there be light, and there was light." Right then. No waiting. Thereafter the continuing light travels at the speed light is known to travel.
- The occasions I found most daring used several phrases common to Judeo-Christian faiths: "Thou shalt not," "manna from heaven," and the "*story* (dismissing it by implication that it was folklore) of Noah and the great flood." Tyson also refers to the "scripture" of the DNA. The instances degrading religion and religious beliefs run throughout; they are sometimes blatant, sometimes subliminal.

Dr. Tyson is the most extraordinary Pied Piper I have encountered. He is a noted scientist. He is also an excellent actor, lending credibility and appeal to the presentation. His physical stature and deep, mellifluous voice charm the viewer to "come along with me." You cannot expect your kids to catch the ways their minds are being led astray by this beautifully produced video when the falsehoods are deftly woven in with true scientific information.

Checking the library

I searched for evolution in my County Public Library system, specifying "books" and "juvenile." I isolated the results to books that had one hundred pages or less, because that generally indicates a lower reading level. Nineteen titles matched those criteria. They were shelved under Science.

I searched for creation using the same search parameters. My results gave me twenty-seven book titles that fit the criteria. That's pretty good, don't you think, considering there were nineteen evolution books? However, seventeen of them were identified *in the title* as "mythology." All were shelved in the Religion or Folklore sections.

I wondered if there were any evolution rebuttal books at all shelved in Science. My last search was for books about intelligent design. There were none that fit the criteria. There was no science rebuttal to evolution for children under the age of ten.

When the new Next Generation Science Standards (NGSS) were released, not as an integral part of Common Core, but sharing similar objectives, I went to the NGSS section on evolution and searched for intelligent design. There were no results found.

A *Scientific American* article, July 5, 2013, titled, "Evolution and Climate Science Make the Grade in State Education Standards" points out:

- Five states have adopted the NGSS, which emphasize beginning studies of climate change science and evolution in elementary school.
- State Boards of Education in Rhode Island, Kentucky, Kansas, Maryland, and Vermont approved the standards with little opposition.
- Some states have avoided teaching climate change and evolution in the past, but are still moving toward adoption of the standards. (Climate change is discussed in chapter 3.)
- Most states begin teaching the concepts of evolution in high school biology. The NGSS guidelines advocate teaching it in elementary school.

An April 15, 2013 article in *U.S. News & World Report* gave the opinion that even though twenty-six of the states had some form of input while the Next Generation Science Standards were being written, they may not all adopt them. The article expresses concerns that the evolution and climate change curriculum mandates may prove serious obstacles. One must wonder what the state input was, and how highly it was valued.

By the end of 2014, a year and a half after their release, only thirteen states and the District of Columbia had adopted the NGSS. Acceptance is slow for a number of reasons. An article in *The Verge* (theverge.com) dated May 19, 2014 reports a number of states simply don't agree with what they must teach. The main difficulties lie with the requirements to teach evolution and man-made global warming.

Just as Common Core is strongly opposed by some, there are those who are actively trying to impede the NGSS. Go to nature.com to see a chart titled "By Design" which shows the state legislative activity from 2004 through 2013, introducing "academic freedom" bills to allow educators to teach creationism.

The website for the National Center for Science Education at ncse.com listed two bills (among many) regarding the teaching of evolution in Iowa and Oklahoma: the "Antiscience bill in Iowa"[11] and the "Antiscience bill dies in Oklahoma."[12] The Iowa bill would have stopped the implementation of NGSS, partly because of the treatment of evolution and climate change. It died in committee. The website states that the Oklahoma bill "would, if enacted, have deprived administrators of the ability to prevent teachers from *miseducating* students about 'scientific controversies.'" (Emphasis mine.)

What are WE teaching our kids?

"In the beginning . . ."

Before you go any further into Genesis, help your kids understand these words from Genesis 1:1. This was not the beginning of God. This was the beginning of the universe, of the world, of all the flora and fauna on the earth, and—in His image—man. It was the point when God established and identified the function of time, for time is limiting and God is limitless. God *created the beginning itself!*

When both you and your kids have wrapped your minds around that really big concept, let them continue reading what events took place on each of the six days of creation.

Obviously, there are many excellent books for young children about creation, published by companies that promote primarily Christian material. Parents have no problem making such material available for their children to read at home. Why then should the library search results remain a matter of concern?

Public school libraries generally buy the same material bought by public community libraries, albeit on a smaller scale. Therefore, if your child is studying evolution in a science class, what choices are offered for outside reading? Do you think they will be directed to the Religion section? Is there even a Religion section in public elementary school libraries? Those are not meant to be rhetorical questions. Do you know if your elementary school library has a Religion section? If it does, do you know if kids are directed to it while studying evolution? I'm quite certain most of the libraries will have a Folklore section. Are they directed there to learn other views of the origin of life?

There is little doubt your children will be taught the theory of evolution. You must be able to put it in the proper context for them. Variations can, and do, occur within a species (microevolution), but one species cannot evolve into an entirely new species (macroevolution). It simply doesn't happen.

In "The Origin of the Species" Charles Darwin states, "If it could be demonstrated that any complex organ existed, which could not possibly have been formed by numerous, successive, slight modifications, my theory would absolutely break down. But I can find no such case."

I think today even Darwin would be willing to admit that many biochemists, as well as scientists in other disciplines, have scientifically broken down his theory (starting with irreducible complexity, which I mentioned earlier).

There are ample materials available for both adults and children that tear apart the credibility of Darwin's theory. I included a brief bibliography at the end of this chapter. It includes books, videos, and websites with which I am familiar, and can recommend. If they are not available from your library, I suggest you buy them. Perhaps a group from your church could share the cost, and pass the materials around.

You can't discuss the subject with your children unless *you* are informed. Your children cannot refute the "science" of evolution unless they know the facts of intelligent design. Yes, I know I did not say creation. Creation as the work of God is a matter of faith. We should not try to argue creationism in a secular setting; we have abundant scientific evidence of *intelligent design*. However, our children are unlikely to hear anything positive about intelligent design in a public school, if they hear anything at all. Most evolutionists regard the concept of intelligent design as a type of religion-based creationism, masquerading under a different name.

When your children are ready to go beyond what we call the Creation Story in Genesis, I recommend reading Job 38–41. These chapters overwhelm me as the most amazing view of God's power, and knowledge, and superiority in the entire Bible.

Apparently Job felt ashamed of his own arrogance after the dressing down God gave him, because in Chapter 42:3 Job says, "You asked, 'Who is this that obscures my plans without knowledge?' Surely I spoke of things I did not understand, things too wonderful for me to know." After young people are able to read those chapters and truly understand the full scope of what God is saying, the weak conclusions of the evolutionists will seem foolish.

Where can you learn more?

Read about irreducible complexity in Michael Behe's *Darwin's Black Box*. Remember his mouse trap example? It's an easy way to explain it to your kids.

However, if you just want a good start into the evolution vs.

creation debate, I recommend *The Case for A Creator* by Lee Strobel. I highly recommend all of Strobel's *Case for* . . . books, but as we're talking about evolution now, start with this one. Lee Strobel is a journalist by profession, making his writing very readable, and his research authoritative.

My next recommendation, albeit with reservation, is *The Politically Incorrect Guide to Darwinism and Intelligent Design* by Jonathan Wells. This book is at times sluggish, but you can skip those parts and get to some of the good (and readable) information it presents. One of the quotes Wells uses is a statement by evolutionary biologist Henry Gee:

> No fossil is buried with its birth certificate. That, and the scarcity of fossils, means that it is effectively impossible to link fossils into chains of cause and effect in any valid way . . . To take a line of fossils and claim that they represent a lineage is not a scientific hypothesis that can be tested, but an assertion that carries the same validity as a bedtime story—amusing, perhaps even instructive, but not scientific.

I was pleasantly surprised to find a book in the library for ages eleven and up titled, *The Evolution Debate: Darwinism vs. Intelligent Design* by Sherri Mabry Gordon. The author discusses both sides of the debate with clarity, and little obvious bias. She includes references to Michael Behe and his scientific conclusions on eleven of the book's 128 pages. The book shows the image of the mousetrap and identifies other examples of irreducible complexity. She also refers to a statement by Lee Strobel.

Gordon includes the nineteenth century drawings of Haeckel which advance the idea that significant similarities exist between animal and human embryos. This drawing is often used in textbooks as evidence of evolution. To its credit, Gordon's book states below the image: "However, Haeckel's work in this area has been discredited, and it is not currently used to support the theory of evolution." (Still, there remain textbooks that promote Haeckel's embryo drawings as "evidence" of evolution, and others that use a variation of them.) Overall, I think Gordon has presented as fair an examination of both sides as one might hope for.

Embryos show evidence of evolution

Let's peek behind the curtain and see how the wizards are manipulating facts to make your kids believe embryos are proof of macroevolution.

A good place to start is with a closer investigation of Haeckel drawings. He put forth his belief that because embryos are so similar, all creatures evolved from the same root. The problem is that in their earliest stages embryos are quite different from one another. Then, as the embryos develop further, they are again very different from one another. However, at one point in the development some embryos have similarities. But not all animal embryos exhibit those similarities. Haeckel chose those embryos that most resemble the human embryo at that one stage of development, chose only the embryos that would exhibit those characteristics, and then manipulated the drawings to further enhance the likeness. The March 2000 issue of *Natural History* carried an article by Stephen Gould that stated, "[Haeckel] exaggerated the similarities by idealizations and omissions," and he called the drawings "outright falsification."

Did all scientists in the nineteenth century agree with Haeckel's theory? Not quite. As early as 1894 Adam Sedgwick, an embryologist, said that Haeckel's drawings were "not in accordance with the facts of development." He emphasized his opinion: "There is no stage of development in which the unaided eye would fail to distinguish between them with ease." Do your kids' textbooks tell them that side of the story?

Behind the curtain, those who wrote the textbooks preferred not to include the words of dissenters. When the knowledge became widespread, many textbooks began using a slightly different version of embryo comparisons by embryologist Karl Ernst von Baer hoping to curb the criticism.

Still others switched to using photographs of embryos. Who could dispute photographs? Surely the camera doesn't lie. No, a camera doesn't lie, but those behind the curtain manipulated the results by again choosing only those embryos that would show the greatest similarities to the human embryo, and photographed them at the one small slice of time in the development when those similarities were present.

There is an entire chapter on this subject in *Icons of Evolution* by Jonathan Wells, who has a PhD in cell and developmental biology. This would only be readable if your kids are starting or presently in college level classes. If your kids are younger, you can read it and be ready to explain how the misdirection is used, and why they cannot always trust textbooks or those with advanced degrees in science.

All hope is not lost

My library search led me to a pleasant surprise. I found a picture book in the public library titled, *Creation* by Gerald McDermott, published by a secular publisher, Dutton Children's Books. It is simply written, beautifully illustrated, and follows the biblical account in Genesis. What may escape all but Christians familiar with the terminology appears on the last page, in all caps, "I AM." However, even though this is a secular publisher, I wonder if it will be found on the shelves of public school libraries.

As a cautionary statement, none of the material listed below is indisputable. Flawed humans are responsible for the content, so you may not agree with everything. Read or view it with discernment.

Obviously, I've just touched on the evolution/creation/intelligent design debate; there are many books and articles about it. If you are going to teach your kids the errors to watch out for, you're going to have to do some studying. I've given examples of innuendos, misleading information, misinformation, and outright lies that your kids will face in the following areas:

- textbooks
- magazines
- library books
- television programs
- government agencies

Now it's up to you to teach your kids how to recognize errors, and be discerning.

✝

"And the Lord's servant must not be quarrelsome but must be kind to everyone, able to teach, not resentful. Opponents must be gently instructed, in the hope that God will grant them repentance leading them to a knowledge of the truth, and that they will come to their senses and escape from the trap of the devil, who has taken them captive to do his will" (2 Timothy 2:24–26).

Chapter Challenge

Choose one from each of the mediums listed below and start to learn more about the subjects your kids will be taught in school.

Resources for teaching your child about creation, evolution, and intelligent design

Please note I do recommend teaching your kids about evolution. It is my belief that they cannot reasonably refute the theory of evolution unless they understand it. And you can't explain it to them unless you understand it. For more resources visit my website at DibsOnYourKids.com.

Books

- Behe, Michael J. *Darwin's Black Box: The Biochemical Challenge to Evolution*. 1996. Second ed. New York: Free Press, 2006.
- Gordon, Sherri Mabry. *The Evolution Debate: Darwinism vs. Intelligent Design*. Issues in Focus Today. Berkeley Heights: Enslow, 2009. (Juvenile/Young Adult)
- McDermott, Gerald. *Creation*. New York: Dutton Children's Books, 2003. (Picture Book)
- Strobel, Lee. *The Case for a Creator*. Grand Rapids: Zondervan, 2004.

Videos

- 2014. *Cosmos: A Spacetime Odyssey*. 20th Century Fox. Narrated by Neil deGrasse Tyson.
- Martin, Dr. Jobe. *Incredible Creatures That Defy Evolution I, II & III. Perf. Martin, Dr. Jobe. DVD Color. Reel Productions.*
- Strobel, Lee. *The Case for a Creator*. Perf. Strobel, Lee. DVD Color. Illustra Media: Lionsgate Films.2006.

Websites

- Answers in Genesis - Creation, Evolution, Christian Apologetics. (2013). http://www.answersingenesis.org/.
- Creation Studies Institute - Creation, Science, Evolution, and Origins from a Creationist and Biblical perspective. (2013). http://www.creationstudies.org/.
- Institute for Creation Research. 2009, http://www.icr.org/.
- Lutheran Science Institute. 13 Jan 2010). 2009, http://www.lutheranscience.org/index.html.

Disclaimer: I do not agree with every statement made in these books, videos and websites, but I do believe they contain much valuable information.

Who's Got Dibs on Your Kids' ENVIRONMENT?

Global Warming - Climate Change What's Going On?

"God blessed them and said to them,. 'Be fruitful and increase in number; fill the earth and subdue it. Rule over the fish in the sea and the birds in the sky and over every living creature that moves on the ground'" (Genesis 1:28).

✝

When I was about five or six years old, my brother and I were in the back yard while my parents prepared the planting beds for spring. My father dug the spade into the rich, loamy ground, and as he turned it over a worm sat on top—cut in half. My brother, with the speed of a bird's beak, picked up both halves of that worm and threw them at me. I screamed, and screamed, and screamed. I hate worms.

I also hate snakes. But I don't hate worms and snakes as much as I hate bugs. I choose to subdue them with large and frequent applications of bug killers, although I don't think that's what God had in mind when he gave instructions to Adam and Eve to subdue the earth.

The biblical quote leading this chapter is from the New International Version. I wondered what other translations would show for the word "subdue." I found "take control," "take charge," "be its master," "bring under control," and the one that seems to me to express it best, "using all its vast resources in the service of God and man."

Not everyone agrees with that. We hear about the crisis we face from global warming if we don't immediately and severely cut back on our use of fossil fuels. Your kids are taught that as a "fact" in school and in almost every other area of their lives.

Where do your kids learn about climate change?

Every place your kids turn they hear and read about climate change. The *Cosmos* science series primarily deals with evolution, but several episodes take a rather strange side trip into climate change and air pollution. In those global warming side trips, they again provide much factual information with an infusion of speculation. The book *Climate Confusion* by Roy W. Spencer is excellent to read as you are watching those climate episodes of *Cosmos*. Spencer is a Principal Research Scientist at the University of Alabama in Huntsville, with a Ph.D. in Meteorology. He was also a Senior Scientist for Climate Studies at NASA. Even with Dr. Spencer by your side, Neil deGrasse Tyson, the consummate Pied Piper, will lure you and your kids into his world through the beautifully produced *Cosmos*.

Libraries abound with books for every age level about global warming and climate change. A search in my library's records, juvenile through adolescent, shows sixty-four possible selections. They range from books, videos, and baseball card adventures, to electronic sources in both fiction and nonfiction. I found only two that gave anything other than a cataclysmic crisis view. The good thing, of course, is that there were at least two.

There are choices

A refreshing change is the book *The Sky's Not Falling!* For kids 9–12, it claims to be a "balanced alternative to Scholastic's fear-inducing global warming kids' book." I recommend you take a look at this one.

A book that will help your older kids with their critical thinking skills (see Chapter Challenge) is *Global Warming: Opposing Viewpoints* published by Greenhaven Press. You can find it in Young Adult books. They published this book in 2002, 2006, and 2010.

I have an extensive list of books and other media on my website at DibsOnYourKids.com.

Earth Day

If your kids are in school they have probably participated in what is now promoted around the world as Earth Day. At earthday.org their mission statement reads: "Earth Day Network's year-round mission is to *broaden, diversify and activate the environmental movement* worldwide, through a combination of education, *public policy*, and consumer campaigns." (Emphasis mine.)

The Earth Day Network claims to have 22,000 partners and organizations in 192 countries. They intend to "green" all of America's K–12 schools within a generation. What does that mean? Among other goals, one of the elements that makes a school "green" is that there is science-based environmental and civic education in the classroom. They are saying, in their own let's-change-the-world-speak, that only what *they* claim is based on science is true—there is no opportunity for dialogue—and if we don't voluntarily make the changes they see as necessary, they will force them on us through government-enacted laws.

Science-based environmental and civic education

The Earth Day Network furnishes lessons teachers can, or in their view should, use in class. One of their classroom lessons addresses cars idling for 30 seconds or more. They want the kids to carry home and tell you, their parents, how bad it is to sit with the car idling while you are waiting to pick up your kids. In Arizona, temperatures are often over 100°F. How long do you want to wait without the air conditioning running? And in the cold climates with temperatures below 0°F? Let's be serious here. And your kids, if not explicitly, are implicitly convinced through this lesson that you are a bad person if you wait with the car idling.

This lesson states: "At the conclusion of this lesson, students will be able to communicate information about idling at your school and the impact of idling on air pollution and will begin a campaign of education and awareness at your school."

But forget for a moment about how uncomfortable you'll feel. How much pollution is going into the air? Let's take a brief side trip into carbon dioxide

A look at carbon dioxide (CO_2)

There is a lot of disagreement between scholars and scientists about the levels of CO_2 in our atmosphere. The level of CO_2 is rising. *Slightly*. It has increased eighty-three parts per million, from about 317 ppm in 1960 to about 400 ppm today.[1] That means CO_2 is at a tiny 40/1,000ths of one percent of all of the gases in our atmosphere—and it is not only good for all living things, we can't live without it.

Some are certain the levels are rising because of our use of carbon dioxide-producing fossil fuels. They believe their use will certainly cause great harm to the earth. This is known as an "anthropogenic" reason for the increase in CO_2—caused by something people do. Those scientists, and others who agree with that theory, admit there has always been carbon dioxide in our atmosphere, but the amount has been increasing, and they believe it has reached levels we need to do something about immediately. They are convinced we must reduce our "carbon footprint."

Other scholars and scientists point out that carbon dioxide is a naturally occurring gas. It is colorless and odorless. Humans and animals exhale carbon dioxide as they breathe. Plants take in carbon dioxide. Humans and animals eat plants. If there were no carbon dioxide, our planet couldn't exist as we know it.

With increased $CO_{2,}$ plants grow better.[2] World-wide population is soaring. There were about one billion people at the beginning of the industrial revolution, and by July 2015 the world population was expected to reach 7.325 billion.[3] It seems to make sense to do as God told us, and use all of our earth's vast resources in the service of God and man, including growing more food for the increasing population. I don't believe that option is discussed in your kids' science classes.

Don't lose sight of good stewardship

This might be a good place to be forthright about the place of the "green" movement in my own life. My husband and I have one container in our kitchen for trash and one for items that can be recycled. When we shop we make a list of what we need, where we need to go, and decide on the most efficient route to take. Exclusive of our lawn, where we use regular sprinklers, all of our outdoor plantings are on a drip system. We don't start our dishwasher until it is full. We keep our cars in good mechanical condition for best performance. In other words, we try to be good stewards of God's blessings.

We have driven through Gary, Indiana, when the air was so thick with pollutants we were happy we didn't need to have the windows down. We have visited southern California when you couldn't see the mountains from I-10. We like our air to be as clean as possible so we can breathe it without dire consequences.

However, we do not follow blindly after the global warming Pied

Pipers, who would have businesses close, coal miners out of work, prices sky-rocket, and tax-payer money wasted on alternative energy companies because they have determined for reasons of their own it should be so. It's important to remember CO_2 is a colorless, odorless gas. The pollution we see in the air is not carbon dioxide.

Next Generation Science Standards

In case you believe what you heard or read, that the Common Core State Standards (CCSS) and The Next Generation Science Standards (NGSS) are state driven, you should check out the NGSS website. Here are a couple of sentences from the first paragraph of the Appendix D page:

> The Next Generation Science Standards (NGSS) are being developed at a historic time when major changes in education are occurring at the *national* level . . . On the other hand, *national* initiatives are emerging for a new wave of standards through the NGSS as well as Common Core State Standards (CCSS) for English language arts and literacy and for mathematics.[4] (Emphasis mine.)

Previously referred to as "global warming," the designation morphed into "climate change." NGSS standards *require* climate change instruction. Some of the directions the courses take are valid areas of study, but others are overtly promoting and instilling the belief in your kids that *we* are the major transgressors where climate change is occurring. Here is one of the high school course descriptions: "Use a computational representation to illustrate the relationships among Earth systems and how those relationships are being modified due to human activity." Please note this does not ask the student to determine *if* Earth systems are being modified by human activity, but *how*.

As I mentioned before, climate change, as it is *required* to be taught to our kids, is a major stumbling block for some states. To understand why there is such pushback, we need to look briefly into what some are trying to teach as scientific fact, and the opposition.

Climate change is indisputable

A vast amount of evidence confirms the world went through an extended Ice Age. There was also a time when the world was warmer overall than it is today. Why else do you think the largest island in the world is called *Green*land? Yet two-thirds of the island sits inside the Arctic Circle. What can explain this?

An article in *Science Magazine*[5] says the Arctic Ocean is a puzzlement when predicting climate change. Scientists wanted to see how the ice in the Arctic had reacted in the past and use that data to predict the future. They drilled down 400 meters (about 1300 feet) under the Arctic seafloor, which they believed would give them information about the ice, according to their calculations, fifty-six million years ago. What they learned was startling—there was no ice in the Arctic at that time. The conclusion was our earth must have thrown some more coal in the furnace because the temperature of the Arctic Ocean was in the mid-60°F *before* the warming began, and rose to an almost bathwater temperature of 73°F. They think methane released from the deep ocean floor, or volcanoes erupting, might have been the cause. (No anthropogenic causes were inferred from the data.)

A Medieval Warm Period occurred during the ninth to the thirteenth centuries. People began to settle Greenland. They abandoned their settlements after that time because of the onslaught of the Little Ice Age. Actions of humans caused neither of those wild temperature swings.

The label "climate change denier"

"Climate change deniers" has a different ring to it than "global warming deniers." It lumps those opposing the global warming theory in with "flat-earthers." This approach shuts down all legitimate discussion.

I stand with the "climate change deniers," although I firmly believe in historic and present climate change. I disagree that changes occurring are caused by human actions, except that with our population explosion more people are exhaling carbon dioxide. My beliefs are in accord with many scientists. There are many facts to back up those beliefs, but your kids will never hear them in most public schools. It is likely your kids will never have the opportunity to ask questions that could lead to an informative discussion of climate change. Many teachers will not permit any questioning of the "facts."

Before the vote which ultimately rejected NGSS in Oklahoma, state Representative Mark McCullough asked the science director of Oklahoma's state Board of Education if the Next Generation Science Standards might indoctrinate students with "a fairly-one sided view as to that controversial subject [climate change], a subject that is very much in dispute even among even the academics."

That sounds like a hypothetical question needing no response, because the answer is so obvious—of course the students will be taught a "one-sided view." That's the point. The supporters of anthropogenic climate change don't want them to learn that there is another scientifically-supported viewpoint. NGSS does not permit teaching your kids any viewpoint other than its own.

National Geographic's position

In the article "Age of Disbelief" in *National Geographic*'s March 2015 issue, the author states: "In the U.S., climate change skeptics have achieved their fundamental goal of halting legislative action to combat global warming. They haven't had to win the debate on the merits; they've merely had to fog the room enough to keep laws governing greenhouse gas (GHG) emissions from being enacted." Note the author, Joel Achenbach, uses the same misleading device, calling opponents "climate change skeptics" rather than "anthropogenic" climate change skeptics. This subtle way of demeaning and diminishing your opponents prevents the controversy from focusing on that important aspect of whether climate change is or is not due to human activities.

Although Congress may be reluctant to pass laws that overburden our society, the Administration has not been. From January 2009 to June 2014, the Environmental Protection Agency (EPA) issued 2,827 new final regulations covering, among other issues, greenhouse gases, air quality, emissions, and hazardous substances.

Vice President Joe Biden gave his view of climate change skeptics: "I think it's close to mindless. I think it's like, you know, almost like denying gravity now."

What are some of the facts in this controversy?

Al Gore's claims

Al Gore was a prominent representative, senator, and Vice-President of the United States. Now an environmental activist, he has exceeded all his former notoriety with his subsequent zeal regarding global warming. Although it won many awards, his movie *An Inconvenient Truth* did not provoke universal and unequivocal acceptance. The film's producer Laurie David had her offer of 50,000 free copies rejected by the National Science Teachers Association (NSTA). One commentator was appalled, and stated NSTA "is squandering a golden opportunity to educate tens of millions of youth in the United States!"

Why would a science teachers' association spurn such an opportunity? They said they wanted to stay away from something political in nature, although I don't remember *An Inconvenient Truth* ever advertised as a political movie. The NSTA also said they saw "little, if any benefit to NSTA or its members." After the rejection elicited a great deal of negative comment, NSTA went on record as saying they would try to find another way to put the DVDs into the classrooms that didn't fall afoul of their policies. (The original NSTA press release dated November 30, 2006, was updated September 5, 2007, and the link to the letter from NSTA to Laurie David is not functioning.[6])

Some said the initial objection was occasioned by the fear of losing money from contributors such as Exxon. So, is the acceptance or rejection of teaching materials for your kids based on good science or political expediency? I can't answer for the NSTA, but I can help you take a closer look at what was reputed to be the impending environmental collapse of earth.

The hockey stick graph

Al Gore introduced the hockey stick graph in his film by saying, "Incidentally, this is the first time anybody outside of a small group of scientists have seen this image." Of course, Gore was partially right—the graph that showed our earth's temperature zooming up to unparalleled ranges had only recently found the light of day. But it was faked![7]

The cause of this dramatic rise in temperature, according to the graph-makers, was due to humankind's use of fossil fuels adding unendurable quantities of carbon dioxide to the air. Keep in mind that this and other climate change graphs are models—what the scientists think is going to happen based on their data—not actual temperatures. Apparently they sometimes do "backward" modeling as well.

The "hockey stick" virtually eliminates the Medieval Warm Period and the Little Ice Age. That bit of deceit should be enough for an honest scientist to disregard the graph in its entirety. There is ample evidence that there *was* a Medieval Warming Period and a Little Ice Age. Those who constructed the hockey stick graph chose to ignore that. Perhaps it didn't fit their scenario.

Reliable data from marine studies

Sea life found in the sediment on the floor of the Sargasso Sea and in the Caribbean showed the temperature was about 2°F cooler during the Little Ice Age. In the ocean off West Africa, temperatures dropped three to four degrees.

A study of marine organisms in the Bermuda Triangle area showed temperatures before 500 BC were as much as 4°F *warmer than today*. And guess what? Those people weren't racing around the streets in fossil-fuel-consuming vehicles.

The South African Journal of Science carried a report that stated "The climate of the interior of South Africa was around 1°C (1.8°F) cooler in the Little Ice Age and may have been more than 3°C (5.4°F) higher than at present during the extremes of the Medieval Warm Period."[8]

The primary author of the paper containing the "hockey stick" is Michael Mann, who held an adjunct faculty position in the Department of Geosciences at the University of Massachusetts, and after receiving his PhD became an Assistant Professor at the University of Virginia in the Department of Environmental Sciences. He has to be a smart man. Why did he choose to foster a lie?

The most inconvenient truth

The most inconvenient truth is that *An Inconvenient Truth* is a packet of lies. Lies? That's a strong word. Not many people want to use it today. It's offensive. But aren't the lies themselves really what is offensive?

The High Court in London said it would send a corrected guidance note to all the secondary schools in England, making clear the mainstream scientific position on the nine errors it had identified in *An Inconvenient Truth*. The Court said if it had not issued that guidance, the judge "would have made a finding that the Government's distribution of the film and the first draft of the guidance note earlier in 2007 to all English secondary schools had been an unlawful contravention of an Act of Parliament *prohibiting the political indoctrination of children.*" (Emphasis mine.)

The Science & Public Policy Institute carries a report by Christopher Monckton, dated October 18, 2007 that claims there are thirty-five errors in the movie.[9] Here are a few:

- Sea level rising—If the West Antarctica and Greenland ice sheets both melted, they would add only about 2.5 inches to the sea level—not the six meters (almost 20 feet) Al Gore trumpeted.
- Increased levels of carbon dioxide caused rising temperatures—Instead, the scientific papers on which Al Gore said he relied made it clear that temperature changes *preceded* the change in levels of CO_2 by anywhere from 800 to 2,800 years.
- Snows of Kilimanjaro are melting because of global warming —The melting of the Furtwangler Glacier at the summit of the mountain began 125 years ago.

What is behind the climate change furor?

The United States government spends $22 billion each year on global warming initiatives.[10] That's twice as much as it spends to protect our borders. Where is all that money going? Who is benefiting?

Wind subsidies

The federal government subsidizes wind power. Congress voted in 2013 not to extend this subsidy for wind farms, but the IRS extended it. It had been costing the taxpayers about $5 billion a year for twenty-three years. That adds up to about $115 billion. The IRS's extension (not authorized by Congress) will add another $13 billion.

Wind energy supplied only 1.6% of all of the energy used in the United States in 2014. The Department of Energy wants a *permanent* subsidy to make certain the wind farms don't go bankrupt while trying to reach their goal of 20%.

Warren Buffett said, "[W]e get a tax credit if we build a lot of wind farms. That's the only reason to build them. They don't make sense without the tax credit."[11]

Letting the sun shine in on solar subsidies

I am a big fan of using the sun's energy. That's as close to sustainable as you can get—until you realize that you just can't use the sun all by itself to power your car or produce electricity for your home. It needs "stuff" to help it. And up to this time, that stuff has just been too expensive to be practical. In spite of our federal government pouring about $39 billion in solar subsidies into the industry in the last five years, only one-half of one percent of all the electricity generated in the United States in the first ten months of 2014 came from solar.[12]

The Ivanpah Solar Electric Generating System in the Mojave Desert is the largest solar power plant of its kind in the world. There are three towers, each surrounded by mirrors. The mirrors convert the sun's energy to heat (800°F.) The heat converts water into steam, and the steam generates electricity.

But—and this is hard to imagine—the sun in the *desert* doesn't always shine enough to do the job. The generating system has to rely on natural gas to heat the water when sunlight takes a vacation. (You can't make this stuff up.)

Ivanpah asked for permission from the state of California to burn more natural gas. This additional use of natural gas to produce the power will increase the amount of carbon dioxide to almost 95,000 tons emitted each year into the atmosphere—that's something like running more than 16,000 cars on traditional gasoline. It's enough to supply the needs of over one-third of the homes this solar plant is supposed to furnish with power. The cost of the Ivanpah Generating Station was $2.2 billion. A gas turbine power plant, designed to produce the equivalent amount of power would cost about $630 million.[13]

Diana Furchtgott-Roth, who was a chief economist at the U. S. Department of Labor, said that if you replace the electricity generated by natural gas with electricity generated by solar power, we'd see our electric bills increase about 25%.

The solar panel manufacturer Solyndra declared bankruptcy after receiving a government loan of $527 million. Solyndra wasn't the only company to receive funds from the federal government and fail. An Internet search for "what solar companies received money from government" will provide a list. Click on the Free Republic's "List of Failed Obama Green Energy & Solar Companies in the Billions."

If federal tax credits, grants, guaranteed loans, and various other subsidies weren't enough, there are forty-three tax breaks available related to solar power and 538 state and local green energy rebate programs.[14] It isn't working. That "stuff" the sun needs is still too expensive for most people to bite.

I believe in using solar energy. I truly wish the technology could live up to expectations.

Ethanol subsidies

The federal government has a way of moving forward those ventures it deems valuable. The method most often used is to subsidize them. In the "real" world known as capitalism, one gets an idea for a product or service, develops it at personal expense, and hopes at some point it will prove successful enough to return the investment and a profit.

The government gets an idea for a product or service, pays people to develop it, gives loans to keep the businesses up and running, and quite often they declare bankruptcy rather than a profit. That is the way green energy products have been brought to market. Congress seldom dares to oppose such subsidies, because each one of the beneficiaries is a prospective voter when the time for reelection comes around. And some contribute significantly to that reelection effort. (For lack of space, I decided to put some of the information I've uncovered about subsidies on my website at DibsOnYourKids.com.)

As alternative fuels, most particularly ethanol, are such a large part of what your kids learn in the classes on saving our environment, I do want to point out a few errors in what they may be learning about ethanol:

- There is not enough arable land to grow the crops used for ethanol that EPA directives require.
- The cost of producing ethanol is high. It cannot be competitive with oil unless the government helps pay for it.
- In the United States, per unit of energy produced, biofuels made from corn and other crops get twenty-five times the amount of subsidies as fossil fuels.
- Corn ethanol does not provide as much energy as an equal amount of gasoline.
- Two-thirds of the sugars in the crops are emitted as carbon dioxide
- In 2013 the United States used 40% of the entire harvest of corn to produce ethanol fuel.
- Unless switchgrass or cellulosics are used, there are many energy inputs required to grow the crops (fertilizer, water, etc.)
- A 2014 report issued by The Intergovernmental Panel on Climate Change (IPCC), admits that some biofuels' indirect emissions can actually produce greater total emissions than petroleum (fossil fuel) products.
- The summary of the same IPCC report states, "Increasing bioenergy crop cultivation poses risks to ecosystems and biodiversity."

That information is most likely not available to your kids as they study the environment, and the effect of the use of fossil fuels. Yet, it turns the production and use of corn ethanol or soybean biodiesel on its head. And those I've listed don't even address the additional problems that occur when using land to grow corn for ethanol that should be growing food crops.

A brief look at sustainability

In order to properly evaluate claims that certain alternative fuels are sustainable, you must understand some basics about sustainability. Many elementary classrooms feature sustainability as being desirable in our alternative fuels, but most kids don't really know what "sustainable" means.

To be sustainable a product must be able to be produced as far into the future as can be imagined without a declining supply. The environment must continue forever without damage caused by producing that product, and without making either the fuel or other products needed, such as food, cost more.

Fuel produced from corn is renewable but not sustainable because of:

- the detrimental effect it has on the land and waterways
- the constantly increasing need for fertilizer
- the reduction of the availability of land to be used to produce food
- the resultant increased cost of food.

> In 2008, while Barack Obama was a presidential candidate, he said, "So if somebody wants to build a coal-powered plant, they can; it's just that it will bankrupt them, because they're going to be charged a huge sum for all that greenhouse gas that's being emitted. Under my plan of a cap-and-trade system, electricity rates would necessarily skyrocket. Even regardless of what I say about whether coal is good or bad. Because I'm capping greenhouse gases, coal power plants, you know, natural gas, you name it—whatever the plants were, whatever the industry was, they would have to, uh, retrofit their operations. That will cost money. They will pass that money on to consumers."

Cap-and-trade

Your kids probably won't study cap-and-trade in school—but they might, depending on what age they are. And it's important that you know a little about it if you don't already. The sidebar quotes then-candidate Barack Obama speaking about his support of cap-and-trade. What is "cap-and-trade"?

To take it down to its bare essentials, some entities get permission to spew forth greenhouse gases up to a certain amount. That is the "cap" part. Then these entities can buy or sell those emission rights on the open market. That's the "trade" part. The regulated firms could buy "carbon offsets" instead of actually cutting back on their emissions. This process would end up, as Candidate Obama promised, significantly raising prices. The low- and middle-income households, the ones who can afford it least, would end up paying most—between $31 and $512 more every year because of higher prices.[15]

Ottmar Edenhofer, a co-chairman of the IPCC, stated in 2010, "But one must say clearly that we redistribute de facto the world's wealth by climate policy."

The Bolivarian Alliance for the Peoples of Our America has a graph with a subheading, "Need to cut emissions by at least 50% and transfer resources to fund a global green future." It shows by 2025, by their reasoning, the United States must cut emissions 57%, the European Union 54%, Japan 58%, and the United Kingdom 54%. It also gives an amount of funding from each of those countries to go to sixteen nations that would amount to over *one trillion dollars*.[16]

Renewable electrical energy standards

The cap-and-trade program creates renewable electricity standards. The big utility companies are required to produce an ever-increasing portion of their electricity from renewable sources. Let's take a look at how that's working.

The U.S. Energy Information Administration (EIA) report for 2014 tells us approximately 67% of the electricity generated in 2014 was from fossil fuels (coal, natural gas, and petroleum). Following those sources, 19% came from nuclear, 6% from hydropower, 4.4% from wind, 1.7% from biomass, 0.4% from geothermal, and 0.4% from solar. That totals 6.9% produced from wind, biomass, geothermal, and solar—those determined to be "renewable" sources.

The 6% hydropower isn't included in the total, because by environmentalist proponents' own standards, it is not a desirable source of energy. They are trying to shut down dams and prevent the building of future dams. According to the 2009 EIA standards, the amount of electricity those renewable sources should be producing by 2025 is 25%. We have a way to go.

Don't forget that Warren Buffett said that if it weren't for the subsidies there would be no point in having wind farms at all—and wind is the largest producer (4.4%) of our "renewable" electricity.

In 2009, at the beginning of President Barack Obama's first term, the EPA was going to give a recommendation for regulating carbon dioxide using the means of cap-and-trade. It asked Alan Carlin PhD, a 38- year employee of the EPA, to head the preparation of a report. Carlin's report was suppressed, and the EPA went ahead with its recommendations. They told Carlin "The administrator and the administration has decided to move forward . . . and your comments do not help the legal or policy case for this decision."

What had Carlin reported that drew the ire of the EPA? He said, "My personal view is that there is not currently any reason to regulate carbon dioxide. There may be in the future. *But global temperatures are roughly where they were in the mid-20th century. They're not going up, and if anything they're going down.*" (Emphasis mine.)

But we're having the highest temperatures ever

No, we're not! Yes, the National Oceanic and Atmospheric Administration (NOAA) and the National Aeronautics and Space Administration (NASA) recently reported that 2014 was the hottest in 135 years of keeping the records.

> If every person on the planet were allotted the same amount of energy consumption and carbon emission, according to the Stockholm Environment Institute's "equity" evaluations, to get to sustainable levels the United States would have to cut CO_2 emissions by over 90% just to meet their lowest requirement.[17]

Isn't that proof of catastrophic global warming? *No.*

That rise in temperature is a move up of 1/100th of a degree. It went from an average 58.45°F to 58.46°F. Climatologist Judith Curry said, "With 2014 essentially tied with 2005 and 2010 for hottest year, this implies that there has been essentially no trend in warming over the past decade."[18] NOAA and NASA disagreed. NOAA said the average temperature was 58.24°, and NASA said it was 58.42° degrees. I don't know who relayed the data to those two agencies or if that was a typo, but they are both cooler than the scorching 58.45° average.

Additional statistics show that the global mean surface temperature has not gone up for the last eighteen consecutive years. Ask your kids if they are learning that in their science classes. If we believe the data that CO_2 levels have risen 9% in the last eighteen years, why hasn't the temperature gone up with it, as our global warming advocates claim it should, has, and will continue to do?

What else throws cold water on global warming?

- In December 2013 Cairo, Egypt, had its first snowfall in 100 years.
- In December 2013 Oregon, along with other states, had the coldest temperatures in forty years.
- Again in December 2013, Antarctica's temperature was the coldest ever recorded anywhere on planet earth—ever!
- In January 2014 Chicago temperatures were the coldest ever recorded for that city.
- December 2014 brought reports that the North Polar ice cap is increasing in size. NASA's satellite images indicate it could be anywhere from 43% to 63% growth.
- In 2015 Boston broke its seasonal snowfall record with 108.6 inches.
- The *USA Today* section of the April 12, 2015 *Arizona Republic* newspaper ran a headline "2nd-straight below-average hurricane season seen." The article stated, "The tropical Atlantic

has anomalously cooled over the past several months . . ."

In light of those statistics, how do you evaluate Al Gore's statement in his Nobel Prize acceptance speech in 2007 for his global warming initiative? He said, "The North Polar ice cap is falling off a cliff. It could be completely gone in summer in as little as seven years. Seven years from now."

He didn't ever think of backing down. In a speech in 2009 he said, "The entire north polar ice cap during some of the summer months could be completely ice-free within the next five to seven years."

In December 2014 Dr. Benny Peiser, from the Global Warming Policy Forum (GWPF), commented on the latest research data, saying the supposed effects of global warming are unpredictable. "The Antarctic is actually growing and all the evidence in the last few months suggests many assumptions about the poles were wrong. Global sea ice is at a record high, another key indicator that something is working in the opposite direction of what was predicted. . . . Most people think the poles are melting . . . they're not. This is a huge inconvenience that reality is now catching up with climate alarmists, who were predicting that the poles would be melting fairly soon."

If you follow things on Twitter, you may have read President Obama's tweet on May 16, 2014: "97% of scientists agree: climate change is real, man-made and dangerous."

Not well publicized are comments from some of the scientific-type global warming champions that refute their own stated beliefs. An e-mail from Kevin Trenberth, who is in the Climate Analysis Section of the USA National Center for Atmospheric Research read: "The fact is that we can't account for the lack of warming at the moment and it is a travesty we can't."

The man who may have started the whole global warming brouhaha, Claude Allegre, recently said he could no longer support the idea that any global warming can be attributed to human activities. His revised opinion has made no difference at all in the pro-global warming enthusiasts' pursuit of monumental change in the quality of life of the population of the world.

There is a breath of fresh air. In April 2015 the West Virginia Board of Education passed a resolution to end what had been months of dispute regarding climate change studies. They agreed to change the teaching standards to permit students to consider both sides of arguments regarding climate change. They stated that "science is never settled" and debating the subject "will lead students into a deeper understanding of the issue." It is probably no surprise that the groups holding a pro-global warming stance were a bit upset.

The changes don't seem all that dramatic. Originally students could only consider *rises* in temperature. The standards replaced the word "rises" with "changes." They also can now give consideration to "natural forces" in addition to human activity when evaluating climate changes.

I want to make clear that I am not a climatologist who can say with certainty that there presently is no global warming. I also cannot say with certainty that our climate is not being affected by the way humans are living on this earth, although that is what I believe. From what I have read, and listened to, and studied, I believe climate change will happen in the natural course of things, and that we should be good stewards of the great and beautiful earth God prepared for us. It is my sincere hope that your kids (and all people) are not being misled. Let us at least have a dialogue.

✝

"Rather, we have renounced secret and shameful ways; we do not use deception, nor do we distort the word of God. On the contrary, by setting forth the truth plainly we commend ourselves to everyone's conscience in the sight of God" (2 Corinthians 4:2).

Chapter Challenge

Check your kids' textbooks to see what their science classes will be teaching about global warming and climate change. Ask their teachers if they will be teaching what is in the book and if there will be opportunity to offer dissenting opinions. If not, press harder. Go to the principal, the school board, your state's Board of Education. Teaching without opportunity for discussion is brainwashing.

Use the example of the people in West Virginia, and when nothing else works, make an effort to change the laws of your state. In that case students at the University of West Virginia and Marshall University testified before the Board, and CFACT readers (cfact.org) sent the Board their comments. You can read the e-mail comment CFACT sent on their website.

Go to the National Center for Policy Analysis (ncpa.org) and under the Research tab, search for an article dated January 23, 1998, titled "Who's Afraid of CO2."[19] Granted it is relatively old, but the science on which the article is based hasn't changed. Make copies of it to pass around.

Choose one from each of the mediums listed below and start to learn more about the subjects your kids are being taught in school.

Resources for teaching your kids about climate change

Please note that I recommend you teach your kids about climate change. As with evolution, they cannot reasonably refute the theory of catastrophic climate change unless they know more than they will learn in school and various mediums. It follows that you can't explain it to them unless you understand it.

Books

- 2006. *Global Warming*. Edited by Cynthia A. Bily, Opposing Viewpoints. New York: Greenhaven Press.
- Spencer, Roy W. 2008. *Climate Confusion: How Global*

Warming Hysteria Leads to Bad Science, Pandering Politicians, and Misguided Policies That Hurt the Poor. New York: Encounter Books.

- Sussman, Brian. 2010. *Climategate: A Veteran Meteorologist Exposes the Global Warming Scam*. First ed: WND Books.

Videos and Movies

- Durkin, Martin. 2007. *The Great Global Warming Swindle* (DVD). Wag TV.
- Guggenheim, Davis. 2006. *An Inconvenient Truth*. Paramount.

Websites

- Climate Depot: A project of CFACT – http://www.climatedepot.com/.
- Humanbeingsfirst – http://print-humanbeingsfirst.blogspot.com/2009/11/let-co-conspiracy-theorist-climategate.html.
- Monckton, Christopher. The Viscount Monckton of Brenchley. 2013. "The Logical Case Against Climate Panic." Online: Science & Public Policy Institute. http://scienceandpublicpolicy.org/images/stories/papers/originals/logical_case.pdf. This one is certain to drive climate alarmists nuts. They can't stand Lord Monckton or anything he has to say. If you read this report and like his style, check out other of his reports. He's an interesting man.
- Watts Up With That?: The world's most viewed site on global warming and climate change. http://wattsupwiththat.com.

Who's Got Dibs on Your Kids' MORALITY?

Is 'Saving Yourself for Marriage' Obsolete?

"As for you, see that what you have heard from the beginning remains in you. If it does, you also will remain in the Son and in the Father. And this is what he promised us—eternal life. I am writing these things to you about those who are trying to lead you astray" (1 John 2:24-26).

This chapter needs a caveat. I am not comfortable with much of what is contained in this chapter. The problem is that everything in this chapter may be presented to your kids! If you would rather not confront this material, I understand. Just be aware that, as offensive as it is, your kids may be dealing with it, and unless they tell you about it you may never know what is going on.

♈

We'd decided to take a small vacation and do some rock hunting. Our first, and at that time only son, was about four years old, and a day's driving had him itching to relieve his restlessness. A motel perched high on a hill with separate cabins and a lot of green space between them beckoned us. Pulling into the parking area, we let our son out of his seat, and unrestrained, he took off running. We called to him to stop—stop now! But he was four after all, and his daddy was in hot pursuit. Great fun.

What we could see, and he couldn't, and couldn't possibly understand the danger, was a two-rail white fence that bordered the property, and on the other side of it was a deep chasm. He was running straight for it. Suddenly his feet slipped on the long wet grass. He went sliding right under the lower rail, and was already dangling over the edge of the precipice when my husband grabbed him by the hand and pulled him back to safety. Our son never realized how close he came to death—but we did. It changed the way we let him out of the car, and when and how we let him roam from that time forward. I still thank God that we were in time that day.

A child seems to be born with a desire for danger, for living on the edge. Push your kids on a swing and they'll cry, "Higher! Higher!" They want to slide down the steepest part of the snowy hill on their sleds. They find it impossible to not put the tip of a finger on something that has a "Don't Touch—Wet Paint" sign. You may remember feeling that way, too. There is something very exciting about danger. You are not always there to shout "Stop—stop *now*!"

The Pied Pipers of impurity know that's how your kids feel, and they will exploit it every chance they get—and if they don't see a ready opportunity, they'll make one.

As a Christian, you may wonder why anyone would want to charm your kids into a life of sin. I know I do. The only answer I can come up with is that Satan is at work, ceaselessly, to bring everyone he can down with him. One cliché that still has real meaning is "misery loves company." Satan's followers hate it when God's Word stands before them like a 1,000 watt spotlight. It makes them and all who see them in that light painfully aware of their sin, shame, and degradation.

If your kids are in public school they may be taught that immorality is not only expected, but it is good. An article just crossed my desk with the headline, "Media Blitz to 'Normalize' Transgenderism." You can't rest easy even if you have chosen a private or parochial school, or if you homeschool, if there is a concerted media blitz.

I'll get to how the media influences your kids later, but first let's see what in store for kids in school. We'll start early, because that's where the Pied Pipers of immorality will be starting.

ABCs, 123s, and *What*?!?

In 2010, the Helena, Montana, school board adopted a program called "Health Enhancement Curriculum" teaching about sex to kindergarteners.[1] The sex education the school board designed would teach the proper name for body parts—all of them—in kindergarten. They introduce the concept in first grade that love doesn't have to be between a man and a woman, but it can also be between two men, or two women. Oh, don't worry though, they don't actually teach homosexuality until fifth grade.

In fifth grade the kids also learn that sexual intercourse "includes but is not limited to vaginal, oral, or anal penetration." (Maybe it's just me, but I don't think this is what I'd want my ten-year-old focusing on.) In 2011, and again in 2013, the State legislature passed a bill to allow parents to "opt in" for their kids to receive the controversial sex education. Both times the sitting Montana governor vetoed it.

In 2013, Chicago passed a law to provide sex education to kindergarteners. Most schools at that time began sex education in fifth grade. The CEO of the Chicago Public School System, Stephanie A. Whyte, was quoted as saying, "By implementing a new sexual health education policy, we will be helping them to *build a foundation of knowledge* that can guide them not just in the preadolescent and adolescent years, but throughout their lives." (Emphasis mine.) The law mandates at least 300 minutes a year of sex education for kindergarten through fourth grade, and 675 minutes for fifth through twelfth grades.

She also stated, "It is important that we provide *students of all ages* with *accurate* and *appropriate information so they can make healthy choices* in regards to *their social interactions, behaviors and relationships*." Again the emphasis is mine, but I want you to be aware of the significance of this. *They* will be building the foundation of knowledge. Not you, the parent. Not the church and Sunday School they attend. The Chicago Public School System will build Chicago's kids' foundation of knowledge.

This new sex education program covers all grades, and it intentionally falls into line with President Obama's national HIV/AIDS policy. Even if you don't live in Chicago, this kind of sex education may be coming to a school near you.

An article I read gave details of what was included in Chicago's fifth grade sex education because parents were appalled both by the language and the graphics. However, it was so shocking to me I will not repeat it here. The article called it "raunchy." Nevertheless Chicago's ten-year-olds will get the full dose unless their parents use the opt out prerogative.

The promoters of this sex education program quote the statistics that over 50% of the students in the Chicago public school system claim to have had sexual intercourse, and 12% of those started before they were thirteen years old. More than one-third said they didn't use condoms, emphasizing that Cook County has more cases of sexually transmitted diseases than any place else in the United States. Those statistics are stunning, but I go back to God's Word that instructs us to abstain from sexual immorality. Peter exhorts us to live Godly lives in a pagan society: "Dear friends, I urge you, as foreigners and exiles, to abstain from sinful desires, which wage war against your soul" (1 Peter 2:11). Public schools seldom teach abstinence.

The Sexuality Information and Education Council of the United States (SIECUS) produced a 112-page publication, *Guidelines for Comprehensive Sexuality Education: Kindergarten through 12th Grade – 3rd Edition.*[2] The intent is that it be used by educators as a tool to see how good their present sex education programs are, and develop new ones. If you start looking into the various entities providing resources for sex education, you'll run across SIECUS and Planned Parenthood frequently. They're big players in the sex education market.

A list of the twenty members of the Task Force that worked on *Guidelines* identifies two as having represented the reporting organization SIECUS. Three were with Planned Parenthood. Three were Independent Sexuality Education Consultants. Three represented public schools in Missouri, New Jersey, and Connecticut. One was with New York University, and one with Indiana University. The remaining had a variety of applicable interests; one of each were with the March of Dimes Birth Defects Foundation, National School Boards Association, Centers for Disease Control and Prevention, New Jersey Medical School, American School Health Association, American Medical Association, and National Education Association.

As a matter of background and introduction, *Guidelines* states while parents should be the kids main source of information about sex and sexuality, they need outside help which can come from faith-based institutions, organizations, and schools. If you read that list of participants in the Task Force carefully you may have noticed it included persons affiliated with a variety of organizations and schools—but not a single faith-based institution. Not surprisingly, the National Abstinence Education Association was also absent.

Think back to the 1990s. What were you doing then? Were you happy? Getting along fairly well? No matter, SIECUS decided you were badly suffering from a lack of first-rate sex education. They had to do something. The first *Guidelines* was issued in 1991. Parents all across America could breathe a sigh of relief. The sex education of you and your kids would now be in good hands.

Some behaviors that *Guidelines* lists as desirable are paraphrased here:

- Decide what sex you are, and don't hassle others about what they think their sex is.
- After you find out that you don't have to do things the way society has always felt was "normal," you can decide if you want to get married or not; to which sex; have abortions because it was just an accident and you don't want to take care of a kid—what they consider "informed" choices.
- Have sex. Just make sure you both agree to it, you don't somehow take advantage of the other person (they call it "non-exploitative"), that you're honest about where you think this is all going, whether you have HIV/AIDS, that it is "pleasurable," and that you use protection.
- Know how to protect yourself properly and do it, so you don't get pregnant.
- Decide how you feel, what "your own values are" about killing your baby if you do accidentally get pregnant.

But parents can opt their child out of these classes, can't they? Perhaps, perhaps not. I'll talk more about the "opt out" process later.

Aside from sex education classes, is there a sexually oriented picture book on the reading shelves in your youngest kids' classrooms? Have you ever checked the books on the shelves in the classrooms and school libraries? It might be time to do that.

Planned Parenthood propaganda

Planned Parenthood is often accused of receiving federal money to be used for abortions. They respond with firm denials. Money from the government would never be used for abortions. Planned Parenthood claims abortions are only 3% of the services they provide; a different source says abortions amount to 94% of their services. The true assessment probably lies somewhere in-between, but as the company does not provide all the statistics needed, any number is just a guess.[3] Whatever part abortions play in Planned Parenthood's services, you should be aware of how another big piece of the monetary pie is used. In 2013 the federal government gave Planned Parenthood a large chunk of the $75 million allocated for Personal Responsibility Education Programs. Abby Johnson, a former Planned Parenthood clinic director, said that "part of Planned Parenthood's curriculum is to demonstrate different sexual positions with stuffed animals to children *in kindergarten*."[4] If that is true, it borders on pedophilia.

Unclothed anatomically correct cloth boy and girl dolls, including pubic hair, are also used for sex education. The female doll has a baby attached with a cord issuing from between its legs[5]

Early in 2015 a California school district's use of representatives from Planned Parenthood for their sex-education courses for thirteen- and fourteen-year-olds was exposed. One describes herself as a "pleasure activist." Another, when not speaking to your kids, provides demonstrations at a sex-toy porn store. I know outside speakers are not required to have teaching credentials, but this seems a bit much.

In these sex lessons, young teens were told that their gender was not necessarily fixed. They were given a checklist on how to prepare for having sex. And lest the boys be guilty of rape, (although it's not clear they were taught about statutory rape) they were instructed to ask if it was "okay if I take off my pants?"[6]

Parents found out about these rather unusual teachers and a clamor arose. The school district said, "Two schools within our district are using highly trained educators from Planned Parenthood this year to assist in the delivery of sexual health and HIV/AIDS prevention education under the direct supervision of the credentialed classroom teacher and within the requirements and parameters of the Education Code." They also claimed that "the value of abstinence is emphasized." I'd like them to verify that. The school district does not do background checks on the "educators" they bring in from outside. Does yours?

If your kids don't get enough of the information they are looking for at school, they can always go into a Planned Parenthood clinic. One woman, posing as a fifteen-year-old girl, was told about men getting pleasure from whips and being tied by their sex partner, even walking them on a leash like an animal. The Planned Parenthood counselor said it would "be helpful if you guys [the pretend fifteen-year-old] read the book [*Fifty Shades of Grey*]."[7]

See, all Planned Parenthood's money from our government *doesn't* go to abortions!

This is "textbook"

Do your high-school-age kids have a textbook for sex education? If so, have you read it? The Fremont Unified School District in California chose to use *Your Health Today* for the 2014-2015 school year. Some of the parents looked at it and were up in arms. According to the local television station the book covers masturbation, bondage, orgasms, the use of vibrators, and how to buy and use condoms. It also uses photographs and diagrams "that parents think are too explicit for their teens."[8]

Not exactly a textbook, but in a middle school in Pennsylvania kids were given word-search puzzles based on *Fifty Shades of Grey*.

I have not read the book, much less the trilogy, but I understand it contains a lot of graphic sexual material. What good could a word-search puzzle based on that do for a middle-schooler? This was not some early-teenager's weird joke. The puzzles were handed out to the class by the teacher. A school board member said the teacher had distributed them "by mistake."

And then there's the uproar that occurred in a Board of Education meeting in Texas back in 2004. The Board was considering using sex education textbooks that stress "abstinence, and not much else." The Board was trying to decide which of four textbooks to use. Only one, ever so briefly, mentioned condoms. Many parents thought it should at least bring up condoms to help prevent sexually transmitted diseases (STDs) and pregnancy.

A young girl at that meeting, a student at a Catholic school, voiced her opinion that telling kids about contraceptives gives them a false sense of security. She said, "It's false information. Our book would be lying to us, our teachers would be lying to us. Abstinence is the only thing that's 100% effective." Smart girl. Don't you wish all members of Boards of Education, parents, and teachers were that smart?

A teacher had a different viewpoint: "Sex is a part of being a person, and we need to teach all of the facts and details that kids need to know to protect themselves. Kids who are on their second pregnancy, kids who have botched abortions, kids who get married at 13, none of these are good solutions to the problem." I agree *in part*. Those troubled kids do need a different kind of help. They need to hear that what they have done is wrong, but also that God is ready to forgive them, and to help them put their lives back on a God-pleasing path. Abstinence would be both God-pleasing and would keep their problems from escalating. Do you participate in your kids' schools' Board of Education meetings? It sounds like they could get interesting.

Planned Parenthood stated that polls in Arizona, and national polls as well, show most parents want their kids to take sex education classes in school. A 2013 survey of 700 Arizona households indicated that 70% of those contacted were in favor of "medically accurate, age appropriate" sex education in secondary schools. It did not ask, or at least indicate a response, about the desirability of sex education in middle grade and lower classes. The survey was conducted by Planned Parenthood Arizona and the Phoenix-based Behavior Research Center.

Promiscuity

I agree with Thomas Sowell, who questioned in one of his Washington Times columns, why it takes "years and years" to teach school children sex education. He answered his own question: "Obviously it does not. What takes years and years is to wear down the values they were taught at home and lead them [Pied Piperish] toward wholly different attitudes and wholly different conceptions of the world."

Many of the schools sex education programs say they teach abstinence as a way to prevent unwanted pregnancies, but it may be something as weak as "Of course the only certain way to avoid pregnancy and sexually transmitted diseases is abstinence, but we know you're all going to do it anyway, so you may as well learn the safe way." That is an interpretation, but "Abstinence Only vs. Comprehensive Sex Education"[9] lists what is included in the Abstinence-Plus Education program:

- Promote abstinence from sex
- Acknowledge that many teenagers will become sexually active
- Teach about contraception and condom use
- Include discussions about contraception, abortion, sexually transmitted diseases and HIV

What part does the government play?

Perhaps a look at the views of Cass Sunstein, the administrator of the Office of Information and Regulatory Affairs 2009–2012, (often called the regulatory czar) will give us additional insight about what is planned for your kids. In his book *The Partial Constitution* he states, "Restrictions on abortion, surrogacy and free availability of pornography are troublesome . . ." and in a 2003 book review, Sunstein argued there is no moral concern regarding cloning human beings since human embryos, which develop into a baby, are "only a handful of cells." Do the views held by an unelected member of the President's administration filter into law? You have to stay alert, and be aware of outside forces that may affect your kids' attitudes and lives.

If the school your kids attend makes condoms available, you should know about the 1996 case, *Curtis v. School Committee of Falmouth* (Case No. 95-617). The U.S. Supreme Court declined to hear it so the lower Court ruling stood. That case was decided *against* the parents who objected to the Falmouth, Massachusetts school district's policy of not allowing parents to exclude their children from condom distribution, or to require parents be notified if their kids request a condom. These contraceptive devices are provided free to junior and senior high school students.

In 2013 the Boston Public School Committee voted 5–0 to expand their condom distribution from nineteen high schools to all thirty-two in the district. Parents in this case can refuse to let them be provided to their kids "by notifying the school when they complete the family information forms at the beginning of the school year."

In spring of 2014 the mayor of Chicago called the decision to distribute condoms in twenty-eight of the Chicago public high schools "a bow to reality." The program started in fall 2014, paid for by a $20 million federal grant. The Chicago Health Commissioner called this distribution "one tool" to help students make "educated decisions" before having sex.

As of December 2012, there were twenty-two Philadelphia high schools distributing free condoms. Washington, D.C. public high schools gave away 200,000 condoms in 2011. That's about sixteen to each student.

In 2014 Gervais County, Oregon, schools began giving condoms away to both high school and *middle school* students. They did not find themselves up against much objection from parents.

Do the schools your kids attend distribute free condoms? If they do, and you are okay with that, fine. If you don't like the idea, try to eliminate the program or at least push for a parental "opt in" process. Failing that, at least see that there is an "opt out" available.

The day after a day that can't have a do-over

Is your daughter at risk of having an abortion without your knowledge or approval? Are you at risk of losing a grandchild you will never see? If you think that's not possible, not in your life, consider the fact that since Roe v. Wade almost 60 million babies have been aborted.[10] Of that number, 18% of the mothers-to-be are ages fifteen to nineteen. That's almost 10,800,000 babies. They could have been born. They could have been cared for by the mother or grandmother. They could have been adopted. But they are gone. And in many instances, schools are facilitating the abortions.

Earlier this chapter covered the sex education material designed by the Sexuality Information and Education Council of the United States (SIECUS). Their document of *Guidelines*, a framework for sex education curriculum from kindergarten through grade twelve, divided into Levels by age ranges, also addresses abortion. The indoctrination for kindergarteners reads: "Abortion . . . When a woman becomes pregnant and chooses not to have a child, she has the option of having an abortion."[11] A "Developmental Message" in Level 1 tells the kindergarteners "Sometimes women become pregnant when they do not want to be or are unable to care for a child." Level 1 is to be used for kids ages five to eight.

There has been a lot of outrage about teaching masturbation in kindergarten, and while the *Guidelines* definitely address it, Chicago says they are not going to do that. Apparently they move it to Level 2.

Level 2 covers kids nine through twelve, Level 3 ages twelve through fifteen, and Level 4 ages fifteen through eighteen. Let's take a short stroll down Level Lane.

Level 2 tells your kids that if a woman gets pregnant and doesn't want to be she can carry the baby to term and raise it, give it up for adoption, or have an abortion. It confirms that abortion is legal up to a certain point in the pregnancy, it must be done by a doctor or other licensed healthcare provider, and a legal abortion is very safe. The material states, "People have a variety of beliefs about the ethics and morality of abortion."

Level 3 explains that the way people feel about abortion is based on their religious, cultural, and family values—some religions support a woman's right to have an abortion and others do not. It acknowledges having an abortion is a difficult decision to make, and teenagers "can"—not "should"—talk with "parents, other family members, religious leaders, counselors, healthcare providers, or other trusted adults."

Level 3 also makes sure the girls know that their right to have an abortion is guaranteed by the Supreme Court with some state restrictions. Some states require a waiting period, permission from the parents, or permission from a judge. They assure the girls that no one can force them to have an abortion, abortions are safest in the first twelve weeks of the pregnancy, and after twenty-four weeks they can only have an abortion if their life is in danger. Finally, they confidently state that "having a legal abortion rarely interferes with a woman's ability to become pregnant or give birth in the future."

Level 4 builds on Levels 1, 2, and 3, informing your kids that they can have either a medical or surgical abortion, and "Emergency contraception (the morning-after pill) is *not* a method of abortion." (Emphasis mine.)

What are the risks associated with abortion?

Let's go back to that claim that "a legal abortion rarely interferes with a woman's ability to become pregnant or give birth in the future," and examine some of the associated hazards that your kids are seldom, if ever, told.

According to an article in the British Journal of Psychiatry,[12] women who had an abortion ran an 81% greater risk of mental health problems and a 59% greater risk of suicide than those who had not had an abortion. The risk of mental health problems goes up to 138% if compared to women who chose to carry a baby to full term.

Hope After Abortion's website at hopeafterabortion.com breaks the numbers down even more. Increased rates of problems in women with a history of abortion, compared to those who have not had an abortion, are startling.

Anxiety	34% Higher rate
Depression	37% Higher rate
Alcohol use and misuse	110% Higher rate
Marijuana use	230% Higher rate
Suicidal behavior	155% Higher rate

In the year after an abortion, *women are three times more likely to commit suicide* than all women of a reproductive age, and six times more likely to commit suicide than women who gave birth.[13]

The National Right to Life website informs us that surgical abortions can damage the uterus or cervix, which could present problems in future pregnancies. It also says that chemical abortions are "bloody, painful, and dangerous" and no one knows what the long term effects may be. The same fact sheet says that the risk of never being able to have a baby in the future is doubled. If a woman has more than one abortion, the risk of having a tubal pregnancy in the future is almost twice as high, and the possibility of a miscarriage of a future pregnancy is heightened.[14]

Parents, this goes beyond trying to stop the government and government schools from lying to your kids, and fostering the idea in your kids that abortion is okay. Look at those statistics. Whether it's your daughter or someone else's who has had an abortion, they need your help. Consider what must go through their minds the day after, and the day after that, and the day after that: *I let somebody kill my baby. My own baby. What kind of a horrible person am I? God can never forgive me. I think I'll kill myself, too.*

> "Tell me, Mellon, when did we let evil become stronger than us?"
>
> The Hobbit:
> The Desolation of Smaug

You know God forgives all sins. He loves your daughters and your daughters' friends, and wants them to end up with Him in heaven. You must let them know that, and try to put an end to abortion's resultant anxiety, depression, alcoholism, drug use, and suicides. Tell them to ask for His forgiveness. Tell them God has great things still in store for them: "'For I know the plans I have for you,' declares the Lord, 'plans to prosper you and not to harm you, plans to give you hope and a future'" (Jeremiah 29:11).

Don't let those Pied Pipers lead them until the door in the mountain-side shuts fast. God said, "For I will forgive their wickedness and will remember their sins no more" (Hebrews 8:12).

How do your kids get an abortion?

The ways in which kids can get an abortion depend on where you live. Thirty-eight states require some parental involvement; with most of those it means that only one parent has to consent or just be notified the abortion is about to take place. Some states let your kids substitute the approval of a grandparent or another adult relative. So, if your daughter finds out she is pregnant, and doesn't want you to know about it, she might be able to go to a twenty-one-year-old cousin to get approval for an abortion. Check your state's laws.

Most states have what is called a "judicial bypass" through which a judge can give approval for the abortion. There are specific criteria the judge is supposed to use in deciding whether to grant it. These criteria include considering the child's intelligence, her emotional stability, her understanding of the possible consequences of having an abortion, etc. While the criteria seem specific, it would seem the judge has great latitude in assessing them.

Some states, fortunately, make the judge have "clear and convincing evidence" that the girl is mature enough to make this life-changing decision. I cannot reconcile the explanations that college students go on spring break and overindulge in drinking and sex because they don't at that stage have the capability of using good judgment, but much younger girls *can* decide to have an abortion.

If your kids go online they will find on Planned Parenthood's website specific information relating to obtaining an abortion. Planned Parenthood makes the information very personal. An example is in the Delaware information where it is specifically addressing young girls: "Your state requires that one of *your* parents, a grandparent or a mental health professional be told of *your* decision 24 hours before *your* abortion. *A judge can excuse you* from this requirement. This law only applies to girls younger than 16." (Emphasis mine.)

The Guttmacher Institute provides an up-to-date chart on abortion laws by state, with a column indicating if a minor needs some sort of parental involvement in the decision making.[15] I found one website with a subheading on a page stating "Mandating Parental Involvement Jeopardizes Teenagers' Health."[16] The proposition that your involvement with your kids, in their best interest, jeopardizes their health is startling.

How much is taken out of your hands by your kid's school? Do an Internet search for "Can a school take a girl for an abortion?" and look at the results. An article titled "Schools arrange secret abortions" reports that a sixteen-year-old had an abortion arranged by a school counselor. The mother was appalled when she found out—four days later. Her daughter had been crying but she told her mother it was just normal teenage emotions, until the mother talked to some of her daughter's friends. The mother says the only consent form she signed permitted the school to treat her daughter at the school's health center for minor problems like a headache, or to give physical exams for sports. She was positive that the form did not in any way mention the possibility of abortion. Be very careful about signing any permission forms. They can be, and often are, misused.

Free speech comes at a price

Some kids have decided they want to fight back. I admire their courage. When the Gay Straight Alliance (GSA) hung posters in Wilson High School in Tacoma, Washington, that showed conjoined male symbols and conjoined female symbols and carried the statement "Love knows no limits," the school's Wilson Students for Life (WSFL) decided to hang posters of their own. One was a picture of a milk carton and the word "missing" over a baby's picture. Thc poster's caption read "Since Roe v. Wade 1/3 of our generation has been aborted."[17] The school refused to permit WSFL to hang it.

Another poster WSFL could not hang carried a Ronald Reagan quote: "I've noticed that everyone who is for abortion is already born." The federal Equal Access Act required that schools give each student group the same opportunities without discriminating against any group. The school thought it had the right to censor any message they considered offensive. Apparently homosexuality is not offensive, but keeping babies from being aborted is. The school lost in court, and now must permit WSFL to have similar events as are allowed the GSA. The school, however, has decided to prohibit all groups from hanging "opinion" posters.

In 2013 the Alliance Defending Freedom (ADF) got into the act on behalf of a sixth-grader who was kept from handing out fliers that took a pro-life stance. She was not distributing them during class time but only in the lunch period to other kids who seemed interested. One of the handouts said, "Save the baby humans. Stop Abortion."[18] Some students apparently found the fliers offensive, and the principal told the student she had to stop. The school's executive director sent an email to the girl's parents saying, "such political activism is limited to students in the School of Rhetoric [the high school] only. The school has a right to censor students without violating their free speech. In short, public schools have every right to prohibit student speech." *Wrong*! After ADF filed the federal lawsuit, the Nova Classical Academy revised its literature distribution policy. These handouts are now okay to give to fellow students and the school agrees that pro-life expression must be allowed.[19]

In 2015 there was a run-in at the University of Oregon between students and an anti-abortion preacher. The students snatched the preacher's "graphic" sign, ripped it up, and stomped on it. One of the students exclaimed, "This is not part of your First Amendment right." A campus cop told the preacher he could talk about abortion if he hid the sign and didn't compare abortion to the Holocaust.

One of the students who had grabbed the sign said, "I realized it was his property, but it was a piece of paper. I considered the sign obscene and offensive and intending to anger and start a scene. I didn't want to look at that obscenity." She also said she felt "emotionally threatened" by the sign. The incident was settled when another cop came along and said everyone could shout at each other as much as they wanted as long as there was no physical violence."[20]

You win some, you lose some

Some evangelical high school kids didn't fare so well. They tried to distribute "fetus dolls" that had a pro-life message attached. A three-judge panel in the U.S.Tenth Circuit Court of Appeals agreed that the school district had the right to not allow the kids to give out the dolls. In this case the problem was not that the message was about abortion, but because the dolls were causing a lot of disruption. The judges ruled against them and their dolls.

The Supreme Court said schools have the right to censor vulgar or obscene student speech in a school-sponsored context such as a newspaper. Also, schools can censor the kids' religious or political speech if they can show definitively that it would substantially disrupt the school or interfere with the rights of others. Think about that. In ordinary circumstances your kids and you, their parents, do not intentionally "substantially disrupt" classes or events if pro-abortion, pro-promiscuity, pro-homosexuality material is taught, displayed, or distributed. You would approach the teacher, the principal, or the Board of Education, but you would not demonstrate in a way to disrupt anything. The up-in-arms disruptive behavior seems always to be retaliatory, and initiated by the other side when opposing your views. That means that *your* views become those that are *causing* the disruption, and *your* views and efforts that will be forbidden!

In an article in *The Telegraph* in November 2014, Tim Stanley tells about accepting an invitation from the Oxford University Students for Life to debate the subject "This House believes Britain's Abortion Culture Hurts Us All." His reaction to what he encountered was, "I've discovered that you're only allowed to debate abortion there if a) you're a woman and b) you're all for it. Any other approach to the subject is liable to attract a mob." And attract a mob, he did. About sixty signed up to attend the debate, but 300 showed up to protest.

Are the Girls Scouts good for girls?

The Girl Scout Law, that the members are to live by, says they will be honest, fair, friendly, helpful, considerate, caring, courageous, strong, responsible, respectful, use resources wisely and make the world a better place. Although the Boy Scouts oath swears that they will remain "morally straight," the Girl Scouts pledge no such thing.

A Catholic priest has called one of the Planned Parenthood's programs their "Girl Scout Project," advocating "the contraceptive mentality—sex without conscience or consequence." Many parents are completely unaware that the Girls Scouts' program now includes family planning. Although the Girl Scouts website emphatically says they don't have anything to do with Planned Parenthood, they praise the founder of Planned Parenthood, Margaret Sanger, as an "eloquent woman." Some examples of how the Girls Scouts and Planned Parenthood interact are provided on the Fellowship of the Minds website:

- Girl Scouts of Northern California refers "at risk" girls to Planned Parenthood for help with "family planning."
- Girl Scouts of San Diego featured a Planned Parenthood speaker.
- Girl Scouts of Western New York works with Planned Parenthood and other pro-abortion groups in programs aimed at tween and teen girls "to reduce teen pregnancy."

Planned Parenthood in Waco, Texas, held an annual "Nobody's Fool" day for twenty-three years. "Nobody's Fool" was a sex education program for kids going into grades five through nine. Waco's Bluebonnet Girl Scout Council sponsored it for several years. What finally ended the program? A boycott against Girl Scout cookies.

The GSUSA held a workshop along with several other groups at the United Nations in 2010. Only girls could get in—no adults allowed. One of the booklets available was *Healthy, Happy and Hot: a Young Person's Guide to Their Rights, Sexuality and Living with HIV*. It contained the advice that "there are lots of different ways to have sex and lots of different types of sex. . . . Just have fun, explore, and be yourself."

Any girl who is a Girl Scout or Girl Guide is automatically a member of the World Association of Girl Guides and Girl Scouts (WAGGGS). WAGGGS has a strong advocacy for sexual and abortion rights. In 2012 WAGGGS participated in a Global Youth Forum where a "Declaration" was put together that demands unrestricted access to abortion, comprehensive sexuality education "free of religious intolerance" and the decriminalization of sex work.[21]

The national Girl Scouts organization is also part of other groups that promote abortions. One of those, The Coalition for Adolescent Girls, is now publicizing an event that will address teen intimate partner violence. Another member of that Coalition is Institute for Reproductive Health (IRH) at Georgetown University. Their statement reads, "IRH is committed to meeting the evolving family planning needs of women and couples throughout the lifecycle by ensuring they have access to a broad range of options within an informed choice context."

I'm saddened it has come to this. I think many girls derived great benefit from the Girl Scouts. I'm also saddened that I can no longer buy Girl Scout cookies. I love those cookies and look forward to them every year, but I cannot in good conscience support what the Girl Scouts of the United States of America has become.

In 2010, Congress cut off the funding for over 169 studies on the effectiveness of abstinence education. The studies were in different phases when the plug was pulled. Not only was the research ended, but all the community abstinence programs that were up and running stopped as well—and they were beginning to produce the hoped-for results.[22]

If your children learn about any and all aspects of love from any sources but you, compare what you think those sources might teach with what God says:

✝

"For everything in the world—the lust of the flesh, the lust of the eyes, and the pride of life—comes not from the Father but from the world" (1 John 2:16).

Chapter Challenge

Check your kids' textbooks and find out what they will be teaching about moral issues in general and sexual issues in particular. I've said this before, but it's so important it bears repeating—ask their teachers if they will be teaching what is in the book, and if there will be opportunity to offer dissenting opinions. If not, press harder. Again, go to the principal, the school board, your state's Board of Education. Determine the methods available to remove your child from the classes if it seems warranted.

You must pay attention to forms that the school wants you to sign. Look at the forms (assuming you kept copies of them) that you signed at the start of school last fall. Read them carefully. Find out about their opt in and opt out rules. Be sure to caution your kids to bring home every form from the school and hand it to you so you know it's there. Some forms are designed so that if the school doesn't hear from you, the school has the right to assume that you have given approval. If you haven't kept copies of these forms before, start that practice immediately.

Have a discussion with your kids, and find out what their school teaches about moral issues. Ask how they feel about it.

Check The Heritage Foundation website for additional information on promiscuity. The page "The Effectiveness of Abstinence Education Programs in Reducing Sexual Activity Among Youth" by Robert Rector affirms and amplifies much of what this chapter contains. Also look into the National Abstinence Education Association.

This chapter makes no attempt to thoroughly cover all of the moral issues your kids face today. There is a great deal of information available about each of the topics it touches on. Some of them you might want to access for more in-depth material:

Books

- *From Crayons to Condoms: The Ugly Truth about America's Public Schools* edited by Steve Baldwin and Karen Holgate
- *IndoctriNation: Public Schools and the Decline of Christianity* edited by Charles Laverdiere. Master Books.
- *You're Teaching My Child What?: A Physician Exposes the Lies of Sex Ed and How They Harm Your Child* by Miriam Grossman M.D.

Videos and Movies

- Gunn, Colin, and Joaquin Fernandez. *Indoctrination: Public Schools and the Decline of Christianity in America*. Gunn Productions, 2011. DVD.

Websites

- "Laws Restricting Teenagers' Access to Abortion." American Civil Liberties Union (ACLU), https://www.aclu.org/laws-restricting-teenagers-access-abortion. 4 May, 2015.
- "State Policies in Brief: Parental Involvement in Minors' Abortions." Guttmacher Institute, http://www.guttmacher.org/statecenter/spibs/spib_PIMA.pdf.4 May 2015.

Who's Got Dibs on Your Kids' GENDER?

The Evolution of Conscience

"All Scripture is God-breathed and is useful for teaching, rebuking, correcting and training in righteousness, so that the servant of God may be thoroughly equipped for every good work" (2 Timothy 3:16–17).

The year 2015 was troubling. January brought the Charlie Hebdo terrorist attack in Paris and the hotel shooting in Libya. As spring approached, there was a shooting in a museum in Tunisia. In May an attack was thwarted, but two men said to be "soldiers of the caliphate" opened fire at a Prophet Muhammad cartoon contest in Texas. Tunisia was hit again in June when thirty-eight people at a beach resort were shot. Still, 2015 had not had the last of terrorist attacks. In October an onboard bomb exploded on a Russian plane killing 244 people, and November was shattered by multiple simultaneous attacks in Paris at a concert, a sporting event, and cafes.

Then the unimaginable happened. A man born in the United States, along with his wife from the Middle East, shot and killed fourteen of the man's co-workers at a Christmas party in San Bernardino, California.[1]

The United States had been hit before by terrorists—no one will forget September 11, 2001—but those terrorists came from another country. Now, we realized, the threat was in our midst. The cry grew louder and louder for President Obama and his administration to call it what it was: Islamic extremist terrorism. You couldn't fight the enemy, it was claimed, unless you properly identified it—called it by its name.

Another troubling force has attacked our country, and it may even have infiltrated your own family. The promotion and widespread acceptance of homosexuality may not provide the visual carnage that shootings and bombings do, but it may be as harmful to our society. It is another enemy that cannot be turned from its destructive path unless we call it what it is. Your kids may be physically healthy, but their spiritual lives may be in grave danger.

If you don't identify it, you can't fight it

Lest you get caught up in euphemisms, a man having sex with a man, or a woman having sex with a woman is homosexuality. That sexual desire is not "gay" and the rainbow doesn't make it any prettier. There is definitely no pot of gold at the end. However, your kids aren't hearing that.

Surveys show that the approval or acceptance of same-sex marriage is growing every year. That should not surprise anyone. The homosexual agenda has been pushed in schools for decades, with the result that every year we have more reaching adulthood who have been nurtured in this deviant behavior. Let's look at what your kids have thrown at them. I use the word "thrown" intentionally—picture the information they see and hear as garbage. God tells us "It would be better for them to be thrown into the sea with a millstone tied around their neck than to cause one of these little ones to stumble" (Luke 17:2).

Where does the United States government stand on homosexuality? A book titled *Believer: My Forty Years in Politics* by David Axelrod, published in 2015, gives some insight. Mr. Axelrod was the political strategist for Barack Obama, and directed the campaigns that got the community organizer elected to the Senate in 2005 and president of the United States in 2008. In his book he states that Obama lied about his views on homosexuality when he was running for office. Axelrod says he knew Obama was in favor of same-sex marriage, but at that time he was vocal in his opposition to it.

A couple of government-sponsored Pied Pipers

From the very beginning of the Obama Administration, Education Secretary Arne Duncan headed up the United States Department of Education. Prior to that appointment, Duncan was the head of Chicago Public Schools (CPS). In that position, Duncan recommended a new school designed specifically to cater to gay, lesbian and transgender students, called the School for Social Justice Pride Campus.

Duncan announced that beginning with the 2014–2015 federal student aid form, all the language in it would be gender neutral. No longer will parents be identified as mother and father, but as "parent one" and "parent two" to lessen problems for students raised by either two mothers or two fathers.

October 2014 found Duncan in Los Angeles where he compared government-funded universal preschool to the civil rights issue of gay marriage, advancing the idea that universal public preschool would become a civil rights issue. "At the end of the day," he said, "for me this is really a social movement."[2]

In his May 2015 speech at the National Summit on Youth Violence Prevention in Crystal City, Virginia, Duncan made another rather startling statement about his desire to take full charge of at least some children twenty-four hours a day: "There's [sic] just certain kids we should have 24/7 to really create a safe environment and give them a chance to be successful." His concern was when "we have some children where there's not a mom, there's not a dad, there's not a grandma, there's just nobody at home." Most people didn't give a thought about what the government would be teaching those at-risk kids "24/7." If such a law would be passed, as he suggests, how long would it be before they were putting other kids—possibly your kids—into what they are calling "public boarding schools?"[3]

Another telling appointment of the Obama administration was Kevin Jennings, known as the "Safe Schools Czar." (Immediately upon becoming president, Barack Obama began appointing "czars"—unelected people who operate with impunity, and are accountable to no one except the administration. Within six months of his inauguration, Obama had an estimated thirty-two such czars.) Kevin Jennings was previously a schoolteacher, and admits to drug abuse. He is outspokenly contemptuous of religion, and advocates promoting homosexuality in schools. While a teacher, Jennings founded the Gay, Lesbian and Straight Education Network (GLSEN). It has almost forty chapters nationwide.[4] The Administration's unnoticed leaning toward advancing homosexual rights had begun.

History tells us they don't want your kids inoculated

Schools require students be inoculated against a wide variety of diseases. The purpose of such vaccinations is to prevent your child from either acquiring the disease, or spreading it. What government schools don't want your kids inoculated against are immorality, promiscuity, and the denigration of Christianity. Parents must teach kids at an early age not only God's Word, but also the beliefs of the enemies of God—inoculating them—so that when they start school their minds and hearts have formed an immune system. It will, as the Center for Disease Control states: ". . . defend against thousands of attacks every day, doing it so naturally that [they] are not even aware it is happening."

With the reminder from Solomon, "What has been will be again, what has been done will be done again; there is nothing new under the sun" (Ecclesiastes 1:9), it seems like a good idea to check history to see what authoritarian governments and radical reformers advocated in the past.

In 1937 Adolf Hitler said:

> The youth of today is ever the people of tomorrow. For this reason we have set before ourselves the task of *inoculating our youth* with the spirit of this community of the people *at a very early age, at an age when human beings are still unperverted and therefore unspoiled*. This Reich stands, and it is building itself up for the future, upon its youth. *And this new Reich will give its youth to no one, but will itself take youth and give to youth its own education and its own upbringing*. (Emphasis mine.)

Read that paragraph again, slowly. Grasp what Hitler was saying. He used the word, "inoculating." Words matter. Inoculation immunizes against an unwanted agent. It started me wondering: did other leaders in times past see the necessity of taking over the minds and hearts of the children? You bet they did!

Let's check out a few of Vladimir Lenin's principles. "Give me four years to teach the children, and the seed I have sown will never be uprooted."

He also stated, "Give us the child for eight years and it will be a Bolshevik forever." It looks like he wasn't ready to let go of the kids after four years; eight would definitely be preferable.

And what was part of Lenin's curriculum? He tells us himself: "Our program necessarily includes the propaganda of atheism."

But what did our Founding Fathers believe regarding education? The following is a quote from an article by scientist, teacher, attorney, and writer, Diane Rufino:

> In our young nation, the Bible was used as a text book for the purpose of teaching children moral principles to live by. As time went on, the Bible was gradually replaced by other text books such as Noah Webster's Primer. Webster's Primer taught children to spell but was also filled with moral Bible verses. In the front of this book was Mr. Webster's picture, accompanied by the inscription: "Noah Webster, who taught millions to read but not one to sin."[5]

More recently, President Theodore Roosevelt said, "To educate a person in the mind but not in morals is to educate a menace to society."

As part of President Obama's determination to deliver government-provided high-quality preschool to your kids, he wants a new string of "investments" for that education from the time they are born through age five, when they will enter government-provided pre-kindergarten.[6]

So are we closer today to the intent of our Founding Fathers, or to those intents of Hitler and Lenin? Please bear in mind; I am not suggesting our government is anything like Hitler's Nazism or the Communism of Lenin. I am only comparing the determination to educate children at an early age to conform to the moral philosophies of the government, and what those philosophies were and are.

Are there similarities in the United States today?

On June 8, 2011, cnsnews.com reported:

> This first-ever "Federal LGBT Youth Summit" was sponsored by the U.S. Department of Education and held at the Washington Court Hotel in Washington, D.C., on Monday and Tuesday. "My commitment to LGBT students is unequivocal and it goes back to when I first supported a charter school for LGBT students in Chicago," Arne Duncan said in a video. "Our Department here has taken concrete steps to protect LGBT students.[7]

The Humanist magazine carried an article by writer John Dunphy in its January/February 1983 issue that still resonates today. In it he advocated: "They [public school teachers] will be ministers of another sort, utilizing a classroom instead of a pulpit to convey humanist values in whatever subject they teach, regardless of the education level: preschool, day care, or large state university."

He went on to say, with what he himself called, "all the subtlety of a charging rhinoceros," that "*The classroom must and will become an arena of conflict between the old and the new—the rotting corpse of Christianity, together with all its adjacent evils and misery,* and the new faith of humanism."[8] (Emphasis mine.) Dunphy bragged eleven years later about all the attention that essay got.

Martin Luther said, "I am afraid that the schools will prove the very gates of hell, unless they diligently labor in explaining the Holy Scriptures and engraving them in the heart of the youth."

As I said before, it is important to teach God's Word to your kids, and also to do some serious inoculating. Tell them about the misinformation they may hear; be sure they'll recognize it as "foreign invaders." Make sure they recognize both truth and falsehood. If you don't make them aware of the sinful views on promiscuity, homosexuality, abortion, etc.—the views that in school they will learn as good, and normal—they will most likely view their teacher as the voice of authority. After all, isn't that what they go to school believing? (Does "But Mom, teacher said . . ." sound familiar?)

Do you cringe when you think of telling your kids about those subjects? I would, if I were a parent of a young child now. But the government schools will have no qualms about introducing them to that material!

Something is all mixed up

The Southern Poverty Law Center (SPLC) is an activist group that has been linked to domestic terrorism in federal court. In October 2012 one of their projects called "Teaching Tolerance" exploded in 2,000 schools across the United States. It was billed as Mix It Up at Lunch Day (MIU), and was the first in what is intended to be an annual event. The idea seems really simple, and kind of nice. Your kids are encouraged to get "out of their comfort zones and connect with someone new over lunch." The American Family Association (AFA) looked into the event and said it was intended "to bully-push its gay agenda, and at the same time intimidate and silence students who have a Biblical view of homosexuality." Anti-bullying policies themselves may have turned into bullying techniques against students whose religious beliefs oppose homosexuality.

In 2014 a case went to court when a college student was kicked out of class for expressing her views in an assignment that was to be a critique of a lesbian romance film, *Desert Hearts*. The syllabus apparently described the course as "all views are welcome" but the judge described it as "only those views with which I [the professor] agree are acceptable." The professor called the student's critique inflammatory, offensive, and hate speech. The case was decided in favor of the student, and the judge said, "[V]iews opposing homosexuality are protected by the First Amendment and that the government is not free to interfere with speech for no better reason than promoting an approved message or discouraging a disfavored one."[9] So your stand against homosexuality can win—but you have to be willing to fight for it.

"Reading is Fundamental" – depending on what you read

A picture book titled *Who's in a Family* by Robert Skutch, conveys the idea that a homosexual family is no different morally than other types of families. To whom do you think a picture book would be designed to appeal? Your first guess is probably right. Amazon shows it as appropriate for ages 3–7, or preschool through second grade. The fact that this book was published in 1997 shows that the drive toward universal acceptance of alternate lifestyles is not new. However, most parents are still not aware of its relentless advance.

In an interview on NPR's "Here and Now" May 3, 2005, the author stated: "The whole purpose of the book (back in 1997 remember) was *to get the subject out into the minds and the awareness of children before they are old enough to have been convinced that there's another way of looking at life*." (Emphasis mine.)

If your preschooler is taught in class that there is no moral difference between homosexuals and heterosexuals, how would he know homosexuality is wrong? Would he know what God says about the subject? Some believe God addresses the subject only in the Old Testament. That's a common misunderstanding; we read some pretty strong language in the New Testament:

> We know that the law is good if one uses it properly. We also know that the law is made not for the righteous but for lawbreakers and rebels, the ungodly and sinful, the unholy and irreligious, for those who kill

> their fathers or mothers, for murderers, for the sexually immoral, for those practicing homosexuality, for slave traders and liars and perjurers—and for whatever else is contrary to the sound doctrine that conforms to the gospel concerning the glory of the blessed God, which he entrusted to me (1Timothy 1:8–11).

And in 1 Corinthians 6:9–10:

> Or do you not know that wrongdoers will not inherit the kingdom of God? Do not be deceived: Neither the sexually immoral nor idolaters nor adulterers nor men who have sex with men nor thieves nor the greedy nor drunkards nor slanderers nor swindlers will inherit the kingdom of God.

First Corinthians continues with the good news that if your kids have already begun following the rainbow-clad Pied Pipers that lead them into sexual immorality, there is hope. Verse 11 gives us comfort: "And such were some of you. But you were washed, you were sanctified, you were justified in the name of the Lord Jesus Christ and by the Spirit of our God."

If you thought 1997 was a long way back for this thought-train to have gotten on track, the picture book *Heather Has Two Mommies* was first published in 1990 and "celebrated" with a 10th Anniversary Edition in June 2000. *Daddy's Roommate* by Michael Willhoite came out in 1994. Some of you younger parents may have been introduced to these picture books yourself as a bright-eyed, rosy-cheeked kindergartner.

The beat goes on. Jazz Jennings, born in 2000, co-wrote a picture book titled *I Am Jazz* about being born a boy but always feeling like a girl. The picture book informs us Jazz is now a girl—her father says he just wants his child to be happy. (Jazz's parents started videotaping Jazz's transgender activities when she was seven years old and posted them on YouTube.[10]) Amazon states this book is for ages 4–8 and from preschool through third grade. Without notifying parents in advance, a guidance counselor in Maine read *I Am Jazz* to kids in the first grade. When schools are dealing with this sensitive a subject, parents should be informed about the book ahead of time so they could preview it, and decide whether to let their kids participate in the reading.

The *School Library Journal*, May 12, 2015, carried an article titled "Evaluating Transgender Picture Books; Calling for Better Ones."[11] The author, Kyle Lukoff, said that when he took his new position as an elementary school librarian he discovered there were no picture books with transgenders in the leading role. He immediately ordered four picture books supporting that life-view.

Mr. Lukoff said there weren't many picture books that talk to your kids about transgenderism. He says *10,000 Dresses* by Marcus Ewert, however, has been very successful. In that book, Bailey—a boy/girl—likes to design dresses. Ewert says that the statement by Bailey's brother, "Get out of here, before I kick you!" isn't "quite dramatic enough" for his taste. It is stunning that teachers do not protest this language and attitude. Remember this is a picture book, designated by Amazon for ages five through nine.

Lukoff calls *Be Who You Are* by Jennifer Carr a "sweet and supportive story about a child coming out as transgender." He commends publisher Flamingo Rampant, for its mission "to produce feminist, racially diverse, LGBTQ-positive children's books."

Even if your kids' library has not carried transgender themed books, you might want to check every so often. They might hire a new librarian.

Crossover has nothing to do with busy streets

Somehow, in my naiveté, I long believed that one could count on a degree of safety and privacy in public restrooms. Called "landmark legislation," Governor of California Jerry Brown signed a bill into law that lets boys and girls use one another's locker rooms and restrooms. It gives students the right "to participate in sex-segregated programs, activities and facilities" based on their self-perception and regardless of their birth gender." If I had a daughter in school now, I'd be worried. How many young males might feel like a girl-for-a-day, go into the locker room and showers, and molest the girls in there? Who's to decide who's really cross-gendering or who's having a little fun with it? And parents or students who don't like this idea are called—you guessed it—bigots!

Well, you might say, they're a little different in California. That could never happen where we live. Parents in Massachusetts probably thought that, too, until a similar law was passed there, but it even goes further. There is an eleven-page directive from the Massachusetts Department of Education that gives bathroom rules, bans gender exclusivity on sports teams (you are what you say you are), eliminates gender-based clothing, and a teacher can't even say that boys should form up in one line, and girls form another line. It actually says that after age four, the best person to say whether they are male or female is that person himself, or herself. And no one can question their decision. This law is to protect transgender students. Who protects the "straight" students?

To top it off, Andrew Beckwith, the general counsel of the Massachusetts Family Institute, said that a kid could choose to be one gender at home, and a different one at school. The school, however, can't tell parents which gender their kid is choosing to be at school. If your kids want to call someone who looks like a boy a boy, but that boy says he's a girl, your kids can be punished for saying "him" or "he." If a girl doesn't want to use a restroom with a boy in the next stall, and complains about it, she's in trouble because she won't acknowledge that the boy is a girl. They say it's "bullying." Beckwith said, "It's affecting students as young as those in kindergarten."[12]

Do you know the Genderbread Man?

This strains credulity, but some high schools are actually using images that resemble the Gingerbread Man, called the Genderbread Man (or Person), to teach high school kids about transgenderism. It's a drawing that looks a lot like the Christmas cookie gingerbread man, and is taken from a book titled *The Social Justice Advocate's Handbook: A Guide to Gender* by Sam Killerman. The drawing and accompanying worksheet teach that "gender isn't binary." Besides being a social justice advocate, Killerman is a comedian of sorts, but the Genderbread Man/Person isn't funny. It shows the kids how they can think of themselves as a "woman, man, two-spirit, genderqueer, or genderless." Then they can express themselves as "male, female, intersex, female self ID, or male self ID."

There are several worksheets that accompany Mr. Genderbread Man. One of them has a checklist so the kids can see if they are ready for sex. Knowing what the material contained, one man said he'd challenge anyone to read some of the stuff, and try to defend their use with thirteen and fourteen year old kids. After Planned Parenthood handed out the worksheets, the parents of some of the students who were presented with this material said it made their kids feel pressured to have sex.

Kids will no longer have gender-based dress codes for the National Honor Society, proms, or other special events. All gender-based distinctions are going to be gone with the wind—and this wind is blowing no good that I can see.

Both California and Maryland have laws that prevent anyone from offending people claiming to be a transgender person.

We've gone from the West Coast to the East Coast, so let's travel to somewhere in-between like Idaho. In a middle school, a transgender boy was allowed to use the girls' bathroom. One mom and dad pulled their daughter out of school because of it and put her in a private school.

How about the Southwest? LGBT activists have forced the Tucson Unified School District to allow transgender students to use any and all facilities designated by sex as they choose. This covers all kids from kindergarten through high school. An attorney with Alliance Defending Freedom says the school district didn't have to cave. In 2009, the Ninth Circuit Court of Appeals issued a ruling that confirmed public schools do have the right to restrict the use of bathrooms or changing areas to members of the same sex only.

In a Colorado high school, girls said a boy claiming to be a girl used their bathrooms and he/she made sexually harassing comments about their figures or what they were wearing. The girls were told not to talk about their constitutional privacy rights, or they may find they can't be on the school's athletic teams.

Rasmussen did a poll about this new trend. Not surprisingly, since you may have been taught this in school, 46% of American adults favor laws banning any discrimination against transgenders. But if they are asked if men claiming to be women should be allowed to use women's bathrooms and showers, the support drops precipitously to only 24% and opposition rises from 34% to 56%.

Brian Camenker, with Mass*Resistance*, an organization opposing homosexuality, spoke at a pro-family rally in Jamaica in December 2013. He outlined what he determined is the homosexual agenda.

- Legalize homosexuality
- Promote gay pride parades
- Demand non-discrimination laws
- Insist on homosexuals' adoption of children
- Push the homosexual agenda in schools
- Force "gay marriage" on society
- Demand public funding to deal with increased homosexual-related social problems
- Promote the transgender agenda

- Impose a large-scale loss of free speech
- Ban counseling for kids confused by homosexual issues
- Attack churches

Evaluate how far this scheme has already taken hold in the United States.

On my honor I will do my best . . .

The Boy Scouts regularly take an oath that ends "to keep myself physically strong, mentally awake, and morally straight." The Scouts have been around forever and have provided many wonderful experiences for boys. Over the last decade a new experience seems to be added—sexuality.

That organization's national policy says that while they do not inquire about the sexual lives of their volunteers, employees, or members, they won't accept members "who are open or avowed homosexuals or who engage in behavior that would become a distraction to the mission of the BSA [Boy Scouts of America]." How long is that stand going to last? In 2013 the national BSA voted to extend membership to boys who are openly homosexual, and they put that into action in 2014.

You may remember Robert Gates, former Secretary of Defense. He was elected president of the Boy Scouts in 2014, and said regarding reversing the ban, "In all candor, I would have supported going further, as I did in opening the way for gays to serve in CIA and in the military." Only thirty of the approximately 300 BSA councils have said they don't want the discrimination against homosexuals to continue in their organization. In April 2015 *USA Today* reported that BSA's New York council hired an openly gay camp leader. He's an eighteen-year-old Eagle Scout. New York sent the Eagle Scout's application to be camp leader to the National BSA which, knowing all the information, accepted it.

CNN reported July 28, 2015 that the executive board of BSA ratified a resolution to remove the national restriction on openly gay leaders and employees. Advocacy groups for homosexual rights thought it was a step in the right direction, but it didn't go far enough. Human Rights Campaign President Chad Griffin said, "An exemption for troops sponsored by religious organizations undermines and diminishes the historic nature of today's decision. Discrimination should have no place in the Boy Scouts, period."[13]

My husband and I fly our country's flag on the special occasion days of the year. Several years ago our neighbor who has a son in scouting asked if we'd participate in their fund-raising project of putting up flags in front yards. We were delighted, and enjoyed seeing all the flags waving along our street ten times a year. My husband recently talked to our neighbor and said we wouldn't be able to participate in that any longer. We can't in good conscience contribute funds to support an organization that welcomes homosexuality in their leaders. He understood our feelings. What a shame to take that wonderful patriotic service of young boys and turn it into fundraising that will ultimately be applied to homosexual advancement.

The Girl Scouts website states that they do admit transgenders if the child and its parents believe the child is a girl, rather than the boy that the physical appearance indicates. In May 2015 the American Family Association (AFA) started a petition to stop that policy and had over 38,000 signatures within a week. Regarding the Girl Scouts' policy, the AFA said, "This means *girls in the organization will be forced to recognize and accept transgenderism as a normal lifestyle*. Boys in skirts, boys in make-up and boys in tents will become a part of the program. This change will put young innocent girls at risk." (Emphasis mine.)

Who are the Pied Pipers leading this parade?

In 2014, at Brock University in St. Catharines, Ontario, Canada, a bunch of professors whose main purpose in life is to study gender identity got together to discuss what the world considers "normal."[14] One said, "Gender independent children are all the rage again." (Again? Did I miss the first go-round?) Looking at all of North America, they came to the conclusion that transgender issues will soon be the civil rights movement du jour. The gender gurus seem to think that as far as male and female identification goes, there may no longer be black and white definitions. They think our society is ready for all those shades in-between.

A book considered the handbook for the "gay agenda" is *After the Ball*. Two homosexual Harvard-trained psychologists, Marshall Kirk and Hunter Madsen, tell gay rights organizers not to present themselves to the public as antagonistic opponents, but as victims. This produces "jamming" which smears Christians and anyone else who doesn't agree with them. Their strategy states: "In any campaign to win over the public, gays must be portrayed as victims in need of protection so that straights will be inclined by reflex to adopt the role of protector. The purpose of victim imagery is to make straight people feel very uncomfortable." David Kupelian, in his book *The Marketing of Evil*, acknowledges that Kirk and Madsen were exceptionally brilliant men. Kirk designed aptitude tests for adults with 200+ IQs, and Madsen "was an expert on public persuasion tactics and social marketing."

Many organizations support gay-rights and same-sex marriage. The Gay, Lesbian, and Straight Education Network (GLSEN), co-sponsored a workshop where "instructors encouraged children as young as 14 years of age to engage in life-threatening sex acts."[15] GLSEN tries to get into schools by saying that homosexual and transgender students need to feel safe and, because those students have a high rate of suicide, they need a support group. I am surprised they admit the suicide potential is significant enough to require support. If that argument fails, their go-to guy is the American Civil

Liberties Union. It has volunteered its services to impose the homosexual agenda through civil action.

Where is the exit?

In every movie theater, auditorium, hospital, and just about every place you might go except for your home, the law mandates an "EXIT" sign. Hotels even post a floor plan on the door of your room to show you the path to the quickest way out. So where is the exit route for anyone who has feelings of homosexuality, or has engaged in it, but knows it is not the life to lead? In most cases the light in that EXIT sign is turned off. In some states it is even illegal for a parent to take their own child to a counselor for the reason of exiting homosexuality.

While there is no problem with access to books advancing the homosexual lifestyle, librarians in school and community libraries often refuse to purchase or even accept donations of books for children that speak of exiting the "gay" scene.

In 2009 the group Parents and Friends of Ex-Gays & Gays (PFOX) tried to place "ex-gay" books in a number of libraries. Regina Griggs, Executive Director of PFOX, said they were trying to get information to anyone who was wrestling with an attraction to the same sex about options that are available. PFOX told Foxnews.com they "offered the same books to Montgomery County, Maryland, and Arlington and Fairfax Counties in Virginia. We e-mailed all publicly funded universities nationwide that have a GLBTQ center. Our offer to donate ex-gay books and brochures, we were rejected by all."[16]

Maybe going directly to the American Library Association (ALA) would get things moving. Griggs wanted the ALA to send a request to schools not to put the ex-gay books on their "banned books" list. That didn't work. Nor did asking they be included in ALA's stand for intellectual freedom under their diversity policy. It's interesting to note that this association's "Library Bill of Rights" states quite clearly that libraries should make material available on all points of view of a subject. That bill of rights also tells libraries that they are to "cooperate with all persons and groups concerned with resisting abridgment of free expression and free access to ideas."[17]

Some of the reasons for rejecting the ex-gay material included that they had not been reviewed by the proper institutions, and they had objections to the ideas the books promote. What was so objectionable that they wouldn't let the books in their library? It was the idea that homosexuality is a treatable condition. They contend that learning about that could be psychologically damaging to homosexuals.

In 2013 ALA refused to acknowledge that it routinely bans ex-gay books. But, apparently, it does. The advocacy group Voice of the Voiceless (VoV) compared the censorship to child abuse. VoV helps former homosexuals and individuals with unwanted same-sex attractions (SSA) and their families. The president of VoV is a former homosexual and a victim of childhood sexual abuse. He said reading something that gave him hope that he could emotionally heal, and leave the homosexual lifestyle, would have been very valuable to him.

Hayley Gorenberg, the Deputy Legal Director of Lambda Legal (a homosexual rights group), compared ex-gay materials to the flat-earth theory—they are not in line with current science.

Let's take a look at current science

Medicare (bear in mind, that's health insurance for people ages sixty-five and older, those who have permanent disabilities, and end-stage renal disease) now covers transgenders' reassignment surgery, even though a prominent psychiatrist says it's not possible to do that. Dr. Paul R. McHugh was the psychiatrist-in-chief for Johns Hopkins Hospital, and its current Distinguished Service Professor of Psychiatry. He says transgenderism is a "mental disorder" that can and should be treated, and that sex change is "biologically impossible."[18] He also warns those who promote or engage in reassignment surgery are working with the knowledge that they are encouraging a mental disorder.

Among the adverse effects of reassignment surgery is a suicide rate that is twenty times higher than in non-transgender people. Also, of the children who thought they had transgender feelings, 70%–80% "spontaneously lost those feelings."

A study in Sweden[19] done over a period of thirty years (1973–2003) looked at both surgical reassignment and treatments with hormones. It came to the conclusion that after sex reassignment transsexuals have considerably higher risks for suicide, death from complications from the surgery (or other causes such as AIDS) and mental illness. Females who changed to males had higher risk for criminal convictions.

Based on the results, it was determined that even though the surgery or hormonal treatments to change from one sex to another might accomplish that goal, it was *not* a satisfactory treatment for transsexualism. The patients needed follow-up treatment for both mental and physical conditions. It was not clear if this study established that the conditions were exhibited prior to sex reassignment, resulted from it, or both.

One man who became a woman went back to being a man. Certainly the first decision to have a sex reassignment was not an easy one, but reversing it all? That must have been monumental. How do you admit to yourself, and all those who know you that you made a really bad mistake? And the surgery itself is not a minor consideration.

This forty-two-year-old man was married, happily by all accounts, and the father of two kids. That was when he decided he wanted to be a woman. Eight years later, miserable, he once again became a man. He said he had felt like he was supposed to have been a girl since he was five years old. After the surgery, it seems, he was euphoric. That soon changed, and reality set in. He finally realized that his disappointment with being a male came from something traumatic that happened to him as a child, not a genetic disorder. He now trumpets to all who will listen that his gender confusion was caused by his environment and family relationships. He says being dissatisfied with who you are is a psychological condition that doctors aren't paying enough attention to.

One genome study twenty years ago claimed it gave the first direct evidence of a "gay gene." That study, and its results, have never been replicated. Therefore the theory has no validity.[20]

Who is responsible for restrictive laws?

Both California and New Jersey have laws forbidding psychologists to provide what is called "gay conversion therapy." This legislation prevents state-licensed therapists from counseling children to lead them out of a life of homosexuality. The American Psychiatric Association, the American Academy of Pediatrics, and the American Psychological Association have called such therapy detrimental, and they "call on their members to respect a person's right to self-determination." In others words, "Parents, leave your kids alone!"

Fortunately the laws in both California and New Jersey don't prevent parents from getting conversion therapy for their kids when religious leaders or groups provide it.

Washington, D. C., our nation's capital, the seat of our liberty, voted unanimously in December 2014 to ban conversion therapy that "seeks to turn gay teenagers into heterosexuals." An article in the Washington Post commented that as legal challenges to bans in California and New Jersey failed, more states are expected to follow with similar legislation.

Maryland tried to get this law passed, but it was withdrawn because of concerns that it wouldn't pass the General Assembly. That doesn't mean the gay and gay-supportive politicians have given up. They are looking for ways to effect it through changes in regulations. Similar bills have also been defeated or died in committee in

Colorado, Hawaii, and Virginia.

In 2015, Arizona, Connecticut, Massachusetts, Minnesota, Ohio, Florida, Pennsylvania, and Vermont had bills pending, but there doesn't seem to have been much movement on them.

In April 2015 the Assembly of New York State voted 94–23 to ban conversion therapy for minors. There is still hope there that it will not become law, however, as the Senate is expected to vote against it.

In May 2015, Oregon's Governor Kate Brown, the first openly bisexual governor in the United States, signed a bill into law that bans conversion therapy for LGBT children. The Oregon House overwhelmingly passed the bill, and it passed in their Senate twenty-one to eight. Some parents and religious groups protested, but their efforts proved fruitless. The law applies only to state-licensed medical professionals. Apparently enough politicians thought parents could still take their kids to their pastors and priests if they wanted to.

Still alive and kicking are bills banning the conversion therapy in Illinois, Iowa, Nevada, Rhode Island, and Texas. The bill in Texas was introduced in their legislature even though the Texas Republican Party adopted a plank defending such treatment by stating "We recognize the legitimacy and efficacy of counseling, which offers reparative therapy and treatment for those patients seeking healing and wholeness from their homosexual lifestyle. No laws or executive orders shall be imposed to limit or restrict access to this type of therapy."

Why do some actively pursue homosexuality?

Many deny the Judeo-Christian values because to admit there is a God would result in their having to also admit that they are accountable to that God. And that would significantly impact their lifestyle and approach to moral matters.

Both socialism and communism have atheism at their base. Many of the people now espousing homosexuality, same-sex marriage, and revisionism in textbooks have turned from God, and are, wittingly or unwittingly, constructing a path to either socialism or communism.

Let's take a brief look at these "isms."

Communism has only one class, in theory, and that is the working class. Nobody is rich; nobody is poor. Everyone is equal. What the people's work produces, be it in factories or on farms, is distributed based on need—it has nothing to do with how long or how hard you worked, or if you worked at all. Today we call it "social justice," except that the government doesn't own everything. Obviously, with this system there are no rights of inheritance. Everything belongs to the government.

Socialism is much like communism but not quite as severe. With socialism, the government owns all the factories, farms, etc. and pays workers a wage. Examples of this in our society are the U.S. Post Office, Amtrak, "Obamacare" (the Affordable Care Act), and the takeover of General Motors. Think of the often used excuse for government takeover—"too big to fail." In addition to the wages, the government gives every worker the basic necessities of life. Neither communism nor socialism produce any incentive for a worker to work harder, or longer, or even do the work better.

I have reduced the definitions to their essence. However, those are the ways the communist and socialist societies operate—but what are their approaches to religion? Karl Marx, the founder of communism, believed religion was "the opium of the people" and it was useful in keeping the "workers" from revolting.

Later, Vladimir Lenin, still in the communist system, believed religion retarded human development. He wrote, in his book *Religion*, "Atheism is a natural and inseparable part of Marxism, of the theory and practice of scientific socialism."[21]

The website of the Socialist Party of Great Britain gives us a clear insight into what socialism thinks of religion: "Socialists are hostile to all religions. Yet there is a difference between the socialist attitude towards religion and that of the secularist or atheist. The secularist tends to treat religion simply as a set of beliefs which he seeks to demolish by rational and logical criticism. To the socialist this seems a pointless exercise (as pointless as religion itself)."[22]

A precursor to either communism or socialism is humanism. Humanist Manifestos I & II tell us that humanism is "a philosophical, religious, and moral point of view." Secular humanism is not "secular" at all; for all intents and purposes, it is the religion of the atheists. One of the signers of Humanist Manifesto I, Charles Francis Potter, said,

> Education is thus a most powerful ally of humanism, and every American public school is a school of humanism. What can the theistic Sunday schools, meeting for an hour once a week, and teaching only a fraction of the children, do to stem the tide of a five-day program of humanistic teaching?[23]

Perhaps the name Gloria Steinem is familiar to you. She is best known for her work as a feminist organizer. Let's call her the Pied Piper of females. In a quote in the *Saturday Review of Education*, March 1973, she gave us her insight as to why schools are advocating homosexuality, same-sex marriage, promiscuity, abortion, and all the activities and attitudes that God abhors:

> We have to abolish and reform the institution of marriage . . . By the year 2000 we will, I hope, raise our children to believe in human potential, not God . . . We must understand what we are attempting is a revolution, not a public relations movement . . . it is humanism that is the goal.

And from the *New Programme and New Constitution of the Revolutionary Communist Party, USA*, its section on "Women" should leave no doubt about their end game regarding government in the lives of families:

> The right to abortion will be guaranteed . . . As far as the policy toward the family, it will be recognized for what it is: Not some holy or sacred institution to be preserved for all time . . . not only will the family be a secondary form for determining children's upbringing, but its influence in promoting conservatism among its members, especially the women and children, will be actively combatted. . . .
>
> While the parents will still have significant responsibility for their children, this does not mean they are "theirs," and there will be struggle to prevent parents from imposing old values, and conservative, non-revolutionary thinking generally on the children.[24]

Did that send chills down your spine? It did that to me when I read it. They know they have to start with your kids if they want to take over society. They know they must obliterate religion. They know they must eliminate the trust and respect your kids have for you, their parents.

Another section of this communist proposed constitution is titled "The Proletariat, Upon Seizing Power, Will Immediately Take Up The Transformation Of Society." Perhaps you have a habit of skipping over the titles and chapter headings. I often do that to get to the "important stuff." In this case the title *is* the important stuff—at least a significant part of it. It says, ". . . the Transformation of Society." During his first campaign to become president of the United States, Barack Obama used the words, "we are five days away from fundamentally transforming the United States of America." Did he know the hidden implications in that statement, or was he just saying some words that he thought would excite the crowd? Can a president be a Pied Piper? We can only judge him now by his deeds in his two terms as president.

If God, and your kids, and our republic mean anything at all to you, this is not something you can close the covers of this book on and walk away from. Apathy is not the answer. In my heart, I sincerely believe God wants us to fight this.

What does God say about this?

Why do we separate ourselves from things like buying Girl Scout cookies and having the flag put up and taken down? They are insignificant in the overall picture, aren't they? In this battle, consider nothing insignificant. Remember, "So God created mankind in his own image, in the image of God he created them; male and female he created them" (Genesis 1:27). And "The man said, "This is now bone of my bones and flesh of my flesh; she shall be called 'woman,' for she was taken out of man." That is why a man leaves his father and mother and is united to his wife, and they become one flesh." (Genesis 2:23–25).

Go back to the first chapter of this book, "Who's Got Dibs on Your Kids' TRUST?" and reaffirm in your own mind who you will trust to lead you on the right path raising your kids.

✝

"Therefore put on the full armor of God, so that when the day of evil comes, you may be able to stand your ground, and after you have done everything, to stand" (Ephesians 6:13).

Chapter Challenge

As I advised previously, check your kids' textbooks and see what their sex education classes will be teaching about homosexuality. Ask their teachers if they will be teaching what is in the book, and if there will be opportunity to offer dissenting opinions. Ask if there will be outside speakers, and check their backgrounds.

Have a discussion with your kids, and find out what they are taught at school about homosexuality. Ask how they feel about it.

It is impossible for one chapter to cover thoroughly all of the gender issues your kids face. There is much informative material available about each of the topics. Check DibsOnYourKids.com.

Books

- *Forgive Us Our Sins: Homosexuality in the Light of God's Truth* by Scott I. Barefoot and Richard D. Starr.
- *The Marketing of Evil: How Radicals, Elitists, and Pseudo-Experts Sell Us Corruption Disguised As Freedom* by David Kupelian.

Websites

- Chapman, Michael W. "Johns Hopkins Psychiatrist: Transgender Is 'Mental Disorder;' Sex Change 'Biologically Impossible'." *cnsnews.com*. Published electronically 20 Aug 2014. http://cnsnews.com/news/article/michael-w-chapman/johns-hopkins-psychiatrist-transgender-mental-disorder-sex-change. 19 May 2015.
- "Celebrate NEA's Read across America: Lessons for Grades K–5." Gay Lesbian and Straight Education Network (GLSEN), http://www.glsen.org/article/celebrate-neas-read-across-america-lessons-grades-k-5. 28 May 2015.
- Lukoff, Kyle. "Evaluating Transgender Picture Books; Calling for Better Ones." *School Library Journal* no. 12 May. http://www.slj.com/2015/05/diversity/evaluating-transgender-picture-books-requesting-better-ones/.12 May 2015.

Who's Got Dibs on Your Kids' MEDIA?

From Captivated to Captive

"See to it that no one takes you captive through hollow and deceptive philosophy, which depends on human tradition and the elemental spiritual forces of this world rather than on Christ" (Colossians 2:8).

One Saturday afternoon a couple of girls in their early teens rang our doorbell. They told us someone was having a party, and a variant of a scavenger hunt was part of the entertainment. Each pair of guests received an item to start them on their search. Their assignment was to go door to door and give whatever they had to that neighbor; in return they would receive something either bigger or better. My husband and I laughed at the ingenuity, and scoured our brains for a suitable exchange item. Finally we took their two four-inch high votive candleholders, and gave them a smaller but—in our minds at least—better Capodimonte porcelain flower basket.

I wondered how that turned out. What items were exchanged for what bigger or better item? Bigger is easy to discern, but better is often in the eye of the beholder. What item did each team have at the end? How did all the guests feel about the final product of their effort? Did everyone feel what each team displayed actually was bigger or better than what they began with?

Smaller, Bigger, Faster—Better?

That incident led me to the comparison of life in the twenty-first century:

- The first mobile phone entered our culture in 1973 and weighed more than two pounds. Today's versions are around five ounces, and that's including the built-in camera with video. Smaller but better.
- The first computer hard disk drive, IBM's Model 350 Disk File, used twenty-four disks stored in a cabinet about six feet wide, six feet high, and a couple of feet deep. It stored a maximum of five MB of data. Michigan Micro Mote (M3) just introduced a complete operational computer system so small you could put almost 150 of them in a thimble. Smaller, but better? It depends on what you need the computer to do.
- In 1939 people could buy their first television set. The picture tube was five inches by twelve inches. Today you can get a 150-inch screen with mind-blowing resolution . . . or you can strap a "*slightly smaller*" one to your wrist. Bigger and/or smaller, but definitely better.

So, we go merrily on our way, constantly following a lot of Pied Pipers of technology, exchanging things for something bigger, or smaller, or better. But all of this stuff costs money and takes up more and more of our time. At the end, are we better off? To determine that, we'll have to look at what all of our spectacular advances in media are now providing us.

Time in a Bottle

Back in the '70s, Jim Croce wrote a beautiful song that said if he could find a way to save time in a bottle he'd spend every day with the person he loved. How would he have spent those days with the one he loved? Back then, people read newspapers and magazines, watched a little TV at night, answered the phone when it rang, and played games with their kids. Sesame Street started just a few years earlier.

Today, for better or worse, parents put tablets in the hands of their toddlers, or sit them in front of the television, and turn on (still) Sesame Street. Those devices amuse them, acting as a sort of baby-sitting service while Mom or Dad "gets things done." Amazingly, those toddlers know how to use the tablets—and they can serve as a great learning tool—but when does it all become too much? How often are you unaware of the content of some the technology your kids are toying around with? It's harder to keep up with than one might imagine.

If you'd count all the hours your kids spend watching television, playing video games, texting, phone conversations, etc. you'd probably get more than they have non-school, non-sleeping, hours in a day. Hyperbole? Not really. They do it by multi-tasking. They text while watching television and during mealtime. Earplugs drive music into their ears almost non-stop. A Kaiser Family Foundation 2010 survey[1] determined that by using eyes, ears, and fingers, they are able to squeeze ten hours and forty-five minutes of using the various media into an actual time of about seven hours and thirty minutes each and every day.

I know the Croce song referred to love between a man and a woman, but change the context just a bit. Would your kids say the time they spend with you now is the way they'd like to spend eternity with you? Is total technology immersion worth saving in a bottle? What do you share of your person and your personality with each other?

I'm a strong believer in our technological advances. My cell phone is a security blanket for me when I'm driving alone, grocery shopping, or even at a concert. You never know when an emergency will arise that makes you want help *now*! I'm certain I spend about twenty-five out of every twenty-four hours a day in front of my computers. Yes, that's plural. I have more than one computer that I use daily. I also have a Kindle, a Nook, and a tablet. A television set graces the top of our bedroom dresser, stares longingly at us at the breakfast table (the news of the day can't wait), and looms large in the family room where we can actually see the puck moving across the ice in a hockey game. We've cut our newspaper down to two days a week, getting most of our news from TV and the Internet. Fewer magazines weigh down our mail truck than formerly. However, it's just my husband and me now; our kids all are grown and out of the house.

Let's talk

What about you? Do you still have kids at home? How many hours (or minutes) of the day do you spend talking to them? I don't mean the "You can't watch TV until your homework is done" or "Did you pick up that mess in your room yet?" talk. I mean the "What did you learn new or interesting at school today" or "Tell me about last night's sleep-over" or "I heard Joey is having a bad time. What do you think we can do to help?" talks. Not enough time in the day for talking? I'm not surprised.

But there is so much good educational material available on TV and the Internet. The kids are learning a lot! I wish that were entirely true. They're learning a lot, but maybe not what you'd put on the top of your "make sure they see this" list.

The Joan Ganz Cooney Center, based at Sesame Workshop, did a survey in 2013 titled, "Learning at home: families' educational media use in America."[2] The survey results indicate that kids ages two to ten will use a mobile device to *learn* things only about five minutes a day, and only three (three?!) minutes a day with *educational* video games. The older the kids are, the less time is spent on edifying material. No surprise there.

The Pew Research Center's report dated April 9, 2015[3] said that because of the ubiquitousness of smartphones, 92% of teens (ages thirteen to seventeen) are online with them every day, and 24% admit to being online just about 24/7. That's easy for them to accomplish, because about three-quarters of all kids have their own, or have access to, smartphones.

In case we think their digitally adept fingers are limited to smartphones, 55% own, or have access to, a tablet, and 72% of our kids find time to play games on their home's video console.

When I read those statistics, I wondered if the survey had reached only the most affluent of homes, so I turned to our latest (2010) census stats. Nearly two-thirds of what the Census Bureau considers "poor" families have not just television, but either cable or satellite TV. A 2009 survey indicates that one third of the poor families have big-screen plasma or LCD sets. Fifty percent have a computer, and almost 16% have two or more computers. Forty-three percent can connect to the Internet. And over half of poor families with children have at least one video game system!

But all these means of entertainment cost money. Whether families are considered poor or affluent, in many homes both mothers and fathers are working. Sometimes they're both working just so they can give their kids all the "stuff" they want. The question that needs careful consideration is, *at what cost*? Who is there to supervise the amount of time the kids spend in front of the TV or playing video games? Who is there to monitor the quality and type of messaging bombarding the kids? For the most part, no one. No one is the overseer. Unless parents have had a serious talk with their kids about what is and is not appropriate and acceptable, not many kids will say, "Ooh, that's not very nice. I won't watch that." It's the equivalent of the inmates running the asylum.

Who has the channel changer?

So what are the kids spending their time with? It depends on their ages, of course. They probably started—correction, you, the parent, probably started them on something like Sesame Street on television. It's a delightful program. Kids learn a lot watching Sesame Street. But, again, do you know what they are learning? A concern raised its ugly head that homosexuality was being advanced on the program.

Are Bert and Ernie a "gay" couple? There has been a lot of furor about this, but the show absolutely denies it. They are simply best friends. A Christian baker in Newtonabbey got sued because he wouldn't deliver a wedding cake, with those two characters atop it, for two lesbians who were getting married. The thing is, it wasn't because of Bert and Ernie, but because the cake was also supposed to carry the words "support gay marriage."

Some wouldn't mind if they were a gay couple. The British author Philip Hensher said, "Why would anyone mind if gay people were represented in Sesame Street? *Children's television should be about alternative families*. There's no point in switching on the TV and watching characters just like your mummy and daddy and boring older sister. You want a bloke with a zip for a mouth." (Emphasis mine.)

Perhaps parents should forget about Bert and Ernie and check out Sesame Street's guests. They include lesbian comedian Wanda Sykes and Katy Perry of *I Kissed A Girl* fame. The biggest harm in introducing this element is that it normalizes homosexuality in our culture.

Not all objectionable content addresses homosexuality. A lot of parents expressed outrage about *SpongeBob SquarePants*. Some of the descriptive terms they used were "violent," "dark," and "hard for kids to separate fantasy and reality." They objected to the characters calling each other names like idiot and stupid. If you don't regularly watch these programs with your kids, it might be a good idea to tune in occasionally.

Do your kids watch *Glee*, or is reality TV their choice? Probably some of their viewing time is spent on MTV. Is the reality show *16 and Pregnant* a favorite? If so, they'd probably like *Teen Mom 2*. What about *Jersey Shore*? Think that's a good influence? *Yo Mamma* is a competition to see who can do the best trash talking. If you hope they are watching intellectually enriching shows, these won't make the grade.

Have your girls practiced twerking? What is twerking—a new exercise routine? No, it's bending over and shaking your rear end as fast as you can. There is only one way this can be interpreted—sexually tempting and arousing. And instead of being condemned when Miley Cyrus did it in a very erotic way on TV, it has been glorified, emulated, and the term even added to the Oxford English Dictionary.

Come on—what does it hurt?

Forget the media multitasking—actual time kids eight to eighteen spend using various forms of technological media is about six and a half to seven and a half hours per day.[4] Do your kids spend that much time together as a family? Do they spend that much time in school? Do they spend that much time sleeping? Do they spend that much time in church or praying or in Bible studies? It's got a name: media saturation!

So besides the content of what they're so engrossed in, are there any adverse side effects to indulging in media saturation? Of the kids in the survey, about half earned the grade of "C" or lower in school if they were really into heavy use of devices. Less than 25% of the surveyed kids were "light" users. I wonder if poor school grades are the cause or effect. In other words, are kids not understanding the lessons in school, and so turn to devices where they can feel a sense of accomplishment, or don't they have time to study because their heads are in some sort of a screen all the time?

An article in the June 3, 2009, issue of *The Journal of the American Medical Association* (JAMA), called out pediatricians because only half of 365 surveyed would recommend restricting kids to just one or two hours of media use per day, even though that was the policy of The American Academy of Pediatrics (AAP). (Perhaps they realized it would be an effort in futility.) Even worse, only half were even interested in learning more about the effects of media on the kids.

By 2011, however, pediatricians and the AAP were catching up to the kids. They said parents should be aware, because of the nature of social media sites, "not all of them are healthy environments for children and adolescents." They specifically mention cyberbullying, sexting, exposure to "inappropriate content," and something that is apparently so prevalent and dangerous it has been given its own special name, "Facebook depression."[5]

Facebook depression occurs when preteens and teens (and adults?) spend excessive time on social media. Postings by others show them having so much fun, engaged in great activities, and the viewer believes the whole world is having more fun, is prettier, more successful—*everything* is better in the lives of others.

Sometimes they will search for other sites to relieve their feelings of depression. Those sites may be traps in themselves, promoting drugs, promiscuity, unsafe sex, and aggressive or self-destructive behaviors. An extreme example of the seduction of some sites is the number of young people converted to fanatical Islam, some even attempting to go overseas to fight with ISIS.

Many kids are living an extension of their lives—real lives—in their online lives. Some begin to be unable to recognize the difference between them. Verbal and face-to-face communication skills are rapidly diminishing. And kids pick up the technological skills so quickly and easily that parents are hard pressed to keep up with them. That makes it doubly difficult to know what Pied Pipers the kids may be following.

Do your kids ride in cars with someone other than you driving? Of course they do. Other parents will pick them up for sports practice, take them to the mall for a couple of hours, or ride-share to and from school. If their friends are old enough to drive, someone will either have their own car or be able to borrow their parents' ride, and everybody piles in. Our society has moved from urban life with an abundance of bus and rail transportation available, to suburbia where a car is a necessity. Think twice before you let your kids get in. Why? Know who's driving!

Of licensed drivers under the age of sixty-five, almost 70% admitted to using their cell phone to talk or text while driving.[6] Tell your kids it's okay to be proactive—ask the driver if they've taken the ATT pledge "It Can Wait" to not drive and use a cell phone at the same time. If their driver reaches for the phone, your kids can and should tell them, "It can wait." On average, distracted driving kills nine people every day in the United States, and 1,153 people are injured.[7]

As I said before, I use various forms of technology a lot, and I believe proper use can have great benefits for all of us, including your kids. However, media in general *can* be high risk.[8] Some think there may be a link between the violence in TV shows and video games to real-life violent acts, and the amount of airtime TV gives to sexual situations and rather explicit innuendoes encourages earlier involvement in sexual intercourse.

Testimony to the dangers of cyberbullying abound. Sadly, the person being bullied seems to be drawn to reading the cruel posts on social media, dragging the vulnerable deeper and deeper into depression, anxiety, and even suicide.

Outside of sending naked photographs, I wasn't too certain what the term "sexting" referred to. The definition seems to include not only sending, but even receiving and forwarding sexually explicit messages or photographs. It doesn't matter if it's done with a cell phone, computer, or any other digital device. About 20% of our teens have indulged in the act of sexting, and when caught, have run afoul of pornography laws, suspension from school, and created severe distress in others who are victims of such "pranks."

Let's take a breather

Yes, there are dangers with the use of media. But you can kill yourself drinking too much water at one time. Anything in excess is not good. Anything that you (or your kids) sense is not good for them should be avoided, just as you would hesitate to walk in a beautiful garden if you are allergic to bee stings. As in all things, discretion and moderation are key. Paul makes this point in 1 Corinthians 6:12: "'I have the right to do anything,' you say—but not everything is beneficial. 'I have the right to do anything'—but I will not be mastered by anything."

Let's look at the bright side. Media lets kids stay in touch with their friends and family in ways they never could before. Have you moved to a new city? Your kids left some good friends. With media they can still be in touch—every day if they like—with brief tweets, photographs, or sending what used to be "letters" by email—and it doesn't take two weeks to get an answer.

Skype is a great way for grandparents who live far away to get to see their grandkids more often.

If they are artistic, your kids can display their work on sites like deviantart.com. There are many such sites catering to different levels and types of creativity. Or if they want to earn a little extra money, they can post work on fiverr.com and draw something for a client for $5.00.

Do your kids have some activity they're all wound up in? Search for clubs, website groups, etc. to put them in touch with others who have similar pursuits: horses, Irish dance, science competitions, creative writing, decorating gourds—it's all out there at your fingertips.

Browsing the Internet may generate interests your kids didn't know they had. They can find information on ruins that may grow into obtaining a degree in archeology; they can learn about deep sea volcanoes that may lead to a degree in oceanography. As with anything and everything in life, your job as a parent is to guide your kids so that they don't follow the paths of the myriad Pied Pipers tooting their enticing calls. Lead them on a better path.

Back to the battle

Let's get away from the teens for a while and look at the effect technology has on the littlest of your kids.

Both the American Academy of Pediatrics and the Canadian Society of Pediatrics say kids under the age of two should have *no* access to media devices such as smartphones and tablets. Yes, they are fascinated by them. Yes, they learn how to turn them on and navigate very quickly and easily. The problem is that when they are hugging the tablet they aren't crawling after a ball that keeps rolling away from them. They aren't learning how to stack blocks one on top of another, and do it over when it falls down. Strangely, using building blocks as a toddler increases the ability to do math later on in life.

Are *you* being seduced by a Pied Piper? If your baby is fussy, it's far easier and less time consuming to put a tablet in the crib with the little guy than to hold that sweet bundle you waited for so eagerly. Talk softly, sing, or just put him on your hip as you get other work done. That tablet in the crib doesn't teach your child personal interaction. Research determined that on average kids under two years of age watched TV anywhere from one to two hours a day, often because it's a peacekeeper, or babysitter while you jump in a quick shower or fix dinner.[9]

If you want your kids to learn to talk early and have a wide vocabulary, talk to them. The AAP policy statement says, "Infant vocabulary growth is directly related to the amount of 'talk time' or the amount of time parents spend speaking to them. Heavy television use in a household can interfere with a child's language development simply because parents likely spend less time talking to the child."

Kids raised with a smartphone or tablet read or get read to less. The result is they are less likely to start school being able to read. Studies have also found that when you let kids do whatever amuses them (excluding the technology stuff)—called "unstructured playtime"—they will be better able to solve problems and be more creative. More kids are starting school now without the ability to properly hold and use crayons or a pencil; they are unable to cut out even the simplest forms with a scissors. These activities develop fine motor skills and your kid's mind; you can and should start them early at home.

At the time the AAP policy statement was written they didn't have much data on the youngest kids. However, they found that preschool and school-aged children who use the various types of media to a high degree have more problems with obesity, shorter attention spans, being aggressive, and have trouble sleeping soundly. They've discovered that if kids don't sleep well it affects their mood, their general behavior, and ability to learn. In spite of what a lot of parents think, watching TV should not "put them to sleep." Turn off the TV at least an hour before bedtime, read to them or, if they're old enough, let them read a non-violent book, or have a devotional time. Reinforce the understanding that it's time to go to sleep—turn out the light, give them a kiss, and say "Good night. I love you."

Eavesdropping versus kids' right to privacy

Something we all learn is that it isn't polite to listen in on a conversation if you aren't intended to be a part of it. It's called "eavesdropping." But isn't that exactly what you're being told parents must do to know what's going on in their kids' lives? Yep, it is.

It's an unfortunate side of our technologically advanced society that much of what goes on using smartphones, tablets, television, and video games. can be both addictive and destructive for your kids. How often have you heard comments after a tragedy like, "She never seemed like that kind of person," or "He was always such a nice, polite, young man." When the life of a kid starts to wander over to the dark side, fangs and horns don't automatically start to grow. Kids are geniuses at hiding things they don't want you to know.

So what should you check, how should you check it, and how often should you do it? It varies. First and foremost, you should set rules and make sure your kids understand them. Those rules, such as when the devices can be used, how much time can be spent on them, and what materials they can access will vary greatly depending on age. Think this out ahead of time so you are prepared and able to defend your decisions. (Not that your kids would ever think of quarreling with them.) Start with their smartphone, and the same principles can be applied to all other devices.

When can the phone be used? Do you consider it a necessity in case of emergency? If so, you might permit it to be carried at all times. Some schools have restrictions; check so your kids don't get into trouble by taking it to class, or using it during class time. Aside from that, do you want your kids making and receiving calls after bedtime? If not, you must have a solution in mind. Either leave it with the backpack, charging overnight, to be picked up on the way out the next morning, or say that you will check the phone bill each month to see when calls were made. There will be a penalty if the rule is broken.

If your kids are able to drive, all use of the cell phone—making or receiving calls, texting, watching a favorite sports event, whatever—must stop when they get behind the wheel, and not resume until the car is parked again and the engine turned off. The time at stop lights should never be used to get a fast text off to someone.

Think about what you consider important, write it down, and start a discussion with your kids. I wouldn't recommend checking up on them without their knowledge. That doesn't mean you can't check when they're not right there with you. Just let them know in advance that their safety and reputation is very important to you, and you will be keeping a close eye out at all times.

I've read the question of whether or not parents should be "allowed" to check their kids used of media. Until your kids are eighteen, you are the one in charge. You are responsible to God and the community for what your kid does both in real space and cyberspace. Of course you have not only the *right*, but the *responsibility* to monitor your kids' behavior. Kids are kids. Every rule set is there to be broken. Here are a few examples (and please don't let it run through your mind that your kids would never do that.)[10]

- 47% of the kids surveyed admitted they've checked out an Internet site their parents wouldn't approve of.
- 46% of tweens and teens said they received either a sexual text or photo that they know Mom and Dad would be upset about.
- 87% of the kids said they saw cyberbullying.
- 43% of the kids ages thirteen to seventeen said they'd been cyberbullied in the past year.
- Slightly less than 25% of the teens said they wouldn't know what to do if someone started harassing or bullying them online.
- Almost 70% admit they hide some of the stuff they read, write, and watch online.

On the more positive side,

- 70% of moms and dads say they look at their teens' text messages.

- 66% of eight- to seventeen-year-olds have rules about how they can use their cellphone, and almost all of them think the rules are fair.
- Most teens say it doesn't bother them at all if Mom or Dad checks up on their cyber use.
- 87% of moms and dads know there are parental restrictions available on the devices.

Social media—the appeal and the aftermath

Just an added word of advice about social media. Kids simply don't think ahead. What they think, do, and say is immediate. They just blurt it out. The thing is, when it's on the Internet it's there forever. A lot of Facebook's entries are as innocuous as what they thought of the half-eaten lunch they just took a picture of and posted. Or "I've got so-o-o much homework to do tonight!" Twitter, Pinterest, and such are pretty much the same—just a cool, quick way to stay in touch with friends.

However, not all posts are that innocent. When they interview for a job, somebody in Human Resources is most likely going to check up on them on the Internet. Were they angry and explosive? Did they use foul language? Was it always "somebody else's fault?" Did they joke about cheating on a test? Did they post some salacious photos? Teenage indiscretions could mean they'll be looking for another job. They may be looking for a long time.

It's now commonplace for a university to have professionals on staff to look into the background of students applying for entry. There is a "Way Back Machine" that will find everything your kids posted on social media in their young-and-foolish days. It could cost them acceptance into the university that has the best program for their interests.

Normal—is it really?

The *Merriam-Webster Dictionary* online defines "normal" as "usual or ordinary: not strange" followed by "mentally and physically healthy."

In the *Original Roget's Thesaurus*, words similar to "normal" are listed under the adjective use of the word "conformity"; some of those are: ordinary, common, average, commonplace, conventional, usual, and representative.

So how could people be made to change their ways—ways that have always been considered "normal"—and vigorously support some far different? The answer: create a belief that what was aberrant (abnormal, unusual, deviant, peculiar, uncharacteristic, eccentric, odd) is actually normal. It is the "new normal."

What you and your kids have now come to believe is normal, is not normal at all! You think it is unremarkable because you have been blasted with the idea that it is from so many different sources, for so long, that you have come to believe you were wrong and they are right. And people who still believe the "old normal" are now labeled weird, bigoted, intolerant, hatemongers, _______(fill in the blank). It's about to happen again.

The "Media Blitz to Normalize Transgenderism" article I mentioned in chapter 4 states ". . . the American public is about to be inundated with journalistic stories, TV shows, books, movies and ads promoting transgenderism."[11] In case you haven't noticed, it has already started.

Bruce (call me Caitlyn) Jenner was spotlighted on and in Vanity Fair magazine, dressed and posed sexually, with full professional makeup, looking like no woman I know born in 1949. And TV news shows ate it up. Most channels celebrated Jenner's change. Now he is considered "normal."

NBC reported April 22, 2015, about how proud California Congressman Mike Honda is of his granddaughter. Did she qualify for the Olympics? Did she win a spelling bee? Did she successfully fight through a disability from a serious car accident? No. Mike Honda is proud of his eight-year-old granddaughter because she is *transgender*! She was born a boy. The article stated his granddaughter ". . . joined what experts say is a growing number of children transitioning at a young age." The new normal. No exact numbers. The number is "growing." NBC's Today Show did a segment on several families who have young transgender children. Soon it will no longer be newsworthy and *you* will believe transgenderism is normal.

CBS, following lockstep in the media blitz, reported on a family that celebrated their "five-year-old son's transgender journey."

Have you watched the new TV series "Transparent?" It's about a family who finds out their father is transgender. It's billed as a comedy-drama. If you can laugh at something, it becomes more acceptable, more "normal."

Another TV series, "TransAmerica," stars transgender model/activist Carmen Carrera. Identified as a "docuseries," it is promoted as an earnest look at millennial women who are transgender. VH1's executive VP of Programming, Susan Levison, said, "This is a show about a group of compelling, gorgeous young friends who are on a unique journey while staying true to their authentic selves. We believe that message resonates."

I wonder how long it will be before the YWCA and the YMCA will have to drop the "W" and the "M" to become just the YCA, as no one will be identified as a woman or man. Oops, keeping Christianity in it won't work anymore either. It will have to be the YA (Young Association). No, that leaves "Young" as a micro-aggression against older people. Let's just all go to the "A."

If you have cereal-eating kids, you must have noticed the Kellogg's promotion, "Wear Your Stripes with PRIDE." (The word PRIDE is rainbow-colored.) Tony the Tiger, with striped arms folded (defiantly?) and a big smile announces, "At Kellogg, we're an evolving culture that respects and accepts employees' sexual orientation, gender identity and gender expression so that all employees can be authentic and fully engaged." Do you really want your kids fed this as they're eating their cereal? Kellogg's was also a corporate sponsor of the Atlanta Gay Pride March and festival in 2014.

The website SLATE (slate.com) had a blog post on October 3, 2014 about General Mills' release of a new commercial starring a gay couple, their adopted daughter, and a bowl of Cheerios. The blogger, Mark Joseph Stern, dubbed the commercial "adorable" and "impossibly cute." As far as I can tell it was made for their Canadian consumers, and has not been broadcast in the United States. You probably remember in 2014, however, when General Mills celebrated Gay Pride Day with all the rainbow colors of Lucky Charms. A video (you can see it on YouTube) tells the kids "We're Lucky. We live in a colorful world full of colorful people. We don't all look the same, believe the same things, or love the same people. And that's a good thing. It makes our world more interesting. Special. Beautiful. Magical." It closes with "Let's celebrate. Share how you make the world colorful with #LuckyToBe." Other than General Mills, who's promoting that campaign? It's the LGBT+ advocacy group GLAAD.

Do your kids like to watch cartoons and animated movies? The cartoon *Clarence* had two gay men kissing (only on the cheek though so don't be alarmed), and *How to Train Your Dragon 2* has a character with a strong implication that he is gay.

How about comic books—do your kids read those? Archie's character Kevin Keller is openly gay. Iceman in "X-Men" is gay. A *Huffington Post* article in December 2013 had the title, "Batman And Robin Go Gay In New 'Erotic Lives Of The Superheroes' Book."

Publishers Weekly (PW) is one of the most highly regarded sources for everything that's happening in publishing. An article dated May 22, 2015, was titled "Transgender Titles for Young Readers: Titles aimed at young readers address the transgender experience."[12] It's worth your time to go to the link shown in the endnotes for this chapter, but here is a copy of their list of the recent and soon-to-be-published books that feature transgender characters and subjects.

Fiction

- *Red: A Crayon's Story* by Michael Hall (Greenwillow, ages 4–8)
- *George* by Alex Gino (Scholastic, Aug. 2015, ages 8–12)
- *Gracefully Grayson* by Ami Polonsky (Disney-Hyperion, ages 10–14)
- *Lily & Dunkin* by Donna Gephart (Random, June 2016, ages 10–up)
- *Beast* by Brie Spangler (Random House, Oct. 2016, ages 12–up)
- *Double Exposure* by Bridget Birdsall (Sky Pony, ages 12–up)
- *Spirit Level* by Sarah Harvey (Orca, spring 2016, ages 12–up)
- *Alex as Well* by Alyssa Brugman, (Holt, ages 14–18)
- *Art of Being Normal* by Lisa Williamson (FSG, spring 2016, ages 14–18)

Nonfiction

- *I Am Jazz* by Jessica Herthel and Jazz Jennings, illus. by Shelagh McNicholas (Dial, ages 4–8)
- *Sex Is a Funny Word* by Cory Silverberg (Seven Stories, July 2015, ages 7–10)
- *This Book Is Gay* by James Dawson (Sourcebooks, ages 14–17)
- *Beyond Magenta: Transgender Teens Speak Out* by Susan Kuklin (Candlewick, ages 14–up)
- *Rethinking Normal* by Katie Rain Hill, (Simon & Schuster, ages 14–up)
- *Some Assembly Required* by Arin Andrews (Simon & Schuster, ages 14–up)

A book that wasn't mentioned in the PW list is *King and King*. This book, banned by some school districts, tells the story of a young man who must marry in order to be crowned king. However, he falls in love with the brother of the princess he was supposed to marry. A homosexual teacher read *King and King* to his eight-year-old students. The parents were not notified in advance that this material was going to be presented. Their reaction apparently was swift and palpable. "These are my children, these are not your children." Now, continues the article, these parents are "tasked with undoing the LGBT indoctrination of their children's minds. . ."

But soon none of this will make a difference. The media blitz is well on the way to doing its job. The Trans Alliance Society (TAS) in Canada wants birth certificates to drop the designation identifying whether the newborn baby is a boy or a girl. The group, along with unnamed others, objects because "we need to stop acting as if doctors can tell the sex of a baby just by looking at the baby's genitals."

> When an opponent declares, "I will not come over to your side," I calmly say, "Your child belongs to us already."
>
> Adolph Hitler

Why is all this going on? Leo Hohmann, the author of the "Media Blitz" article, believes, "Just as economic Marxism had to destroy capitalism before it could rebuild a society under socialist principles, cultural Marxists work to destroy the family and religious institutions so they can usher in a new order based on secularism and brute materialism. Some have called it 'cultural terrorism.'"

Are your kids afraid of something—anything?

What do your kids fear? Being left out of a social circle? Being laughed at because they won't participate in certain activities? Not knowing what's going on because you won't let them use Facebook or Twitter?

Franklin Delano Roosevelt, thirty-second president of the United

States, said in a speech, "Let me assert my firm belief that the only thing we have to fear is fear itself—nameless, unreasoning, unjustified terror which paralyzes needed efforts to convert retreat into advance." He wasn't referring to the assault on Christian morals, but the statement still rings true. Christians cannot let fear of technology, or a socialist agenda, paralyze us into retreat instead of fighting the battle head-on.

God says "The fear of the Lord is the beginning of knowledge" (Proverbs 1:7). When your kids learn to have high regard for the Word of God, they will also begin to understand the place media has in their lives, while many of their friends may not. Impress on them that "The fear of the Lord is the *beginning* of knowledge." There is so much more out there to learn. God gave them good minds to learn all He prepared for them. Help them turn their minds to those things.

It's amazing, but probably shouldn't be, that Solomon's wisdom still is pertinent today. Proverbs starts right off in chapter 1, verse 4, saying you should give kids knowledge and discretion. Discretion—that's such a huge part of growing up, especially today when platters upon platters of delectable enticements are offered up by such a variety of Pied Pipers. And Solomon says in that same verse there's no one too young or too uneducated to understand the necessity of being prudent.

If your kids think "they're so smart," Solomon would say to them, if you're so smart, open your ears up and hear what I'm saying. Learn something. If you understand so much, you know better than anyone that you really do need some guidance in uncharted waters.

Who does Solomon say scorn lessons you try to teach them? Fools! He goes on to tell your kids to listen to what your dad has to say, and don't let your mom's lectures go in one ear and out the other (Proverbs 1:8). Don't use the all-the-other-kids-are-doing-it excuse. In Solomon's own words, "If sinful men entice you, do not give in to them" (Proverbs 1:10). Don't go down the paths Pied Pipers want you to follow, whether they say they are your friends, or movie stars, or singers. There are consequences to doing that.

✝

"For the waywardness of the simple will kill them, and the complacency of fools will destroy them; but whoever listens to me will live in safety and be at ease, without fear of harm" (Proverbs 1:32–33).

Chapter Challenge

As has been my habit, I'm going to encourage you to verify some of what I told you in this chapter. In doing that, you'll also be able to expand your knowledge. After doing your own research, start a discussion with your family and your friends.

Do a little research within your own family. How much time do your kids spend with the various devices? How much of it is school/homework related? How much is frivolous time on social media? Have you become accustomed to everyone having their smartphones at the table during meals (assuming that ancient family gathering called "mealtime" is still alive and well in your home), or do you have a rule that no devices appear at the table at mealtime? Would you be willing to follow that rule yourself? If the phone rings, are you willing to let it drop into voicemail? Do your kids know you are going to be checking their texts and tweets and Facebook posts? Do you have a rule that they can't delete the history from their computer's memory when they walk away from it?

If you don't feel this kind of self-examination is necessary, please re-read this chapter. Take an active role in your kids' cyber lives. Uncomfortable as it might be in the beginning, it will pay off in their *real* lives in the future.

Websites

- "What Christian Parents Need to Know About Facebook" @ stickyJesus, http://stickyjesus.com/2012/01/what-christian-parents-need-to-know-about-facebook/.3 Jun,2015.
- Shellenberger, Susie. "Social Media and Your Teens!" justbetweenus Christian Magazine & Ministry, http://www.justbetweenus.org/pages/page.asp?page_id=236849.3 Jun,2015.

Reports

- "20 Fine Motor Skills Activities for Preschoolers". Kingdom First Homeschool. http://kingdomfirsthomeschool.com/2014/12/fine-motor-skills-activities.html.3 Jun,2015.
- "Media Use by Children Younger Than 2 Years", 17 Oct 2011, American Academy of Pediatrics. http://pediatrics.aappublications.org/content/128/5/1040.full.pdf+html?sid=71cb491b-910a-469f-9f8a-9d5e4d65c1d3, 2 Jun 2015.
- Lenhart, Amanda, *Teens, Social Media & Technology Overview 2015: Mobile Access Shifts Social Media Use and Other Online Activities*, 09 Apr 2015, Pew Research Center. http://www.pewinternet.org/2015/04/09/mobile-access-shifts-social-media-use-and-other-online-activities/, 30 May 2015.
- Rideout, Victoria J., *et al.*, *Generation M2: Media in the Lives of 8- to 18-Year-Olds*, Jan 2010. https://kaiserfamilyfoundation.files.wordpress.com/2013/04/8010.pdf, 30 May 2015.

Videos

- *Run, Jump, Learn! How Exercise can Transform our Schools*. John J. Ratey, MD at TEDxManhattanBeach. https://www.youtube.com/watch?v=hBSVZdTQmDs.

Chapter Seven

Who's Got Dibs on Your Kids' RELIGIOUS BELIEFS?

Where Christian Kids and the Secular World Must Part

"If you hear it said about one of the towns the Lord your God is giving you to live in that troublemakers have arisen among you and have led the people of their town astray, saying, "Let us go and worship other gods" (gods you have not known), then you must inquire, probe and investigate it thoroughly . . ." (Deuteronomy 13:12-14).

✞

Managers' meetings started at 7:00 a.m. and that first Monday morning I dashed out of the house without breakfast, without even a cup of coffee. Little did I know my new job would lead me to a life-long change in my coffee drinking habit.

I slid my briefcase onto the conference table, and smiled as someone placed a steaming hot mug of that aromatic stimulant beside it. I looked around for the creamer, but just then everyone took their seat, and I was left with the option of drinking my coffee black, or not drinking it at all. The rich fresh-brewed smell was intoxicating, and soon the mug was at my lips; I resisted a shudder.

I learned that not only was coffee always ready and waiting at those ridiculously early meetings, it was the custom for whoever wanted a refill to take the pot around filling everyone's cup that had any room for more. Their thoughtfulness created a problem—I drank milk or cream in my coffee, and the various distributors of the liquid jolts brought only coffee. I decided that when I wasn't doing the pouring, I'd drink it black.

Little by little the bitter taste of undiluted coffee became less nasty, and soon I wasn't even thinking about it anymore. Now I don't need or even want cream in my coffee.

That process—a slow, unplanned modification and adaptation—is called incrementalism. Such change is much more than adjusting your palate to a different taste, as with my coffee. According to Merriam-Webster, incrementalism is "a policy, or advocacy of a policy, of political or social change by degrees." And that's what the Pied Pipers of atheism, humanism, and socialism have in mind.

As I look at that last sentence, I realize it suggests I'm a conspiracy theorist. I don't think I am one, but I am a realist. I see the elimination of Christianity from our country and our lives as one of the primary goals of some very highly placed people—people with enough power and money to make it happen. Let's just take a look at the path the United States has followed since its founding.

Where our country's position on religion started

From the time the Puritans came to these shores, God was an integral part of life in this land, especially the education of children. Not all of our Founding Fathers were Christian, but all agreed that the moral principles of Christianity should be the foundation upon which all our laws would be established. The Founding Fathers often referred to the United States as a Christian nation, but that does not mean they thought of it as a theocracy.

Keep in mind, *there is nothing in our Constitution that establishes the so-called separation of Church and State*. The only reference to this at all makes certain that our federal government cannot establish a religion, and it cannot prevent us from exercising our religious beliefs.

- The Massachusetts Act of 1642 required parents and masters to be sure children knew the laws of the land and could read their Bibles.
- The *New England Primer* was what we would call a first-grade textbook. Published about 1690, it used Bible passages to teach the ABCs, and included prayers, the Lord's Prayer, the Ten Commandments, and a short version of a Catechism. This was used in American schools, both public and private for 200 years.
- Congress approved the purchase of Bibles for schools in 1781.
- The first Noah Webster *Speller* (known as the *Blue Back Speller*) was published in 1783. It's opening sentence was "No man may put off the law of God."
- In 1787 Congress passed the Northwest Ordinance. Article 3 of that document required all the territories to establish schools "to teach religion, morality, and knowledge." Almost all states wrote that phrase into their Constitutions. They all used the Bible as the basis for teaching.
- Thomas Jefferson was president of the Washington, D.C. schools in 1802. He required the Bible and the hymnal of Isaac Watts to be used in the classrooms.
- The McGuffey *Eclectic Readers* were published in 1836. They taught the ABCs and Bible verses, along with the fundamentals of grammar, proverbs, and selections of what was

considered the best of English literature.

- In 1844 the Supreme Court, in a lawsuit brought by a school that wanted to teach morals without using the Bible, stated, "Why may not the Bible, and especially the New Testament . . . be read and taught as a divine revelation in the [school]? . . . Where can the purest principals of morality be learned so clearly or perfectly as from the New Testament? . . . Any book teaching good morality would certainly be teaching what the N.T. teaches, so why not use the original source which doesn't change." The unanimous opinion of the Supreme Court also read in part: "Christianity . . . is not to be maliciously and openly reviled and blasphemed against, to the annoyance of believers or the injury of the public."
- In 1892, in Church of the Holy Trinity v. United States, the Supreme Court ruled: "Our laws and our institutions must necessarily be based upon and embody the teachings of the Redeemer of mankind. It is impossible that it should be otherwise; and in this sense and to this extent our civilization and our institutions are emphatically Christian."
- In Updegraph v. the Commonwealth [Pennsylvania], it was decided that, "Christianity, general Christianity, is, and always has been, a part of the common law . . . not Christianity with an established church . . . but Christianity with liberty of conscience to all men."[1]

From the time the Pilgrims landed the intent was for the United Sates to be a nation based on Christian principles. In 1853 a group tried to get Congress to separate church and state because they wanted chaplains out of the military, the congress, etc. After due consideration both the House and the Senate Judiciary Committees made very similar reports:

> Had the people [the Founding Fathers], during the Revolution, had a suspicion of any attempt to war against Christianity, that Revolution would have been strangled in its cradle. At the time of the adoption of the Constitution and the amendments, the universal sentiment was that Christianity should be encouraged, but not any one sect [denomination]. . . . In this age, there can be no substitute for Christianity. . . . That was the religion of the founders of the republic, and they expected it to remain the religion of their descendants.
>
> The great, vital, and conservative element in our system [the thing that holds our system together] is the belief of our people in the pure doctrines and divine truths of the Gospel of Jesus Christ, it eminently becomes the representatives of a people so highly favored to acknowledge in the most public manner their reverence for God.[2]

How our country's position on religion has changed

In 1947, the Supreme Court surprisingly issued the statement that "The First Amendment has erected 'a wall of separation between church and state.' That wall must be kept high and impregnable." Where did that come from?

Dr. William James, known as the father of modern psychology, said about that claim of a wall of separation, "There is nothing so absurd but if you repeat it often enough people will believe it." And repeat it they did! Finally in 1962 the Court made the first ruling that completely separated Christian principles from education.

Contrary to the well-stated intent of our Founding Fathers, our courts took the following actions regarding Christian religion in American Schools from 1948 through 2000.[3]

Understanding the First Amendment clause by clause.

"Congress shall make no law respecting an establishment of religion," – this means Congress can't establish a religion and make it the obligatory religion of our country. Examples of that are Great Britain which our first settlers were running away from, or Germany, where the "official" religion was Lutheranism, or the Roman Empire where Caesar was "god." Lutheranism is still state-sponsored in the Scandinavian countries; many predominately Muslim countries require anyone elected to a high office must be Muslim; Thailand requires the heads of the monarchies be Buddhist. Our Founding Fathers did not want such limitations placed on our citizens.

"or prohibiting the free exercise thereof;" – this in our present context is the important clause, because if a "wall of separation" is put up between our government and the citizens, it is effectively barring the citizens from free exercise of their religion. Why? Because our government is of the *people*, by the *people*, and for the *people*. The people *are* the government. How can you put a wall between them? That supposed wall effectively does prohibit the *free exercise* of their religion in every part of their daily lives, because our work, family, leisure, worship, all overlap with our civic lives and responsibilities.

"or abridging the freedom of speech," – If we, the people, cannot be prohibited from "free exercise" of our religion, it stands to reason that our right to speak of religious matters cannot be restricted. That is simply irrational.

"or of the press; or the right of the people peaceably to assemble, and to petition the Government for a redress of grievances." – As this clause is an extension of the previous clauses, religious published works cannot be labeled "hate speech," students may not be forbidden to have a Bible study club, and all citizens have the same right to appeal to the government when any of the clauses of this Amendment, as well as any other of our rights, are being trampled on by others who disagree with our religious views.

1948 – U.S. Supreme Court rules time set aside for prayer in public schools is unconstitutional. (McCollum v. Board of Education)

1962 – U.S. Supreme Court rules that children may not recite a state-written prayer in school. (Engel v. Vitale).

1963 – U.S. Supreme Court bans individual school prayer (Murray v. Curlett) and Bible reading in public schools. (Abington Township School District v. Schempp)

1965 – U.S. Supreme Court rules that a child may pray silently if no one knows he is praying and his lips do not move.

1980 – U.S. Supreme Court rules that the Ten Commandments cannot be posted in classrooms, "for a child might read them, reflect upon them and then obey them." (Stone v. Graham)

1983 – President Reagan proposes a Constitutional Amendment to allow school prayer. It was defeated in the Senate.

1985 – U.S. Supreme Court strikes down Alabama law requiring schools to have a moment of silent meditation at the beginning of the day.

1987 – U.S. Supreme Court overturns a state law requiring a balanced treatment of creation science and evolution. (Edwards v. Aguillard)

1992 – U.S. Supreme Court rules that clergy may not offer prayer at graduation ceremonies. (Lee v. Weisman)

2000 – U.S. Supreme Court rules student initiated or student led prayer at football games unconstitutional. (Doe v. Santa Fe)

Far from the Founding Fathers

How can a country that separated itself from another with the words in its Declaration of Independence, "We hold these *truths* to be *self-evident*, that all men are *created* equal, that they are *endowed by their Creator* with certain unalienable Rights . . ." (Emphasis mine)—how can that same country prohibit the teaching of God-ordered creation, or even intelligent design, and force upon your kids the "fact" that our origins derived from evolution?

Where else does our slide from the Founding-Father-acknowledged "truths" take us?

A teacher handed long garments to the girls to wear over their clothes. A cloth draped their heads, covering their hair. Some covered their faces except for the eyes. They were wearing the Muslim hijab, sometimes known as a burqa. Was this a scene in a school in the Middle East? No. Was this a scene in a Muslim school in the United States? No. It was in a high school class in Lumberton, Texas

This occurred as part of a CSCOPE study of Islam.[4] (See chapter 8 for more about CSCOPE.) Some of the students became upset that they were forced to participate, but the school pressed them to sign statements that said they did this exercise of their own free will. The children had to sign waivers saying it was all right for them to participate even though they had voiced objections. Yes, you read that right. The *children* had to sign the waivers! No parents were present.

Now some may say it makes no difference for them to wear the hijab—it's just some pieces of clothing to let the kids understand cultural differences.

That's not actually true. I checked it out.

I found a study on the *Oxford University Press* website that makes clear what the Muslim women's garments are. Here are a couple of lines from that report: "Muslim women's clothing [from puberty] must cover the entire body, with the exception of the face and the hands . . . It is asserted, therefore, that the 'hijab is not a [religious] *symbol* but rather *it is a religious obligation* for Muslim women.'" (Emphasis mine.)[5]

So here's the question: Is it right for Christian girls to put on garments that are *a religious obligation of Islam*? You decide.

A mother of one of the students told Fox News, "My biggest thing is not the burqa," she said. "That was the key to opening up the rest. It's scary how far they dove into the Islamic faith. It's scary what they taught my daughter. Who's in charge of this? How did our superintendent let this slip through the cracks?"

Jesus tell us in Matthew 7:15, "Watch out for false prophets. They come to you in sheep's clothing, but inwardly they are ferocious wolves."

Changing your perception of Islam

If asked what the purpose of education is, the answer would probably be to help students acquire knowledge and develop skills so they can be responsible, contributing members of their community. Some believe it extends beyond that to changing attitudes, principles, and social conduct. A *WND* article in February 2013 reported, "One student quoted the teacher as saying, 'We are going to work to change your perception of Islam.'" That teacher assumed knowledge of what the students' present perception of Islam was, and implied that her perception was better.

> "I wouldn't want to create the impression that I wouldn't like the government of the United States to be Islamic sometime in the future, but I'm not going to do anything violent to promote that. I'm going to use education."
>
> Ibrahim Hooper
> Spokesperson for the Council on American-Islamic Relations (CAIR)

The article quoted another student as saying that the teacher in the hajib/burqa lesson also told the class, "I do not necessarily agree with this, but I am supposed to teach you that we are not to call these people terrorists anymore, but freedom fighters."[6] Never mind that the "freedom fighters" are determined to kill all infidels. Infidels are all who do not follow Islam. I fall into that category. Do you?

Students at a high school in Union Grove, Wisconsin, had a writing assignment in World History. The kids were told to put themselves in the shoes of a Muslim living in the United States and describe the "struggles" they face.

The kids were to pretend they were either a Muslim young man or woman living in the U.S. They were to give three examples of what they do every day for Islam, and any difficulties they have because of practicing their religion. The assignment was accompanied by the cautionary statement: "Keep in mind we've been doing work and watching documentaries that have the *facts* needed to write the essay." (Emphasis mine.)

The superintendent ended up facing his own struggles as he was flooded with calls from people objecting to the assignment. A similar writing assignment had also been given on Hinduism. The superintendent acknowledged that no assignment had been given, nor was one planned, for the students to put themselves in the place of a Christian or a Jew living in a predominately Muslim country.[7]

It's happening all over America in different forms. In Mason, Ohio, a high school had what was billed as "A Covered Girl Challenge" day. The idea was promoted by the school's Muslim Student Association (MSA). They wanted all the female students to wear the hijab on that day to "celebrate" diversity and "promote open-mindedness." One blogger asked when the school was going to have a "Cross-wearers Challenge" day, or a "Yamulke-wearer's Challenge" day. As far as I could tell, those never happened.

We should ask ourselves if these examples are instances of a determination to change kids perception of—and possibly belief in—Islam.

Teaching world history and cultures, or teaching religion?

Should your kids be told the true story of Islam, and its commitment to killing all the infidels? It's not going to happen in a government school. Dale Wolverton, a teacher in Texas tried to do that, and handed out brochures detailing Islam's bloody history. He was fired.

John Wood, a former Marine and the father of an eleventh-grader in Maryland, had enough. He engaged the Thomas More Law Center (TMLC) to represent him against his daughter's school. Why? She got a failing grade for not completing her assignments. She refused to do them because, in her opinion, they were all Islamic indoctrination. According to TMLC, the students were "required to write how the prophet Muhammad was visited by the Angel Gabriel, and preached that there is only one true god, who is Allah . . . that Mohammad is the messenger of Allah and that the Qur'an is holy text . . . to affirm that 'Allah is the same god that is worshipped in Christianity and Judaism.'" She also had to affirm "there is no god but Allah" and state the five pillars of Islam. Wood demanded his daughter be given an alternative assignment, but the school refused and banned him from school property.[8]

Well, that's troubling, but certainly we can assume there was balance. The next week's assignment *must* have included memorizing and reciting the Ten Commandments, the Bible passage John 3:16 "For God so loved the world that he gave his one and only Son, that whoever believes in him shall not perish but have eternal life." And surely they learned John 1:2–4 "He was with God in the beginning. Through him all things were made; without him nothing was made that has been made. In him was life, and that life was the light of all mankind." Certainly there was balance? These and other tenets of Judaism and Christianity must have been taught in addition to the five pillars of Islam. Weren't they?

Of course they were *not* taught! Other information the kids *didn't* learn was the treatment of women, homosexuals, Christians, and Jews under Islam's Sharia law.

Keeping it all in con "text"—in textbooks, that is

Some of the indoctrination of Islam is more subtle. Pearson Publishing is probably the largest provider of our textbooks, and for years has been leaning more and more to following the desires of those in the Muslim Brotherhood. To better understand the path Pearson is taking, and will likely continue to take, you must know that one of its largest financial contributors is the Libyan Investment

Authority, founded by Muammar Qaddafi's son, with 26 million shares of Pearson stock. Other large Pearson investors are Turkey, Saudi Arabia, Council on American-Islamic Relations (CAIR), and the Muslim Brotherhood. A statement in an *American New Media News* article reads: "Muslim Brotherhood documents seized by the FBI and presented at the Holy Land Foundation Trial in Texas revealed a plan by the Muslim Brotherhood and their subsidiary organizations like CAIR to penetrate and indoctrinate American K–12 students."[9]

A study by ACT! for America, a non-profit organization that identifies itself as "devoted to promoting national security and defeating terrorism," did a study in 2011 that found Pearson published thirteen book titles that were decidedly slanted toward promoting the Muslim faith.[10]

Of the thirty-eight textbooks ACT! examined, they found "the predominant place given to Islam in these textbooks highlights the issue of proselytization in the classroom." How does that happen? ACT! discovered that three organizations have heavily influenced your kids' textbooks: the Teachers Curriculum Institute (TCI); Arab World and Islamic Resources and School Services (AWAIR); and the Council on Islamic Education (CIE), founded by Shabbir Mansuri, now known as the Institute on Religion and Civic Values (IRCV). CIE/IRCV seems to carry the heaviest influence of those.

The ACT! report quotes Dr. Robert D. Crane, former Chairman of the Center for Understanding Islam and expert on Islamic jurisprudence, as saying:

> Mansuri has rewritten the required textbooks on religion for thirty-seven of America's fifty states, thanks to unlimited funding by America's first homegrown Muslim billionaire, Safi Qureshey. Selecting the appropriate textbook is no longer a problem, because

> once California adopted the set of textbooks that Shabbir [Mansuri] prepared for the various grades, the publishers had to adopt it in order to make a profit.

ACT! found nothing on the CIE or IRCV websites that indicated Mansuri has any qualifications to recommend him as one to rewrite textbooks. Regarding the content of the textbooks they examined, they stated:

> Textbook errors identified in the Report range from egregiously false historical statements to significant omissions and subtle half-truths. Some are blatant and obvious, others are subtle and deceptive. The errors in these textbooks are not grammatical or typographical. They are substantive, significant and often repetitive.

If you think you can trust your kids' teachers to sift out the wheat from the chaff, don't be so confident. Some teacher training programs are funded by Saudi Arabia. Lesson plans and seminars on the Middle East, for United States K–12 teachers, are designed and provided by Middle East Studies, courtesy of Saudi Arabia, without any U. S. government control.[11]

Parents battled the Tennessee Education Committee over textbooks they describe as "anti-Semitic, anti-Christian, anti-Israel and anti-American." The parents wanted to stop the use of those questionable textbooks, and change the textbook adoption process, "due to the inaccurate and biased textbooks from publishers like Pearson Publishing." One of their biggest causes of concern was Pearson/Prentice Hall's *The Cultural Landscape: An Introduction to Human Geography 10th Edition*. If your kids use that textbook, you may want to take a look at it.

Documented in testimony before the Tennessee Senate Education

Committee was the information that Shabbir Mansuri was hired by Pearson/Prentice Hall to oversee the content of their textbooks. The CIE warned educators and public officials to follow their requests (demands?) or be considered "racists, reactionaries, and enemies of Islam."[12]

In the textbook *World History* (Prentice Hall-A Pearson Education Company), *thirty-six pages* are devoted to teaching Islam; *three paragraphs* feature Christianity. Florida State Representative Rich Workman said, "It's remarkably offensive to me. This book very much sugarcoats the rise of Islam to be this wonderful new world order, while teaching that Christianity is dogmatic." Workman believes the book reshapes history so that Islam won't be insulted.

Subtle mind-manipulation occurred by using the word "massacre" when Christians are fighting a battle, and "takeover" when it's a Muslim war.

Representative Workman also took exception to the rewriting of history. He said, "If you don't see it from the eyes of a parent, kids are going to take this book as gospel and believe that Christians and Jews were murderous barbarians and thank God the Muslims came along and the world is great . . . It leaves out that tens of thousands of Jews and non-believers were massacred by Mohammed's armies," he said. "It's a blatant deception."

There are extensive passages quoted from the Koran in that textbook, but none from the Bible. The text states that Mohammed is the "Messenger of God." It does not state or even imply that Jesus is the Son of God. It does mention that "Some believed he [Jesus] was the messiah." It states that Jesus was executed, but not that he rose from the dead.[13]

Varied methods to get the message out

Prayer was banned from public schools by the Supreme Court in 1962. Apparently the Court only meant Christian prayer. In California, seventh-grade students were taught to pray "in the name of Allah, the Compassionate, the Merciful" as well as chant "Praise to Allah, Lord of Creation."[14] In that same three-week intensive course the kids also had to learn the principles of Islam, study the important people of Islam, wear a robe, choose a Muslim name for themselves, and perform their own jihad! Keep in mind, the meaning of "jihad," according to Merriam-Webster, is "a war fought by Muslims to defend or spread their beliefs" or "a holy war waged on behalf of Islam as a religious duty," or "a personal struggle in devotion to Islam especially involving spiritual discipline."

Can you imagine the furor if anyone even suggested this kind of study of Christianity? How can such a curriculum be approved in public schools in the United States? Are you beginning to understand why I believe public schools can be a dangerous Pied Piper, leading our children on a path away from God?

Compare and contrast

The direction often used these days is "compare and contrast." Let's do that now. Let's compare and contrast the following attitudes and actions:

- The superintendent of the school where the girls had to wear burqas did not allow a Bible history class.
- The Springs Charter Schools in Temecula, California, told the librarian to get rid of all books with a Christian message, authored by Christians, or published by a Christian publishing company. The school's superintendent said they do not allow "sectarian materials on our state-authorized shelves." Many textbooks are approved and

> "I am waging a 'bloodless' revolution, promoting world cultures and faiths in America's classrooms."
>
> Shabbir Mansuri, Founder and Director of the Council on Islamic Education (CIE)

often funded by Muslim organizations.

- A student at Forest Heights Community School in Nova Scotia, Canada, was suspended because the statement on his shirt, "Life is wasted without Jesus" is a form of hate speech. His principal said "people would get offended." The school does not have a dress code.
- The Matoaca Middle School, Matoaca, Virginia, banned students from wearing rosary beads until the ACLU stepped in. Someone said it was because the cross might be looked at as a "gang identifier." There was no gang presence at the school.
- At California State University's twenty-three campuses, Christian college clubs are banned if they do not permit non-Christians to lead their groups. They assert a belief-based organization cannot require beliefs from their leaders. Someone suggested, tongue-in-cheek, that Oscar Meyer should be allowed to lead campus chapters of the Ethical Treatment of Animals.
- A student at a northern California university was told she had to take off her two-inch-long-cross necklace because others might find it offensive. The university's mission statement includes "tolerance and inclusivity to all."

The above incidents should not be happening. In Tinker v. Des Moines Independent School District (1969), the United States Supreme Court held that students do not "shed their constitutional rights to freedom of speech or expression at the schoolhouse gate."

Class assignments your kids may get

The *Encarta Dictionary* definition of indoctrination says it is "to teach somebody a belief, doctrine, or ideology thoroughly and systematically, especially with the goal of discouraging independent thought or the acceptance of other opinions." Keep this definition in mind as we look at some class assignments.

Do your littlest kids get pictures to color in class? Make sure they bring them home so you can see them. An atheist group, along with Satanists, is handing out literature in Florida schools, and one piece is an activity and coloring book. It's called "The Satanic Children's Big Book of Activities." One of the activities has the kids drawing an inverted pentagram: "Damian is showing this class the way to make an inverted pentagram. Connect the dots to make one yourself." The pentagram is probably one of the best-known symbols of the occult, used to conjure up spirits.

Are you familiar with Ashtanga yoga? Most people believe yoga is nothing more than a great way to relax. Not so, say the students and parents in a California school district. The program has the students bowing to the sun god.

This form of yoga was being taught and subsequently, because of concerns, removed from classes around the world. Austria has removed yoga from its classrooms, and the Indian Supreme Court is considering if the Ashtanga yoga philosophy "would discriminate against the Muslim and Christian minorities." Yoga is one of the six schools of Hindu religious philosophy. Yet the California schools do not see a problem.[15]

Fighting the California school district on behalf of the parents and students, the National Center for Law & Policy stated, "Courts are especially sensitive to the coercive pressures involved when the government, because education is compulsory and supported by tax dollars, leads young impressionable children with tender consciences through group liturgical/ritual religious exercises or activities including bowing to the sun god."

Even students at parochial schools are not out of danger. A Canadian government study course, "Ethics and Religious Culture," is mandatory for all public and private schools. This course declares all religions, from Christianity to Wiccan, as equally sound. Schools are required to teach the material just that way! It also forbids teachers, including those in Christian schools, to tell the kids that their own school's faith is preferred over the others covered in that course.[16] Granted this occurred in Canada, but we must be alert that it doesn't happen in the United States.

A high school in Jenison, Michigan, took a novel approach to the study of Islam. They gave their tenth-graders an assignment in their world religion class to create a pamphlet that provided the main concepts of Islam. The introduction to the assignment said the "pamphlet should be targeted towards elementary students" with the instruction that it should be understandable by third grade kids. Now, admittedly, the pamphlets were never distributed to the school district's third-graders. Nevertheless, one of the best ways to learn something well is to teach it, and one of the best ways to teach it is reducing it down from a complex form to a more understandable form. I will make a guess that the kids who created those pamphlets will never forget the "facts" they learned in that world religion class.

Not exactly a "class assignment" but part of the school day is the reciting of the Pledge of Allegiance. A furor arises every now and then about the necessity of including the phrase "under God" in the Pledge. However, leaving that phrase out wasn't an option when it was read aloud in Arabic at the Pine Bush High School in Pine Bush, New York. The school's defense was that it was meant to honor National Foreign Language Week. But the school does not even offer classes in the Arabic language.

Rocky Mountain High School in Colorado did the same thing, permitting the Cultural Arms Club to lead the student body in Arabic. What is so important about reciting the Pledge in Arabic? Think about what the words say—"one nation, under God" becomes "one nation, under Allah." Is that what you want your kids to say? I'm certain our God of the Bible would not want us to replace His name anywhere, or pledge that Allah is our country's spiritual guide.

Shouldn't the President of the United States know better?

The President of the United States takes his own liberty with America's important historical and foundational documents. An article in *USA Today*, December 10, 2010, took President Obama to task for some rather unstatesmanlike gaffes:

> The president cannot stop stumbling over the religious maxims that have defined us as a nation.
>
> Earlier this fall [2010], President Obama repeatedly misquoted the Declaration of Independence, saying "We hold these truths to be self-evident, that all men are created equal, that each of us are endowed with certain inalienable rights." Why leave out the "Creator"? Doing this once would have gathered no notice. Twice, and the grumbling began. Three times, and people began to wonder whether he had made a conscious decision to reword this founding document, presumably for the purpose of political correctness.[17]

The *USA Today* article continued with a reference to a speech the president gave in Indonesia in November 2010 where he said the motto of the United States was E Pluribus Unum (Out of Many, One). Since 1956 our motto has been "In God We Trust."

In 2013 President Obama was celebrating the 150th anniversary of Lincoln's Gettysburg Address. He read that famous speech in its entirety—well, almost. Instead of reading "that this nation, under God, shall have a new birth of freedom," he left out the "under God" part. His excuse? Some staffer gave him Lincoln's draft document known as the "Nicolay Version" which did not include those words, instead of the final one. I would have expected a United States president, a constitutional scholar, a man of a race freed from slavery through the efforts of Abraham Lincoln, would have noticed it before he publically read it, and obtained the final, correct version.

One more religious element President Obama has a problem with is in the Bill of Rights. The First Amendment to the Constitution of the United States declares, "Congress shall make no law respecting an establishment of religion, or prohibiting the free exercise thereof." Obama's interpretation of that in a speech recognizing Religious Freedom Day in 2013 was "the freedom to worship as we choose." Why does this matter? The Bill of Rights gives us the *free exercise* of our religion, meaning we can live our lives in accordance with our religious beliefs. We can openly express our faith, both in private and in public. Freedom to *worship* is private, personal; it's what happens between an individual and God, in prayer and in a worship service. There is a big difference between *freedom to exercise* our faith, and the *freedom to worship*.

What did our Founding Fathers intend?

If you wonder what our Founding Fathers intended, just look to James Madison. He said, "The civil rights of none, shall be abridged on account of religious belief or worship, nor shall any national religion be established, *nor shall the full and equal rights of conscience be in any manner, or on any pretext infringed*." (Emphasis mine.) Keep that in mind the next time you read of a baker or florist losing their business because they would not provide their services for a same-sex "marriage."

Words matter

Did you know that people aspiring to become citizens of this country are taught to say "freedom of worship" rather than "freedom of religion?" The Department of Homeland Security made that change in the naturalization materials in 2008. Senator Lankford (R-Oklahoma) wrote a letter of complaint to Jeh Johnson, the Secretary of Homeland

Security, in which he said, "We are doing a great disservice to those seeking citizenship in this great country if we distort our history and fail to teach new citizens about the founding and constitutional principles of this nation . . . your own naturalization materials do not even accurately reflect the constitutional rights of American citizens."

Are your kids studying the Constitution in school? What are they learning about the First Amendment—freedom *of religion* or freedom *to worship*? Check it out. It's important!

By the government's own standards, our schools are not educational

Focus on the Family's James Dobson started another organization, the Family Talk Action Corporation. Its stated purpose was to spread the good news about the saving grace of Jesus Christ, and offer education for parents and children. It would also speak to cultural matters. The Family Talk Action Corporation filed an application for 501C4 tax-exempt status. It was denied.

The IRS agent reviewing the request said, "I don't think your Form 1024 (application for exemption) will be granted because Family Talk Action is *'not educational' because it does not present all views*." She continued saying Family Talk Action sounded like a *"partisan right-wing group"* because *"it only presents conservative viewpoints*." (Emphasis mine.)

By that agent's definition, many of our public schools are not "educational." They present, and permit, only one view (evolution) regarding the beginning of the world. They present, and permit, only one view (a fully acceptable life-style) regarding homosexuality. They present, and permit, only one view (promiscuity) regarding sexual behavior. They present, and permit, only one view (abortion with or without parents' consent) regarding the sanctity of life.

It seems that if, by our government's own characterization, our schools are not "educating" our children, we should shut them all down, and start our own schools that will actually educate.

Football, faith, and flinging the flag

If you had a son who loved football, and made the high school team, you'd want to be there and celebrate with him when he makes his first-ever touchdown. And you'd expect your son to be pretty happy about it as well. That's how Sam Turner, playing for Fort Myers High School felt. And when he crossed the goal line for his very first touchdown he, just for a moment, dropped to one knee, raised his finger toward the sky and prayed, "Thank you, God for this talent you've blessed me with."

And then the official flung the flag. Sam Turner, with his brief, quiet, thanks to God, had cost his team fifteen yards! He was penalized, the ref said, for calling attention to himself. Yes, there is a rule that was occasioned by too many players becoming "overly exuberant" in the end zone. But dropping to one knee and quietly saying a ten-word prayer hardly fits into that category. Fortunately Sam's teammates knew of his faith, and took the penalty with good grace.

Interestingly, the National Football League permits such action in the end zone with some qualification that the player is observing his faith. Sam certainly met that requirement. I have to wonder if that Florida high school ref would have allowed a touchdown celebration of a fist-pump and a shout of "YES! Yes, yes, YES!!."

I don't remember many touchdowns where the player simply crossed the goal line and walked demurely over to hand the ball to the ref—Larry Fitzgerald being a possible exception. So what actually is it that warrants a penalty? Celebrating a touchdown? Or a drop to one knee to thank God?

The pit and the pendulum

It is said that an alcoholic or drug addict can't truly fight the addiction and start back on the path to an alcohol- or drug-free life until hitting bottom. Do you feel as though our nation has followed the atheist/humanist/socialist/Islamist Pied Piper as far into the "vilifying Christianity" pit as it can? Have we hit bottom yet? Can we expect the pendulum to start its way back in the other direction? I hope the answer to those three questions is a resounding "yes." But recovery requires more than just hitting bottom. There has to be the desire, and the effort, to get out of the pit. Only God, not a Pied Piper, must lead us this time.

God has been explicit about parents' responsibility regarding their children's knowledge of the will of God. In Proverbs 22:6 He tells us, "Start children off on the way they should go, and even when they are old they will not turn from it." That is a two-edged sword. Are you training your kids in the way they should go according to God's laws, or are you letting someone else train them to walk a path away from salvation through Jesus Christ? It is a serious question for you to consider, for God himself tells us, "when they are old they will not turn from it."

✝

"This temple will become a heap of rubble. All who pass by will be appalled and say, 'Why has the Lord done such a thing to this land and to this temple?' People will answer, 'Because they have forsaken the Lord, the God of their ancestors, who brought them out of Egypt, and have embraced other gods, worshiping and serving them—that is why he brought all this disaster on them'" (2 Chronicles 7:21–22).

Chapter Challenge

Have members of your group check textbooks, worksheets, and other assignments. Where problems are noted bring copies for comparison. Don't make the assumption that because your school district is highly regarded and wins awards you don't have to worry about what your kids are being taught. Some of you may not face any of the difficulties related in this chapter. If your school district *is* spanking clean, be willing and available to help others who are encountering problems. The fight is not easy, and every bit of assistance you can offer is important.

Ask for help from others in your church who do not have kids in school. Have them review and comment on textbooks. Ask them to attend Board of Education meetings and report back to your group. Ask them to spread the word. They can help tremendously not only with the elements of this chapter, but in bringing to light a variety of insidious ways used by some who are conniving to get dibs on your kids.

God has made you ultimately responsible for the religious education of your kids, but you may need help. Ask your pastor for recommendations of materials appropriate for the ages of your kids. There are many available. Listed here are just a few of the many resources:

- Christ Light materials from Northwestern Publishing are available for three-year-olds through grade twelve. They also carry a wide selection of books for all ages. One of my favorites is the "Little Visits" series. Check them out at http://online.nph.net/s-7-13-books.aspx.
- Concordia Publishing House has a wide range of books and study materials available at http://www.cph.org/c-776-homeschool.aspx?REName=Education&plk=1319.
- LifeWay has a "Kids Ministry 101" web page with links to materials, talking to your kids about difficult subjects and more at http://www.lifeway.com/kidsministry/?type=learn.
- Visit "A Kid's Heart" at http://www.akidsheart.com/ for a variety of suggestions including clip art, puzzles, coloring pages, and more.

Books

There are many good resources for your personal and group study about the ways the Christian religious beliefs are being denigrated, twisted, and eliminated from your kids' lives. Some of those I recommend are:

- Barton, David. *America's Godly Heritage*. Aledo, TX: WallBuilder Press, 1993. This and the following book by David Barton are both small in their number of pages, but loaded with valuable information.
- Barton, David. *Separation of Church and State: What the Founders Meant*. Aledo, TX: WallBuilder Press, 2007.

Reports and Other Referenced Material

- You can download and read the Executive Summary of the report "Islam in Florida's K-12 Textbooks" from the Citizens for National Security website at https://cfns.us/the-cfns-report-on-pro-islam-bias-in-public-schools/.

Videos

- Gunn, Colin, and Joaquin Fernandez. *Indoctrination: Public Schools and the Decline of Christianity in America*. Gunn Productions, 2011.
- Barton, David. *"The American Heritage Series."* 780 minutes (26 episodes of 30 minutes each – 10 discs): WallBuilders, LLC, 2009. I *highly* recommend this series!

Who's Got Dibs on Your Kids' FUTURE?

How Your Kid's Dreams, Goals, and Profession are Manipulated

"They are a nation without sense, there is no discernment in them. If only they were wise and would understand this and discern what their end will be!" (Deuteronomy 32:28–29).

The spring of 2015 brought disturbing events. In Baltimore, Maryland, the police took a black man, Freddie Gray, into custody. According to the police, when they put him in the transport van he was calling for his asthma spray but otherwise seemed in good health. When it was time to remove him from the van and take him into the police station, his neck and spine were so badly injured he died a week later. What happened?

The police tried to assure people that they had not abused him, but the Baltimore community would have none of that. Riots broke out, over one hundred police officers were injured, stores were looted and burned, and the Bloods and the Crips united in common cause. Strange bedfellows indeed.

Out of this mayhem a strikingly wonderful scene erupted. A mother saw her teenage son walking among the protesters. Even worse, in her eyes, he was wearing a black hoodie and face mask. Others could probably not tell who he was, but his mother knew. And she knew she had to get him out of there immediately. That mother ran to her son, shouted at him to go home, and started smacking on him with her hands, forcing him out of the crowds. (I don't think anyone will accuse her of child abuse; her son was a great deal taller than she was.) Although it was obvious he didn't much appreciate what was going on, he walked, stumbled, half-ran, as his mother continued to thrash him. Later that mother said she didn't want her son turning into the kind of person he was with that day.

The kids at his school probably made fun of him getting walloped by his mom in public and on national TV; he was undoubtedly embarrassed. His mother didn't care at all about that—he was her son and she was going to do anything and everything she could to see that he grew up to be a fine, responsible young man. I imagine he will.

That mother was definitely concerned about her son's future. I'm sure you are concerned about your kids' future, too. But how far are you willing to go to protect them from outside influences that in all probability could and would change their destiny? Normally, you would want to make sure they got good grades in school, kept out of trouble, and had a well-rounded life. What could possibly go wrong with that?

Raising kids is no longer that simple. The government has made it next to impossible for parents to help their kids with homework, or to even be aware of what they are being taught. Some of the confusion is by design.

Did you ever run an obstacle course? There are many available, some designed for kids just to have fun, and some that are world-class competitions. The idea is to prevent you from getting to your destination easily or quickly. Hazards and obstacles are designed to make you give up. One major competition course warns that you should expect to get lost at least once. They provide GPS trackers that can transmit a "mayday" signal in emergencies. Your kids' schools do not. The education obstacles the Pied Piper is directing your kids through are planned less to see how many he can lead to success, and more like how many he can sacrifice to secularism, humanism, and atheism on the way. Let's look at some of the hazards your kids may encounter.

Obstacle #1 – Wading through the marshland of Common Core

Studying, homework, tests, and then the Report Card! How are your kids doing? If you live in any but a handful of states, they are struggling their way through the new Common Core method of education. What is this new education marshland?

Common Core State Standards, the official name for this program, is often referred to by its letters CCSS or just Common Core. Although it sounds like it would be referring to *state* standards, it is not. This is a *federal* program mandating what subjects states will teach at which grade level, although it does not dictate specific curricula. The theory is that if it were known to be a federal program, parents would balk at such universal government control over their children—not to mention it being unconstitutional. Call it what you will, the federal government is in control.

CCSS has a copyright, held by the National Governor's Association and the Council of Chief State School Officers. There has been a lot of discussion about whether or not states using Common

Core can make changes to better suit their local needs because of the copyright. Generally, under federal copyright law no one, no school, no Board of Education would be able to modify the Standards in any way. However, states dug into this, and came to the conclusion that because of the nature of the program those copyright restrictions on changes do not apply.

The Standards originally indicated that states could add up to, but not more than, 15% to the Standards. The latest word is that states may add whatever they want, but are encouraged to adhere to the 15% limit or it will undermine the nationwide uniformity of the Standards.

States lined up to get their share

From the outset, forty-six of our fifty states signed on to the idea, although Minnesota got on board for only the English Language Arts portion. Why did so many agree so readily? Federal grant money, connected to Race to the Top, was a big incentive. The Heritage Foundation reported:

> Billions in federal funding was used to create incentives for states to adopt the standards, yet the effort has left state taxpayers to pick up the tab for their implementation, conservatively estimated to cost more than $16 billion. . . . The Department of Education offered $4.35 billion to states in Race to the Top grants, conditioned in part on adoption of "standards common to a significant number of states."

The only standards option that qualified at the time (and currently) was the Common Core State Standards Initiative.[1]

Interestingly, since Common Core was launched in 2009, some of those states that had their hands out for the money are now having second thoughts. Indiana voted to put a temporary halt on the program, even though implementation had begun in some classes. They wanted to look at it more closely. Some in that state believed the Standards were not well written, and their existing standards were already higher than CCSS. They wanted education decisions to be local rather than at the federal level. Further, a cost analysis was not done prior to acceptance, and they feared it would be cost prohibitive. Thanks to the persistent efforts of two moms, Indiana will not be using CCSS in the 2015–2016 school year.[2]

Oklahoma and South Carolina both reversed their adoption of Common Core. Alabama, South Dakota, and Georgia are also having buyer's remorse, and the Michigan legislature recently voted to defund the project. Arizona tried to get out of it—the legislators didn't think it was any better when Governor Jan Brewer renamed it the "AZ College and Career Ready Standards"—but the bill was defeated.

Obstacle #2 – Climbing the high wall of CCSS cost

Pull your pockets inside-out because Common Core may take everything but the lint. New Common Core aligned textbooks cost about $50 each, and as much as $139 for the teacher editions. Multiply that by the number of kids-plus-teachers in your district, and you'll get a pretty hefty figure.

The Standards can be implemented at three different levels, but Fordham's Institute did an analysis and found that the cost to Wisconsin taxpayers would range from a "bare-bones" approach at $62.3 million, to a middle-of-the-road versions at $106.5 million, to an in-all-the-way approach (called the "traditional" model) at a cost of $256.1 million. And don't forget to add on the $23 million going to the new testing needed to comply with Common Core.

The Arizona cost for "essential elements" of Common Core were estimated at $156.6 million, according to a survey performed by the Arizona School Boards Association. The state of Washington is looking at a bill of over $300 million. But hold your breath, California will be on the hook for about *$1.25 billion* to "prepare the way for Common Core."[3] To read the May 2012 Thomas B. Fordham Institute report, and see a chart of costs for implementation broken down by state, go to the Chapter Challenge section for the link.

Keep in mind, the Common Core State Standards have never been tested, evaluated, improved, tested again, or run by the school boards. Nothing. But take their word for it, this is really going to be great. Well worth billions of dollars.

Moreover, not many states have that kind of money floating around looking for a good project. Can you think of anything in your state or school district where that money might serve a better purpose?

Obstacle #3 – The quicksand of "comfortable" math

Has math become a problem for your formerly top student? Do you hear moans about "I just don't understand this" or "This is so *dumb*! Why do I have to do this?" Your kids are okay. It's the new CCSS math that is driving everyone crazy. You can find many instances online, but here are a few doozies:

Example #1: Your kids just can't answer a math problem by writing down 12 – 9 = 3, they have to show *five* different ways you can get to that answer.

Example #2: Ilene Ryan, a math teacher, declared that "Our young learners might not be altogether comfortable thinking about what 9 + 6 is." She actually said that! When was the last time you worried if your kids were "comfortable" when they were learning their math tables? She continued, "They are quite comfortable thinking about their friend, 10." (Aren't you glad to know that "10" is a friend?) "Ten is emphasized in our young grades as we're working in a base 10 system. So if we can partner 9 to a number and anchor 10, we can help our students see what 9 + 6 is."

The kids are supposed to "decompose" the 6 into its parts: 1 and 5. Then the teacher "anchors" the 9 to the 1. She seems to assume the kids can understand that totals 10. Then she adds the 5 (left over from deconstructing the 6) to the 10, and *presto*! You have the answer: 15. She says "That's much more comfortable."

That must have turned on the math lights above every kid's head in class. I don't know whether to laugh or pull my hair out. Try this method the next time you're balancing your check book.

Example #3: This is a video of a teacher training session where the Curriculum Director explains how it would be okay for your kids to arrive at the answer 11 when the problem is 3 × 4, as long as they could explain their reasoning. One teacher asks if they shouldn't correct the student, and the presenter says, "Yes, of course," but that isn't really the way they are going to approach teaching math anymore.[4]

Obviously memorizing the math tables is out. But should it be? A team of neuroscientists says that rote memorization plays a crucial role in the development of your kids' brains. They are quite certain that memorizing the tables makes their brains reorganize so it can handle more complex math. It is a major factor in the process of achieving mathematical reasoning.[5]

Five members of the CCSS Validation Committee refused to put their names to the project when they saw the end-product. One of those four, James Milgram, a Stanford University professor and mathematician (the only mathematician on the Board) said that the math portion will put U.S. students two years behind students in other high-achieving countries. Why did he feel that way? Milgram, along with Sandra Stotsky, the only expert on K–12 English Language

Arts standards, prepared a report.[6] In it they quote Professor Jason Zimba, the lead writer of the Common Core mathematics standards, as saying, "the concept of college readiness is minimal and focuses on non-selective colleges."

In a back-and-forth between Stotsky and Zimba, Zimba conceded that based on their CCSS education, students would most likely have to take remedial courses in math and English to get into even lower ranking colleges and community colleges. "[I]ts college readiness level is not for certain professions or for demanding colleges." In response to Stotsky questioning as to whether high school students would be prepared for STEM (Science, Technology, Engineering, Math) or international competitiveness, Zimba said, "Not only not for STEM, it's also not for selective colleges. For example, for UC Berkeley, whether you are going to be an engineer or not, you'd better have precalculus to get into UC Berkeley."

As a trying-hard-to-be-proud American, I'm embarrassed to learn that a Pew Research Center study shows our fifteen-year-old kids in the United States rank thirty-fifth in the world in math skills! Of the sixty-four countries studied, twenty-eight score "significantly higher" than we do. And it's not that no one was aware. A survey of members of the American Association for the Advancement of Science (AAAS) unveiled the truth that scientists think our STEM education is below average. Not to worry, though. Test results are up. Now only 17% of fourth-graders and 26% of eighth-graders rate in the lowest performance level.

> "In the first place, God made idiots. That was for practice. Then he made school boards."
> Mark Twain

Some of the additional CCSS changes to the study of math are:

- Algebra is introduced in ninth grade instead of eighth grade.
- Division is postponed from fifth grade to sixth grade.
- Traditional geometry is replaced with an experimental, untested, approach.

- Proficiency in addition and subtraction is not expected now until fourth grade.
- Proficiency in basic multiplication is delayed until fifth grade.

If your kids are going to have any chance at success in most college-level courses, both the discipline of and competency in math will be essential. If your kids are getting sucked down into this new math quicksand, you are going to have to take a firm stand. This is no time to throw up your hands and say, "I just can't help you with this." Consider teaching them "real" math at home, or hire a tutor. Then opt out of the standardized tests. I give ways for you to do this in chapter 10.

Obstacle #4 – Belly-crawling under the low rail of informational reading

English did not fare better than math. How could this happen? Stotsky reveals some of the dubious machinations in a report she presented at a conference at the University of Notre Dame in 2013.[7] Twenty-nine members of a "Standards Development Work Group," were divided into a Mathematics Work Group and an English Language Arts (ELA) Work Group. The ELA group had no English professors—none! It didn't even have any high-school English teachers. So who was providing the input as to what kids should be taught? Who would presume to know better than professional English teachers? It would be the lead writers, David Coleman and Susan Pimental. Those two lead writers for ELA standards never taught an English class at any grade level, never published a serious paper on K–12 curriculum and instruction, and had no established reputation for scholarship or research—they had no credentials to qualify them for this job!

There was also a "Feedback Group" which did include one English professor and one high-school English teacher. They were informed theirs would be an advisory role only, and all final decisions rested entirely with the Work Group. The Feedback Group felt that after they had worked hard, the evaluations and recommendations they developed and sent to the appropriate parties just dropped into some deep hole (probably resembling the one in hospitals labeled "Hazardous Material. Do Not Touch".) They were not even given the courtesy of an explanation.

Work Groups were secret, no meetings were open to anyone not in the Group, no minutes of meetings were made available, and there was no means for public comment.

But, breathe a sigh of relief, there was a Validation Committee (VC) of another twenty-nine members in 2009–2010. Oh, sorry, other than Stotsky, the VC had no experts on ELA standards. Stotsky said she was the only one on the VC nationally recognized as an expert on English Language Arts standards, and that recognition was because she had previously worked on some high school ELA exit standards. After she stomped, yelled, and waved her arms enough to get their attention, a high school English teacher was finally added to the VC. Again, all the work of the VC was confidential. They were charged with some actions and activities, but in Stotsky's opinion, "It quickly became clear that the VC existed as window-dressing—to rubber-stamp, not improve, whatever standards were declared as college- and career-readiness and grade-level standards."

The Heritage Foundation published Issue Brief #3800 by Sandra Stotsky titled, "Common Core Standards' Devastating Impact on Literary Study and Analytical Thinking." In it she claims that Common Core is "a step backwards for English standards."

You are not alone if you are concerned about many aspects of the CCSS instruction your kids get in schools. The English Language Arts portion of the Standards requires a continually diminishing portion of reading allocated to literature, and increasing time being spent reading nonfiction and informational material. I've read some reports that classic literature instruction will be reduced to 40%, even possibly 30%, of ELA's reading material in high school.

The designers of Common Core believed that college students read more nonfiction than literary texts and, therefore, will be better prepared to succeed in college. Stotsky pointed out there is no research indicating that path will promote greater college readiness. Instead, she insists, "the decline in readiness for college reading stems in large part from an increasingly incoherent, less challenging literature curriculum from the 1960s onward."

As the continued implementation of CCSS is being assessed, high school English teachers complain that the required amount of instruction time devoted to informational reading leaves only enough time for excerpts from novels, plays or epic poems, or just very short stories and poems. This interferes with students' analytical thinking, which develops when doing in-depth literature studies.

> "We all want progress, but if you're on the wrong road, progress means doing an about-turn and walking back to the right road; in that case, the man who turns back soonest is the most progressive."
>
> C. S. Lewis

Stotsky noted that CCSS will "significantly weaken the intellectual demands on students in the areas of language and literature." She also expressed the concern that students will produce lower scores when they take ACT, the college entrance exam, because literary features such as characters, literary devices, tone, ambiguity, elaboration, structure, intricate language, and unclear intentions are abundant in that test.[8] (Not to worry, Pearson Publishing is rewriting the college entrance exams to conform to CCSS.)

An additional concern is the choice of reading materials for the fiction portion of the course. I refer to it as "fiction" because most of it doesn't deserve to be called "literature." I'll tell you more about that in chapter 9.

Obstacle #5 – Crossing the chasm of the cursive writing void

Tap, tap, tap. Fingers or thumbs fly quickly over keys to send a text message or access a website. "We use the computer at school. I can type it. Why do I need cursive?"

Why should kids today be forced to learn to write, or soon, print? Who needs that?

Your kids do. And it is going to be up to you to insist on it. You know your kids won't.

The Common Core State Standards do not prohibit teaching cursive writing—it's just that there isn't any time for it. Generally, instruction in cursive begins in the third grade. Now, the Pied Piper of technology takes over that time slot for keyboard instruction. Schools are allowed to add 15% of instructive material to the Standards, but what should they choose, and who gets to make the choice? Cursive is called an "ancient skill." (I know I'm getting old, but I don't think of myself as "ancient" yet.)

You might have already bought into the theory that cursive writing is no longer important. Others strongly disagree. William Klemm, D.V.M., Ph.D., says learning cursive enhances cognitive development, and trains a child's brain to develop "functional specialization." Cursive writing affects sensation, movement control, and thinking. Studies show it activates parts of the brain that using a keyboard doesn't stimulate.

When your kids are struggling with learning cursive, Dr. Klemm says, "fine motor control is needed over the fingers. Students have to pay attention, and think about what they are doing and how they are doing it. They have to practice. Brain imaging studies show that cursive activates areas of the brain that do not participate in keyboarding."

Virginia Berninger, a psychologist at the University of Washington, found that if kids composed text by hand, rather than using digital technology, they *wrote more words*, they *wrote them faster*, and they poured out *more ideas*. Those students were in grades two through five. When older students were tested, they were asked for ideas for a composition; the ones with the best cursive handwriting lit up brain areas connected with working memory, as well as stepped up neural activation in all the reading and writing networks.[9]

If you don't think those results are enough to jump-start your kids' future, when students took longhand notes during lectures, they remembered more of the lecture than the ones who entered their notes digitally on tablets or laptops.

As a result of the research, some states have passed a law that requires teaching cursive. By now the negative results of the lack of cursive instruction have become evident. Twelve states have already moved to make it mandatory, and the Ohio House overwhelmingly passed a bill to require cursive instruction to be part of their kindergarten through fifth grade studies.

One argument often used to validate the necessity of your kids learning cursive is that if they don't, at some point no one will be able to read our country's original documents such as the Declaration of Independence, the Constitution, and the Bill of Rights. These are all beautifully written in cursive.

You might be wondering why that would be important. If only a few people can read them—if you or your kids can't read them—how will anyone know if someone with authority over you (Congress or the Supreme Court) is telling you the truth about what they say?

> "Ignorance is the curse of God; knowledge is the wing wherewith we fly to heaven."
> William Shakespeare

Will your kids go through life without ever learning cursive? At what point will they wish they knew it?

Obstacle #6 – Getting stuck in the spider's web of data mining

Consider the web of a spider:

- It's spun carefully with the intent to trap prey
- It's sticky and hard to get disentangled

- It spreads out mazelike in every direction—there is no way out
- The spider sits waiting for the opportune time to pounce

This analogy describes what happens with the longitudinal data mining associated with the Common Core State Standards. You can't find anything in CCSS that specifically says your kids will and must have all of their information collected, processed, and saved digitally. But it's there.

President Obama's Race to the Top initiative provide states with money if they promise to adhere to four specified reforms. However, that's not where you'll find the mandatory data mining. One of the reforms calls for "development of rigorous standards and better assessments." This, of course, is politician-ese for Common Core State Standards. It also says they have to adopt "better data systems to provide schools, teachers, and parents with information about student progress." We're getting close now but, oh, what a tangled web they weave.

The State Fiscal Stabilization Fund gives additional taxpayer dollars for state education, but it requires "progress toward rigorous college- and career-ready standards and high-quality assessments that are valid and reliable for all students." The only standards and assessments that neatly fit that description are the CCSS. It just doesn't come right out and say it. But another requirement is what we're looking for: "The state must assure that it will take actions to … establish and use pre-K-through-college *and career* data systems to track progress and foster continuous improvement." (Emphasis mine.)

Do you understand what that is saying? Your kids will have everything any teacher, principal, and testing agency knows about them entered into a huge data collection system from the time they enter pre-school through college, and beyond! You might think I'm exaggerating about collecting data beyond college. An excerpt from the U.S. Government's document about their Statewide Longitudinal

Data Systems (SLDS) Grant Program reads:

> The SLDS Grant Program is designed to aid state education agencies (SEAs) in the design, development, and implementation of SLDSs through a competitive discretionary grants process. *These data systems securely follow students from early education through the workforce* and facilitate the disaggregation, reporting, and analyses of longitudinal data.[10] (Emphasis mine.)

Who's in charge of gathering the data? It is the Council of Chief State School Officers (CCSSO), a co-holder of the copyright on Common Core State Standards. The data they collect is startling. There are over 400 points of data collected and stored on each and every child.

Data mining of students was originally accomplished by a project called inBloom It was created and funded primarily by the Gates and Carnegie Foundations at a price tag of approximately $100 million. It recorded information about grades, absences, likes, dislikes, whether the student had a scuffle during recess, was caught cheating, took medication for ADHD (may be listed as taking mind-altering drugs), grade-point average, and more. Through questionnaires and "student surveys" it also obtained personal data about the student's family such as family income range, voting status, religious affiliation, and more.[11] The data was stored digitally on an Amazon.com data cloud.[12]

A Home School Legal Defense Association (HSLDA) review of Common Core and data mining tells us:

> The Gates Foundation is collaborating with researchers to explore other methods of "how specific brain activity is correlated with other cognitive and affective indicators that are practical to measure

> in school settings." The study recommends that facial expression cameras, posture analysis seats, pressure computer mice, eye tracking devices, and computer programs to track a student's mood be used in schools. Keeping tabs on the physiological activity of schoolchildren is the trajectory of the data systems developing alongside the Common Core.[13]

I find that chilling!

This data collection continues throughout the student's entire educational career and into the workplace.[14] It is disguised with the designation "P–20" which means pre-kindergarten through workforce. The research company SRI International was referred to in the excerpt as the "researchers." They issued the report "Promoting Grit, Tenacity, and Perseverance: Critical Factors for Success in the 21st Century."[15] In that report's section titled "Measuring Grit, Tenacity, and Perseverance," we read:

> For example, data mining techniques can track students' trajectories of persistence and learning over time, thereby providing actionable feedback to students and teachers. In addition, functional Magnetic Resonance Imaging (fMRI) and physiological indicators offer insight into the biology and neuroscience underlying observed student behaviors.

I read that there was some discussion about doing MRIs on your kids, but the equipment and resources were not yet available for that type of testing of all students. I thought certainly that was nonsense. Maybe not.

We do have some good news. So many parents and privacy advocates complained, they forced school districts to drop the inBloom data collecting in 2014. The company could not give parents the assurance they needed that the kids' data was never going to get into the hands of the wrong people. But what happened to all the data collected? At one point inBloom had information on over a million students in its database—they said they would destroy it all.

However, not all information was collected through inBloom. If your kids are instructed to open a Google account to use Gmail or use the Google Apps for Education technology for class work, it's being sucked into the massive data collection system. How able are the data collection gurus at preventing hackers, sexual predators, big businesses, and any branch of the government from accessing the information?

One of the current data mining companies is Pearson. They acknowledge they share the information they collect with their contractors, and their policy can change without notice. Their contractors have no privacy policy.[16] Yet another company (they are innumerable), Knewton, doesn't analyze only what your kids know, but how they think. One article stated "Thc most adept are scooping up an estimated 10 million unique data points on each child, each day. That's many times more data than Netflix or Facebook or even Google collect on their users."[17]

In July 2015 Senators Blumenthal and Daines introduced a student privacy bill named the "Safe Kids Act." It's not a perfect bill, but one advantage it does have is that it would allow you to delete your kids' personal information if it is collected by vendors and other third parties. You *wouldn't* be able to delete anything in their education records.[18, 19]

What is the point of collecting this data? Obviously, someone plans to use it for some unidentified purpose. The federal government assures us that it will be kept private, but it outlines who may access it: teachers, principals, agencies, universities, outside researchers. It then describes who must review reports before they are *published*.

Interestingly, Federal Statute 20 U.S.C. § 7911 prohibits maintaining a national student database. But if all the states do the data mining, and all the systems are interconnected, you have effectively a national student database.

This would seem impossible with a federal statute prohibiting the collection of student information on a national level, but the Obama administration found a way around it. They took actions *without* congressional approval to issue new rules that reduced privacy restrictions in the Family Education Rights and Privacy Act.[20] This took effect in January 2012, and it's probably a good guess you didn't know anything about it.

While I was considering that "effective national student database" I ran across the PowerPoint presentation titled the "*National* Education Data Model: A project funded by the US Department of Education Coordinated by the Council of Chief State School Officers."[21] (Emphasis mine.) One of the bullet-points answering the question, "Why do we need NEDM?" is "So databases can talk to each other." Who wants to bother with those antiquated privacy laws?

The overview of the National Education Data Model says that it "exists for anyone who uses student information in their work" and that "the uses of NEDM are *practically limitless*."[22] (Emphasis mine.) The Pied Piper of data collection says, "Follow me down this path" or "Let's step over to this part of the web" and all the while the Pied Piper nimbly negotiates that web without getting his own boots stuck once. It seems to me they think they have dibs on your kids' future. That should raise the hairs on the back of the neck of every parent.

Obstacle #7 – The Common Core marshland surrounding the entire obstacle course

The end of the educational obstacle course is not in sight. The CCSS surrounds and encompasses every obstacle we've looked at here, and more.

At the end of the process members of the Validation Committee were asked to sign a letter giving their thumbs-up that the CCSS were all they were supposed to be. As I said before, five members of the twenty-nine member VC refused to put their name to these assertions. Milgram, while refusing to sign, had some very positive statements to make about the Standards. After documenting some of the CCSS weaknesses, he stated, "Overall, only the very best state mathematics standards, those of California, Massachusetts, Indiana and Minnesota are stronger than these standards." Still, in his opinion, the weaknesses were so substantial he could not defend them.

In 2011, the editor of the *AASA Journal of Scholarship & Practice* wrote a twelve-page commentary titled, "Common Core State Standards: An Example of Data-less Decision Making." In it he stated, "Children do not have a seat at the policy-making table. Policy is thrust upon them, not created with them. They are helpless to defend themselves against poor decision making."[23]

Brad McQueen, taught fifth grade for a decade. He has a BA in political science, and a master's in Education. He also worked on the AIMS (Arizona's Instrument to Measure Standards) test for the Arizona State Department of Education.

Arizona sent him to Chicago for a week to evaluate how the reading and writing portions of Common Core would be tested in the PARCC (Partnership for Assessment of Readiness for College and Careers). Brad claims he went in to the assignment with a completely open mind. That changed quickly.

According to this very well-qualified educator, his "handlers" shrugged off his "questions about where the standards came from, who wrote them, who wrote the test questions, etc." The best he could get from them was that teachers—some unidentified teachers—had something to do with it. The odor of a rodent started to waft about the room. Still, he was there to learn, to assess, to evaluate. He put aside his doubts and plugged away, until he asked a question about a student writing sample. His handler snapped at him, "We don't ever care what the kids' opinions are. *If they write what they think or put forth their opinion then they will fail the test*."[24] (Emphasis mine.)

Brad said he always taught his students to think for themselves. He'd provide different views on a topic, and the kids had to decide what their own opinion was, giving reasons for reaching that conclusion. If you explore you will find that one of the stated criteria in Common Core is "critical thinking." I'd call Brad's approach critical thinking, wouldn't you?

Either bored or irritated at being questioned, Brad said the handler sighed and said, "That is the old way of writing. We want students to repeat the opinions of the 'experts' that we expose them to on the test. This is the 'new' way of writing with the Common Core." In other words, follow our Pied Piper all the way. Brad felt, without a doubt, that he and others like him were in Chicago just so the ones holding the CCSS reins could say teachers were involved. Where Common Core is implemented, teachers across the country are quitting because they feel they are unable to help their students be successful in their classes.

Free education is not a constitutional right

States have provisions in their constitutions, usually called the "education article," providing for free education for the kids in that state. It usually covers first through twelfth grade. Education is a matter of state and local government, not to be connected to or governed by federal laws. The Supreme Court confirmed this division of responsibility in 1973 when they determined that education is not a fundamental right under the U.S. Constitution.[25] That's why the Obama Administration continually makes such a point of saying these new standards are Common Core State Standards rather than Common Core National Standards. They emphasize that they originated with the National Governors Association (NGA) and the Council of Chief State School Officers (CCSSO). Both of those groups are simply nonprofit organizations like any business organization. Their members are governors, and leaders in public schools, respectively, but they are not "state" organizations.

The CCSSO declares it "is *committed to transforming our nation's public education system* through the Council's four strategic initiative areas. Our staff has experience working in state education agencies, in education policy, as educators, and in the business community." (Emphasis mine.)

The NGA admits to providing "governors and their senior staff members with services that range from representing states on Capitol Hill and before the Administration on key federal issues to developing and implementing innovative solutions to public policy challenges through the NGA Center for Best Practices." How would one interpret those statements if not to assume the NGA is basically a lobbying group?

Who got the CCSS ball rolling?

Gene Wilhoit, the Executive Director of CCSSO, working together with David Coleman, one of the lead writers of the Common Core State Standards, brainstormed their way to what they thought was a possibility to dramatically alter every public school classroom in the United States. The main roadblock was money. They estimated what they had in mind would cost at least tens of millions of dollars. They didn't have it. The states didn't have it. Local school districts didn't have it. Who did? The gazillionaire, Bill Gates.

Wilhoit and Coleman managed to get a face-to-face meeting with Gates, and after several weeks of serious thinking about it, Gates said he was in. In *big time*. The Bill and Melinda Gates Foundation threw over $200 million into the pot which would be enough to finance the development of CCSS, generate political support for it across the nation, and even persuade states to agree to expensive changes they could ill afford. The name "Gates" carries a lot of weight. The Gates Foundation lavished money on teachers unions, Chambers of Commerce, and political groups of every stripe. All received Gates largess, and bowed at the feet of what some called "one of the swiftest and most remarkable shifts in education policy in U.S. history."[26]

Eventually forty-six of our fifty states signed on to the earth-shattering new standards, which had never been, and never would be, tested before implementation. No one knew empirically whether this new idea was good or bad, and yet almost every school across the nation agreed to throw away everything they had been doing, right or wrong, and embrace the Common Core State Standards. In most states, not a single elected lawmaker was permitted a vote on this massive transformation in education. Even many Catholic schools, the largest provider of education by a religious group, bought in because almost all textbooks were rewritten to the new standards; if you needed new books, there weren't many alternatives.

Back at the White House

Let's do a recap. Gene Wilhoit and David Coleman have their heads together and get this wild idea how they can fundamentally transform education in the United States; Bill Gates listens to their story (remember no precedent, nothing written, nothing tested), and the richest man on the planet, who made his money being a shrewd businessman says, "I'm in"; $200 million gets spread around; states who don't need it and can't afford it, and don't know what to expect from it, say, "We're in"—all this is going on, and the Obama Administration said they had no knowledge of any of it. They claim the reason is that the Constitution says education is the responsibility of the state and local governments. Maybe it's just me, but I find that hard to believe. Especially since waivers from the No Child Left

Behind program were quickly produced. Funding was available for all the states that got on board (carrot) and withheld or withdrawn from those who did not (stick).

Oh, wait. There was something. The Washington Post article said, "And the idea found a major booster in President Obama, whose new administration was populated by former Gates Foundation staffers and associates. The administration designed a special contest using economic stimulus funds to reward states that accepted the standards."[27] Never mind that pesky Constitution.

Schools aren't forced to use a Common Core curriculum

One claim I've read many times is that the Common Core State Standards do not require schools to use any particular curriculum. They are free to use whatever they choose. The Core Standards website makes it very clear:

> The Common Core is not a curriculum. It is a clear set of shared goals and expectations for what knowledge and skills will help our students succeed. Local teachers, principals, superintendents, and others will decide how the standards are to be met. Teachers will continue to devise lesson plans and tailor instruction to the individual needs of the students in their classrooms.[28]

But if, or when, your kids take Common Core aligned tests, they had better know the Common Core information that is going to be the foundation of the questions, or they will fail.

Texas, one of the states that elected not to join the grab for the federal education gold, uses books and materials designed to their own state standards. However, when they received a book order they found a reference to "Common Core Enriched" vocabulary. The

Carnegie Math Grade 6 book, adopted by the Texas State Board of Education and supposedly 100% Texas Education Agency aligned, provided the Common Core standards correlation for every chapter. These materials were additional to those designed and ordered by Texas, and without their knowledge or consent.

About the same time Common Core was beginning its launch, Texas adopted a program called CSCOPE. Those advocating the curriculum said that it provided lesson plans and activities for teachers to use, and as it was totally online it eliminated the cost of textbooks. However, being totally online created one of the problems. No one outside of an exclusive group could get access to it.

Once it was implemented, teachers formed a group called "Teachers Against CSCOPE." The students who were taught the "fact" that "Allah is the almighty god," mentioned in chapter 7 were using the CSCOPE program. The class that mandated the teacher refer to terrorists as "freedom fighters" was in CSCOPE. The program characterized the Boston Tea Party as a terrorist act, called Christopher Columbus an "eco-warrior" and deleted references in his journal that mentioned God or Christianity.[29]

Word was getting out, and Texas parents wanted to see for themselves what was going on. They were told "no," although Texas law states that all parents have the right to see any and all instructional materials used in state classrooms. One of the parents insisted on seeing the science lessons used between September 2012 and 2013. The school district's attorney responded that it would cost her $700 if she wanted to see the material![30]

Eventually there was so much opposition to CSCOPE it was shut down. Hardly anyone noticed it was given a new name and became integrated with Common Core.

✝

"They encourage each other in evil plans, they talk about hiding their snares; they say, 'Who will see it?' They plot injustice and say, 'We have devised a perfect plan!' Surely the human mind and heart are cunning" (Psalm 64:5–6).

Chapter Challenge

An excellent overview of the Common Core State Standards can be found on the The Heritage Foundation website at heritage.org. Search for the April 2012 report titled, "States must reject national education standards while there is still time."

I also recommend the Heritage Foundation Issue Brief #3800 by Sandra Stotsky titled, "Common Core Standards' Devastating Impact on Literary Study and Analytical Thinking."

Check your state's cost of the implementation of Common Core with the Thomas B. Fordham Institute report titled, "Putting a Price Tag on the Common Core: How Much Will Smart Implementation Cost?" at http://www.edexcellencemedia.net/publications/2012/20120530-Putting-A-Price-Tag-on-thc-Common-Core/20120530-Putting-a-Price-Tag-on-the-Common-Core-FINAL.pdf.

Get informed. See what others just like you are doing to stop government interference in their kids' lives. Some websites of those fighting Common Core and data mining are:

- Student Privacy Matters – http://www.studentprivacy-matters.org/.
- HSLDA: Common Core Issues – https://www.hslda.org/commoncore/default.aspx.
- Common Core: Education Without Representation – https://whatiscommoncore.wordpress.com/.

Who's Got Dibs on Your Kids' MINDS?

Mind-Controlling Techniques: From Blatant to Subliminal

"Finally, brothers and sisters, whatever is true, whatever is noble, whatever is right, whatever is pure, whatever is lovely, whatever is admirable—if anything is excellent or praiseworthy—think about such things" (Philippians 4:8).

✝

Carol toyed with her mocha frappe and said, "I hope Amy doesn't bring a pie to our year-end potluck. Last time you could have retreaded tires with the crust."

"And the biscuits she brought to the breakfast—I had one and thought it must have been the stone rolled away from the tomb," said Grace. "She's a disaster waiting to happen in the kitchen."

Sara, the newest member of the Friday-at-the-coffee-shop group, who knew nothing about Amy, must have concluded that Amy was a failure as a cook.

What the women didn't say, so Sara couldn't possibly know, was though Amy lacked baking skills, she pulled the most beautiful Thanksgiving turkey out of the oven every year, and her fragrant stuffing had everyone hoping there was more in the kitchen. Sara didn't know that friends almost enjoyed getting sick because they knew Amy would be at their door with some of her delicious homemade soup.

Sara didn't know Amy was a success in the kitchen, not a failure, *because she had been told only part of the story*. The part she heard was true, nonetheless unkind, but without full information Sara could only come to the wrong conclusion about Amy.

That fictional story demonstrates a similar situation occurring over and over in your kids' textbooks. They're being taught only a part of the whole; the part today's educators want them to learn. They don't have any idea that their beliefs, opinions, and principles are being shaped and determined by incomplete and possibly flawed information.

If you are like most parents, you send your kids to a public school. It's by far the easiest and least expensive path to take. And, if you're fortunate enough, or planned well enough, you live in a highly regarded school district. What could possibly go wrong?

What could go wrong? A lot. We'll look at some of the ways others try, and often succeed, to control your kids' minds.

Mind-controlling techniques can mislead and misstate

In chapter 2 on Origins we looked at the television series *Cosmos*. We saw the blatant words "evolved," "evolution," "big bang," and "billions of years," given as fact. We also noticed some of the subliminal methods used to denigrate religion. Remember, not only have your kids possibly watched *Cosmos* at home, teachers are now eagerly looking forward to using it in their science classes. What wasn't mentioned? The case for intelligent design.

Alexis de Tocqueville, a French historian and political scientist who wrote *Democracy in America* in the 1800s, couldn't praise America and America's values enough. Times have changed. David Coleman, President of the College Board and a writer of Common Core, has forced on your kids the Advanced Placement U.S. History Framework, also known as APUSH. They will no longer learn about our country's outstanding achievements in the fields of military, diplomacy, scholarship, religion, and politics. Those subjects have fallen to the bottom of the educational barrel. The best thing you can say about your kids learning those subjects is that they are deemphasized. The sad truth is those studies have, for the most part, been completely eliminated.

Four of the nine members of the committee that developed APUSH were history professors—experts in the *historical aspects of race, class, and gender*. APUSH classes teach high school students—the brightest, the ones taking advanced placement courses—that America is a place of oppression and persecution.[1]

Bruce Thornton is a Research Fellow at Stanford's Hoover Institution and a Professor of Classics and Humanities at the California State University. He described what is being taught in grades K–12 in an article titled "Is Leftist School Indoctrination Unstoppable?"[2]

> Questionable leftist ideas I had to sit through in graduate seminars turned up regularly in my kids' English and history courses and textbooks. . . . The founding of the United States, then, was not about things like freedom and inalienable rights, but instead reflected the economic interests and power of wealthy white property-owners. The civil war wasn't about freeing

> the slaves or preserving the union, but about economic competition between the industrial north and the plantation south. The settling of the West was not an epic saga of hardships endured to create a civilization in a wilderness, but genocide of the Indians whose lands and resources were stolen to serve capitalist exploitation.

APUSH makes the Pilgrims, James Madison, Thomas Jefferson, Benjamin Franklin, and Abraham Lincoln, along with many other important figures in the history of the United States, disappear like the morning mist. Instead, it focuses on how the settlers brought diseases that wiped out the Indians, exploited many peoples, and, of course, owned slaves. It says that "belief in white superiority" led them "to justify their subjugation of Africans and American Indians."

George who? George Washington, the father of our country, is given a quick passing reference, and the Declaration of Independence is only briefly mentioned twice.

If you were a kid who knew almost nothing about the history of our country, what would be your thoughts and beliefs based on such instruction?

Among those not mentioned in the APUSH document are its authors. Twenty-seven college professors and teachers kept an eye on things as APUSH was developed. The actual authors' names are not made public, nor is the method used to come up with the document.[3]

One man reports that when he was an undergraduate at the University of Texas his professor never once mentioned Thomas Jefferson, Abraham Lincoln, or the Fourteenth Amendment. They spent several weeks, however, "hearing how the Salem Witchcraft Scare reflected oppression of women, blacks, and the poor in Puritan Massachusetts."

A website chronicles the history of slavery with a timeline compiled by Professor Brycchan Carey, Professor of English Literature at Kingston University in London, England. It is very enlightening. Here are a few portions your kids probably aren't learning in school:

> **Before 1400:** Slavery had existed in Europe from Classical times and did not disappear with the collapse of the Roman Empire. Slaves remained common in Europe throughout the early medieval period. . . . In Southern and Eastern Europe, Classical-style slavery remained a normal part of the society and economy and trade across the Mediterranean and the Atlantic seaboard meant that African slaves began to appear in Italy, Spain, Southern France, and Portugal well before the discovery of the New World in 1492. From about the 8th century onwards, an Arab-run slave trade also flourished, with much of this activity taking place in East Africa, Arabia, and the Indian Ocean. In addition, *many African societies themselves had forms of slavery*, although these differed considerably, both from each other and from the European and Arabic forms. (Emphasis mine.)

Part of the timeline on this website shows Spanish merchants started heavily trading slaves in the 1470s, with one Spaniard bringing back 400 slaves from Africa in 1476. In 1486 the Portuguese settled a West African island, planted it with sugarcane, and populated it with African slaves. This was happening well before Christopher Columbus discovered the New World.

In 1660 "The newly restored King Charles II of England charters the 'Royal Adventurers into Africa', the first English state-sponsored slave trading company," but Pennsylvania Colony in the New World was later a center of *anti*slavery.[4] Do your kids learn that in school?

I abhor slavery, but many of our American historians seem to want to make America the only bad actor. Slavery was, and still is in some places, a hideous way to get free labor. APUSH says "The abundance of land, a shortage of indentured servants, the lack of an effective means to enslave native peoples, and the growing European demand for colonial goods led to the emergence of the Atlantic slave trade." You can visit the website and read more about this yourself. Find the link in the Chapter Challenge section.

APUSH is not the only distorter of history. Connecticut is throwing Thomas Jefferson and Andrew Jackson under the school bus. That state's Democratic Party is deleting their names from their annual fundraising dinner because they had ties to slavery.

> There are more human slaves in the world today than ever before in history. Modern slavery is a multi-billion dollar industry with estimates of up to $35 billion generated annually. The United Nations estimates that roughly 27 to 30 million individuals are currently caught in the slave trade industry.
>
> Washington Examiner
> 9/14/2015

APUSH mentions "capitalism" frequently, with a negative connotation. Establishing the idea of victimhood in these young minds, it says "the new governments continued to limit rights to some groups" without elaborating on all the good, right, and beneficial aspects of our fledging country.

Choices: How they affect us and others

There is a phrase, used most often by doctors, nurses, and diet promoters, that says, "You are what you eat." While many of us give no more than lip service to that idea, we all know it is true. Our bodies are designed to be healthiest when we eat food that doesn't negatively affect our systems. Saturated fats and large quantities of sugar and salt are to be avoided. Even though we know this we—at least I—tend to find excuses to consume them anyway. We've developed a desire for them. Our parents probably introduced us to them when we were children.

I'm concerned that schools are doing that with the minds of our kids. I'm particularly referring to a book by Toni Morrison titled *The Bluest Eye*. It has caused a storm of controversy across the nation, primarily because it is on the Common Core's suggested reading list for eleventh grade students. The American Library Association lists it as the fifteenth most banned or opposed book from 2000 to 2009. What are many parents objecting to? You wouldn't have a clue if you only read the curriculum description: "An Eleven-Year-Old African-American Girl In Ohio, In The Early 1940s, Prays For Her Eyes To Turn Blue So That She Will Be Beautiful." What's so terrible about that?

What that description doesn't tell you is that the book contains graphic sex scenes about incest, rape, and pedophilia. In an online article at PolicyMic (mic.com), Alexandra Cardinale said we shouldn't deny teenagers ". . . intellectual and challenging literature because the traditional community is too uncomfortable with taboo subjects like pedophilia and incest [which] only deprives that student of understanding the deeper emotional and psychological complexities behind the taboo."[5] Think back to the Philippians 4:8 Bible passage that leads this chapter: "Whatever is true, whatever is noble, whatever is right, whatever is pure, whatever is lovely, whatever is admirable—if anything is excellent or praiseworthy—think about such things." I don't believe *The Bluest Eye* is what God has in mind. He understands how easily your kids' minds can be programmed.

The Bluest Eye author herself stated she "wanted the reader to feel as though they are a 'co-conspirator' with the rapist. She took pains to make sure she never portrayed the actions as wrong in order to show how everyone has their own problems. She even goes as far as to describe the pedophilia, rape, and incest 'friendly,' 'innocent,' and 'tender.'"

It will not surprise you to learn that *The Bluest Eye* is not the only questionable reading material recommended for your kids. Parents also protested other books, one of which is *The House of the Spirits* by Isabel Allende. They deem it inappropriate as it also contains "graphic descriptions of rape, prostitution, violence, abuse, abortion and death. The book also contains numerous curse words." It has been often challenged across the country. Some protests were lost. Some were won. The Richmond, California, public library removed it from its shelves because it was found to be "immoral and depraved."

The *School Library Journal* reported, "The Kids' Right to Read Project (KRRP) announced that it has urged New Mexico's Alamogordo Public School district to return Neil Gaiman's *Neverwhere* to high school English classrooms." School Superintendent George Straface told a newspaper: "I reviewed the language personally . . . I can see where it could be considered offensive . . . The F-word is used. There is a description of a sexual encounter that is pretty descriptive, and it's between a married man and a single woman." Apparently the *School Library Journal* did not find those elements inappropriate.

By the eleventh grade the Common Core State Standards require reading to be 70% nonfiction and only 30% fiction. With that limited amount of fiction, can the schools not find better literature to interest, instruct and develop young minds? Can we not give them an appetite for healthier reading material? If you are concerned about what sort of programming is being done to your kids' minds, I suggest you carefully check their recommended reading lists.

Libraries tell kids they have a right to read anything

And just when you thought it was safe—to go to a library—the American Library Association has created a brochure for your kids titled *Kids, Know Your Rights! A Young Person's Guide to Intellectual Freedom*. It informs kids that no matter what their parents say, they have the right to read, watch, and listen to anything they choose. It also recommends books that may conflict with your desires for your kids.[6]

Carl Sagan said, "An extraterrestrial being, newly arrived on Earth – scrutinizing what we mainly present to our children in television, radio, movies, newspapers, magazines, the comics, and many books – might easily conclude that we are intent on teaching them murder, rape, cruelty, superstition, credulity, and consumerism. We keep at it, and through constant repetition many of them finally get it." Carl Sagan was wise about many things.

Imparted, infused, and unrefuted

Those who would fill the minds of young people such as marketers and advocates of their specific belief systems, use similar techniques as advertising companies. They use them to promote the theories of the origin of the universe and mankind, promiscuity, homosexuality, and other aberrant views. Successful advertising companies follow five practices routinely.

- **Repetition**: Did you ever try to memorize something? The most effective way is to repeat it over and over again until it sticks in your brain. This is especially effective when you see and hear something at the same time, as you do when watching television.
- **Claims of fact**: In advertising, television commercials and printed ads claim a certain product is the best, the most effective, the only one you should buy, without any proof that what they claim is true. No dissenting opinion is offered.
- **Association**: The use of a person who is considered trustworthy or highly admired to promote the product, such as a prominent athlete, movie star, or musical celebrity, suggests the idea that you surely want to be associated with that special person, if only by using the same product.
- **Belonging**: Called the "bandwagon technique" the target is convinced that everyone else is using the product, or going

to a special resort, and you are really missing out if you don't buy into it.

- **Rewards**: *Free* is a big promotional word in advertising. A reward can come with your purchase, or come later. Either way, you don't get the free "whatever" if you don't buy now. Send in six cereal coupons for a *free* movie ticket. Buy now and get six more *free* crayons in the box. Don't lose out on *free* rewards!

Advertising techniques are used to attract attention, engage minds, trigger emotions, and change what people think. Let's look at just a few ways these techniques are used to refashion the minds of your kids.

Applying the techniques

The programs instilling the view that homosexuality is an acceptable lifestyle are reinforced in many ways. The GLSEN sponsored "Day of Silence" is a statement of protest opposing any dissent about homosexuality. If your kids dare to speak out on that day, they may be ostracized.

The United Nations declared May 4 to be the official Pink Shirt Day, when everyone is supposed to wear a pink shirt, Pink Shirt Day began in Nova Scotia in support of a kid who was tormented for wearing a pink shirt. It is now a full-blown anti-bullying campaign, and is slowly morphing into the International Day of Pink, standing "against homophobia and anti-gay discrimination." One of the sponsors is RainbowYOUTH, a New Zealand charity. It offers services for queer and gender diverse youth. Much like the Day of Silence, it instills a feeling of **belonging** in the kids who participate, and conversely, a feeling of being left out by those who don't.

The push for acceptance of the homosexuality agenda is also an example of **repetition**. The topic is not limited to sex education classes. GLSEN produced what they call a "toolkit "for elementary schools titled "Ready, Set, Respect!" It advises teachers to use teachable moments, incorporating information about homosexuality (GLSEN defines it as "gender diverse families") into varied classroom subjects and schoolwork. A math problem reads, "Rosa and her *dads* were at the store and wanted to buy three boxes of pasta. If each costs $.75, how much will all three boxes cost?" (Emphasis mine.)

Teachers are cautioned: "Make sure the analogies you use when teaching don't rely on hetero-normative or gender-normative images or viewpoints. A hetero-normative viewpoint is one that expresses heterosexuality as a given instead of being one of many possibilities." This is use of the **claims of fact** approach.

Establishing the idea that cross-dressing is normal, "Ready, Set, Respect!" suggests teachers tell their students to draw pictures of their favorite TV or storybook characters (what age do you think this is aimed at?) and "dress them in clothes that are different colors and styles from what they would typically wear." They suggest dressing Cinderella in knight's armor, or putting a magic tiara on Spiderman. This can fall into the **association** category.

The toolkit provides a crossword puzzle titled "That's a Family" that includes the words gay, lesbian, homosexual, transgender, and blended. It also includes heterosexual, and straight. When students work this puzzle, their minds are reinforced in the thinking that gays, lesbians, homosexuals, and transgenders belong in the same family norm as heterosexuals and straights—**repetition**.

Let's go back to the claims of separation of church and state. One of the exercises in the GLSEN toolbox is designed for a history class. The statement, requiring a "true" or "false" answer, is "Jesus condemns homosexuality in the bible [sic]." The answer: "FALSE: Most passages, which are interpreted as condemning homosexuality, are found in the Old Testament, and derived from Hebraic tribal law; all of the few New Testament references are all in the book [sic] written by Paul, who was born decades after Jesus' crucifixion. No condemnations of homosexuality are found in any of the 'Gospels' or books that deal with the life of Jesus." This is an obvious use of **claims of fact**. If kids don't have a strong biblical knowledge base, they could agree with the "False" answer. Christians should be able to refute this with the **facts** that all Scripture is inspired by God, Jesus directly taught Paul, Jesus is the Son of God, and Jesus said, "If you love me, keep my commands" (John 14:15), and "I and the Father are one" (John 10:30). If the Father condemned homosexuality, so did Jesus.

We can't forget Jesus own words in Mark 7:20–23 where He said, "He [Jesus] went on: "What comes out of a person is what defiles them. For it is from within, out of a person's heart, that evil thoughts come—sexual immorality, theft, murder, adultery, greed, malice, deceit, lewdness, envy, slander, arrogance and folly. All these evils come from inside and defile a person." Jesus doesn't list here all the forms of sexual immorality, but it would be more than a little disingenuous to try to infer that He didn't include homosexuality in that statement. Of course, the true/false answers to the GLSEN quiz don't allow for rebuttal.

In 2011 California passed a law requiring public schools to teach the contributions of lesbian, gay, bisexual, and transgender Americans as part of the social sciences curriculum. Governor Jerry Brown said "History should be honest. This bill revises existing laws that prohibit discrimination in education and ensures that the important contributions of Americans from all backgrounds and walks of life are included in our history books." This adjustment will be made to lessons in kindergarten through high school.[7] The law requires textbooks and instructional materials to promote in a positive light LGBT Americans' contributions in the same way schools currently include the contributions of ethnic minorities. It also forbids any informational material or instruction that would show anything other than a positive viewpoint of anyone because of their sexual orientation. The

Christian Post website remarked: "How does this stack up with the governor's statement that "history should be honest?" This **claims of fact** approach is the only one your kids' minds will be absorbing.

Often classes will be **rewarded** when such instruction, silence, or pink shirt day is finished with a cupcake party or something similar. If you have decided not to let your kids participate, they will likely sit in the hall until the celebration is complete. Not only don't they get the **reward**, they lose their sense of **belonging**. Many students are paying a price for voicing opposition to evolution, and many scientists have lost their jobs and their reputations doing it.

Any objection to same-sex "marriage" will be confronted with the statement that it's the law of the land. The Supreme Court said so. This fits nicely into the **claims of fact** category. The problem is the Supreme Court doesn't, and shouldn't, and can't (according to the Constitution) make laws. The Court's opinion is just that—opinion. The decision in the Dred Scott case is ample proof of that, and that it is not carved in stone. The decision can be either ignored or overturned.

Photographs don't lie—or do they?

Another method of creating an opinion is to alter the product through what has become known as "photoshopping," which is digital manipulation of what the camera sees and records. If you want to see how it's used check out the Internet site "13 Mind-Blowing Tricks Advertisers Use to Manipulate Photos" at cracked.com.

Can that happen with science? You learned some actual instances of manipulation of data and visuals in the chapters on climate change and evolution. Al Gore's helpers did a wonderful job shrinking the polar ice for his film. If you've forgotten, the hockey-stick graph was also faked. Turning to evolution, remember the images of embryos by Haeckel. And we can't forget the faked peppered moth photos. It goes without saying that your kids aren't told about this image fakery, but still it's amazing that when the ones who commit the fakery are called out on it they find ways to defend their duplicity.

The Pied Pipers of subliminal suggestion

The art of subliminal advertising is to make you aware of a product, service, or idea without you realizing that you are being "sold." It bypasses our conscious mind and aims directly at the subconscious. This is not a new phenomenon. *The Hidden Persuaders* by Vance Packard was published in 1957. It opened the eyes of the general public to the psychological aspects of advertising. It's politely referred to as "motivational" or "persuasion" advertising.

The inside flap of *Subliminal Persuasion: Influence & Marketing Secrets They Don't Want You To Know* by Dave Lakhani says, "You can choose to believe you're immune, but you can't choose not to be persuaded. The power of subliminal persuasion can move markets and control consumers—and that's a fact." Is it possible to resist such motivated impulses? Can you teach your kids to resist them? Half of the battle is won when you know what's going on.

You've seen some of the visual tricks that can be played on your mind:

- Two lines with arrow-like points on each end, one with the points facing away from the line, and the other with the points facing inward. Which line is longer? They are both the same length, but your mind doesn't see them that way.
- Which spot is larger: The darker colored one or the lighter one? They are both the same but the lighter one will appear larger.

Split-second flashes of images accomplish the result of motivating a viewer to desire something. There are reports of this happening in movie theaters when patrons have an irresistible urge to get ice cream or a soft drink. But *if you know* you might be manipulated, could you . . . would you . . . fight off the urge? I think you can and you would.

One way your kids are manipulated is being told, in one way or another, that "everyone is doing it so it must be okay." Have you noticed the provocative poses of kids in clothing ads? Your kids most likely don't even realize what they are seeing is inappropriate, much less evaluate whether they should make it their lifestyle. By the time they are teens, the "come-on" images have become so common they are part of their culture, and are an accepted part of their behavior.

The math problems I mentioned before in the context of homosexuality are an example of subliminal persuasion. The thoughts of it being normal are insinuated into every facet of your kids' lives. Working crossword puzzles, writing words down, reinforces them without anyone realizing it is happening. However, once your kids are aware of those influences, they will begin to recognize them, and they will have the ability to resist such indoctrination. Clyde Miller, the author of *The Process of Persuasion*, said when we learn to recognize the devices of the "persuaders," we build up a "recognition reflex."

Don't think – just follow the tune being played

In *Subliminal Persuasion*, Dave Lakhani echoes these propaganda techniques. He says they work when they are constantly repeated and reinforced, through many different media, over and over again. The goal is to make the message one the receiver (your kids) can accept, repeat, and then act on. This is most effectively accomplished by providing the information in "sound bites" rather than long, tedious streams of information. One way is to use storytelling; we saw that in the beautiful Cosmos presentation by Neil deGrasse Tyson, and in the many picture books available. Lakhani says, "The goal is to deeply implant and leverage ideas in the subconscious where most thinking is done. Once we've made our impact on the subconscious appropriately, it is very easy to control the outcome of the messages we are sending."[8]

A vital point is that the message they want to convey mustn't be boring. There has to be a "hook"—an element that leaves them with a strong desire to know more. It's what TV shows do to make sure you tune in again next week, or novels that end each chapter with a "cliff-hanger" that keeps you up all night reading. This ingredient isn't overlooked by those designing material for your kids.

Next, there has to be conflict, a shared enemy. You'll find those enemies to their propaganda identified as "climate change *deniers*," "religious *fanatics*," and "homo*phobes*." As we noted before, your kids don't want to be in the camp of the enemy, and be called those names. The result: they are in the camp of the conforming.

Everyone loves facts, and kids are no different. Those with a message layer on the facts, just as GLSEN did with the statement about Jesus and homosexuality. They keep enough of it accurate so that it's believable, and then sauce it up. Hardly anyone checks those **claims of fact** anyway.

Then there's the "secret" they might tell your kids not to tell even you, their parents, about. Secrets are delicious and special. Al Gore knew this when he was speaking to a conference of young people in Washington, D. C. He said, "There are some things about our world that you know that older people don't know. Why would that be? Well in a period of rapid change, the old assumptions sometimes just don't work anymore because they're out of date." In one fell swoop Al Gore put parents in a class of "older people" whose statements and beliefs are "old" and not facts, but "assumptions." Oh yes, you are very much "out of date!"

Evoking strong emotions is important in subliminal messaging. We've seen how they use desire, a need for belonging, and not wanting to be the enemy. These all stimulate strong emotions in your kids. Lakhani says, "When your audience is in an emotional state, they are not focused on critical thinking; they are caught up in the feelings that the emotions create." Then the kids are asked to share their "emotions" (feelings) with the class, and shared emotions bond people together. Those who do not share the same feelings become outsiders.

Endorsements can lend validity. Think about Kellogg's Tony the Tiger, and Sesame Street promoting the homosexual agenda. Stores like Target put statements in newspapers that they support that lifestyle. And if there is something in the background, not obvious, in a movie or television show that was enjoyable, subconsciously the mind stores that background information as valid and enjoyable as well.

Some parents think their kids can be positive influences in their world of misinformation. That's always a possibility—God works in many ways—but it's unlikely. The teachers, and most of the kids in their school, are already "true believers." They can look at a mountain of evidence that their beliefs *aren't* true, and they won't admit it. It is called confirmation bias; they are able to absorb only that information that confirms what they already believe. They completely ignore any evidence disproving it.

Experts and voices of authority

Experts are often brought in, either in person or by video or print, to solidify claims of fact. Al Gore, the former vice-president of the United States, would be such a voice of authority. Neil deGrasse Tyson has an impressive resume, and is imposing to look at and listen to. His stature and voice embody the "voice of authority."

MTV, the young adult cable television network, was promoting the climate change argument. They had data gleaned from the Natural Resources Defense Council. MTV, along with its partners, establish a new belief system: we must change our lifestyle or we'll all die and the planet will implode.

The formula to create new belief systems starts with something that is already accepted, and builds a bridge over to the new information. Then supercharge it. Make it an emotional experience. The mind now believes it must be—it *is*—real. Now bring in the experts to reinforce the new belief. Those experts will take the ideas and boil them down to the bare facts. In math it's called the lowest common denominator. (If you remember *Dragnet*, Joe Friday used to say, "Just the facts, ma'am.") These simplifications are then pounded into the brain with sledge-hammer force. That is followed by repetition delivered in various ways (everyone learns differently) and soon it has been seen and heard so often, it's *true*! Now set up the groups that can reinforce the belief system in each other, and provide some sort of reward or recognition.

Kids often are told they can't wear t-shirts with religious messages, or they must put their cross under their blouse or shirt. These are symbols of belonging, and they must be eliminated. That is not the group-bonding the deliverers of the new belief systems want.

I told you earlier about Google's new Knowledge Vault. This is an excellent tool to redirect minds. For some reason, when we search the Internet we think we control our searches. Most people never go beyond the first page or two for the links they want to visit. It's this reason that people pay good advertising dollars for a top position on the first page. We unreasonably tend to believe what we find on the Internet. Why are we so easily bamboozled?

From now on, be aware of trickery, deception, and various subliminal efforts to manipulate your kids' minds—and your own as well. A statement from important, well-known personalities does not ensure its truthfulness.

Color me black

Your kids probably started using coloring books as soon as you thought they could hold one of those chunky crayons in their little hands. This activity has many benefits, including learning colors, creativity, small muscle motor skills, and identifying objects in the pictures. Depending on your kids, coloring and the other activities could keep them safely occupied and quiet for long periods of time. So coloring books are good, aren't they?

Not if the book is named *The Satanic Children's BIG BOOK of Activities*! I told you a little about this activity book earlier.

This coloring book is provided to schools by The Satanic Temple to be given to your kids. A few examples will open your eyes to how your kids' minds can be programmed by something as innocuous as a coloring book.

At the top of page one is "Find six differences:" There are two pictures with some differences, but in both the central figure is a girl wearing a kind of robe that has a pentagram in a circle on the front. She is standing on a pentagram in a circle with her hands raised as if she were blessing the class. Surrounding her on the floor are a candle, a glass that looks like a wine glass, a bowl, a frog, and something that might be a skull. The text reads: "Annabel is spreading knowledge and helping to dispel fear and ignorance by demonstrating her Satanic ritual for her class. Find six differences to help her."

Let's analyze what your kids read or hear and see. This gives them knowledge – a good thing. It takes away fear and ignorance – a good thing. The implied opposite is that if you don't believe as the Satanists do, you are fearful and ignorant. It defines what the kids are seeing as a ritual. If they ask their teacher what a ritual is, she might say praying before meals is a ritual, or what you do in church are rituals. If they hear that, the kids will believe that Satanic rituals are in the same "good" category. Think about the subtlety this one page uses to program your kids' minds to accept Satanism.

Page two has a word jumble. The accompanying text reads: "These bullies are mad and afraid of things they don't understand. Help Damian use inclusive language to defuse the situation." The jumbled words are: friendship, compassion, respect, empathy, justice, reason, freedom. How bad can Satanism be if it uses words like that? Again, those who are not Satanists are "mad" (worse than angry), fearful and stupid.

Page three says, "Color Annabel's study filled with Satanic literature and philosophy." I think you're getting the idea. The finesse with which this activity book was designed is impressive. Working on the pages, spending time with them, reinforces the message—and the kids don't even know the mind games being played.

The mind: mine or meme?

You've probably heard the word "meme" used often lately. The science of memetics is decades old, but the word "meme" itself has recently become a meme. Do you know what a meme is? The book *Virus of the Mind* says a meme is an idea, a belief, or a behavior that catches on, and is passed from one person's mind to another, until everyone is thinking it, believing it, doing it, saying it. As the title of the book indicates, a meme acts like a virus, replicating itself over and over, and doing the replicating faster and faster, until no one knows or cares how it started, or why it started, or if it even means anything. Perhaps this was the origin of the expression "going viral." It becomes part of the culture. The term "survival of the fittest" applies to a meme that replicates itself most abundantly and quickly.[9]

Can you see how the tried and true methods of advertising, politics, and now teaching, are like the meme? **Repetition** is a vital element. **Association** with others in your class, clique, group of any kind is desirable. A sense of **Belonging** exists when you incorporate the idea, belief, or behavior into your every day life. **Rewards** can be physical such as cupcakes, or exhibit themselves as part of the **Belonging** and **Association**. When do your kids' minds become less *their* mind and more of the meme?

In chapter 6 on Media, we looked at the power and influence entering your kids' lives through technology. You saw how schools are placing ideas and belief systems repetitively into your kids' minds in almost every class. Much of what is being taught your kids today is done with the zeal of an evangelist. The promoters of evolution, promiscuity, and homosexuality are in full "spread the word" mode. You, as the parent, will have to decide if the memes others are spreading are what you want to stay with your kids, or if you want to change those ideas and belief systems to ones you think are better. Chapter 11, "Who's Got Dibs on Your Kids? YOU HAVE!" will give you some options.

It's been planned and executed for a long time

Sexual rights activists Marshall Kirk and Hunter Madsen published a 432-page book in 1990, *After the Ball: How America will conquer its fear & hatred of Gays in the 90's*. Kirk graduated from Harvard with a degree in neuropsychiatry. Madsen also attended Harvard acquiring a doctorate in politics, with expertise as a social scientist in public persuasion tactics and social marketing. He graduated summa cum laude—they are both smart guys!

After the Ball advocates slow and steady manipulation of the public, using strategically coordinated propaganda. It identifies and suggests uses of a variety of subtle psychological coercion techniques. Reading it with an unbiased mind, it is rather startling and informative to see all the ways that have been used to "normalize" homosexuality. In the book, the authors state, "Thus propagandistic advertising can depict all opponents of the gay movement as homophobic bigots . . ." They claim unequivocally that "[T]he person's beliefs can be altered whether he is conscious of the attack or not."

This attitudinal marketing is described well by Paul Rondeau in his paper "Selling Homosexuality to America." He says, "The relationship between education and marketing cannot be overemphasized." Using the meme "gay rights," and getting everyone to accept the term as having validity, framed the issue not as a sexual one, but as a constitutional "rights" issue. (Don't look here—look over there.) And using the term "gay" rather than "homosexual" subliminally has your brain telling itself, "Oh, gay. That's happy. Happy is good. There's nothing here to object to."

How successful was their marketing and promotion of homosexuality? The magazine *Seventeen* polled its readers in 1991, and only 17% of its teenagers considered homosexuality as good or acceptable. Fast forward to 1999—the kids had been inundated with the homosexual propaganda for eight years. How did they respond to that same *Seventeen* poll then? More than triple the number of teens, 54%, then believed homosexuality was absolutely appropriate.[10] The mind-bending is still going on. Do you think it's effective?

✞

"For the time will come when people will not put up with sound doctrine. Instead, to suit their own desires, they will gather around them a great number of teachers to say what their itching ears want to hear. They will turn their ears away from the truth and turn aside to myths" (Timothy 4:3–4).

Chapter Challenge

Your challenge for this chapter is to do what the marketers of errors, lies, and immorality are doing . . . spread the word. Tell every parent you know about how the Pied Pipers of subliminal suggestion are leading your kids and theirs on a path away from God without anyone being aware of it. Then spread the word of truth as aggressively as they are spreading the lies.

That's a short challenge, but it's a big one. You probably don't have the marketing education and skills that your opponents have. That means you will have to work harder, learn what they know, and be willing to put it into action even if it puts you miles outside of your comfort zone.

Books

- *The Marketing of Evil* by David Kupelian is ten years old, but still loaded with pertinent information.

- *Don't Let the Kids Drink the Kool-Aid: Confronting the Left's Assault on Our Families, Faith, and Freedom* by Marybeth Hicks is an excellent book on how your kids are being battered in every area of their lives.

Websites

- You can read the full slavery timeline I quoted from in this chapter and read additional information about slavery, abolition, and emancipation at http://www.brycchancarey.com/slavery/index.htm.
- Read more about *After the Ball* in the online article "The Homosexual Propaganda Campaign in America's Media" at http://www.massresistance.org/docs/issues/gay_strategies/after_the_ball.html.

Who's Got Dibs on Your Kids' PARENTAL RIGHTS?

God Gave Your Kids to YOU - Not the Government!

"Be strong and take heart, all you who hope in the Lord" (Psalm 31:24).

Do you remember when your little darling was about one or two years old, and the strident "NO!" bounced off the walls anytime an unwanted food was approaching, or the car seat became the hated object of the day? Then there was the "I don't want to" accompanied by a foot stomping. Not all kids go through that stage; it isn't very pleasant, but you have to admit it gets attention.

If you are going to exercise your parental rights to protect your kids from unwanted overreaching authority, you are going to have to do a little foot stomping yourself, accompanied with a don't-mess-with-me "NO!"

What the Courts have to say—what you didn't want to hear

In November 2005 the U.S. Court of Appeals for the Ninth Circuit ruled on your rights as a parent to control the way your children are raised, what they are taught, as well as when you let go of your kids' hands and they step foot into the school. The ruling reads, your right "does not extend beyond the threshold of the school door." They also determined the school has the right to teach your kids anything they want to teach: ". . . whatever information it wishes to provide, sexual or otherwise."[1]

> "In order to submerge the individual, and develop ideal citizens, Sparta assembled the males at seven into barracks and intrusted [sic] their subsequent education and training to official guardians."
> Meyer v State of Nebraska (1923)

This court (the case was Fields v. Palmdale School District) upheld a lower court's ruling that your responsibility as a parent, entrusted to you by God, and with the instruction to "bring them up in the training and instruction of the Lord," simply disappears when they go to school. The court said you—the parent—don't have the right "to control the upbringing of their children by introducing them to *matters of and relating to sex in accordance with the personal and religious values and beliefs*." (Emphasis mine.) The ruling continued, "There is no fundamental right of parents to be the exclusive provider of information regarding sexual matters to their children." You also have no right "to override the determinations of public schools as to the information to which their children will be exposed." The court also stated parents' "fundamental right to control the education of their children is, at the least, substantially diminished."

You have been stripped of your parental rights. The government requires school attendance. That requirement carries with it denying your right to direct all forms of education of your kids the moment they pass through the door of a public school.

What started the uproar that ended up in a federal court? The school district had *seven- to ten-year-old kids* complete a questionnaire—asking if they thought about having sex, touching the private parts of others, and committing suicide. What was the purpose of this personal invasion of privacy? The court's decision said the questions were designed "to improve student's ability to learn." *To learn what*?

A permission slip was sent home prior to administering the questionnaire, but it somehow neglected to include information about the deeply personal probing that would take place. It did say if any child felt uncomfortable with it, the school would have a "therapist for further psychological help." Apparently what they were saying was, if you or your kids preferred not to answer these questions about sex and suicide there was obviously some kind of a mental problem, and these little kids needed a mental health therapist.

On the positive side

A law was passed in 1978 stating schools can't ask the students questions about either their own or their parents' political leanings, religious beliefs, sexual actions or thoughts, and a whole bunch of other private actions, thoughts, and beliefs. It's called the Protection of Pupil Rights Amendment.

In November 2005 Congress passed House Resolution 547 with a 320–91 vote, quoting Supreme Court decisions upholding "the fundamental right of parents to direct the education of their children is firmly grounded in the Nation's Constitution and traditions."[2] It's just a Resolution though. It doesn't change a thing. It's a nice statement, but nothing more. It does, however, put on record that in 1923 the Supreme Court stated within the Fourteenth Amendment to the Constitution is the *"power of parents to control the education"* of their kids. (Emphasis mine.)

The courts have also affirmed that not only do parents have rights under the constitution, and that your kids are *your* kids, you also have responsibilities. In 1925 the Supreme Court stated your kid is not "the mere creature of the state; those who nurture him and direct his destiny have the right, *coupled with the high duty, to recognize and prepare him for additional obligations* . . ."[3] (Emphasis mine.)

Apparently courts were adamant about the responsibilities of parents. The Supreme Court referred to the term "additional obligations" again in 1972. "This primary role of the parents in the upbringing of their children is now established beyond debate as an enduring American tradition. . . . The duty to prepare the child for 'additional obligations', referred to by the Court [the 1925 case] must be read to include the inculcation of moral standards, religious beliefs, and elements of good citizenship."[4]

The Supreme Court also determined "The Fourteenth Amendment guarantees the right of the individual . . . to establish a home and bring up children, to worship God according to his own conscience."[5]

It boils down to the government can't interfere with your right as a parent to control your kids' education,[6] and you have the right to privacy in your own home: "This privacy right encompasses and protects the *personal intimacies* of the home, the family, marriage, motherhood, procreation, and child rearing . . ."[7] (Emphasis mine.)

Probably the most definitive statement of all by the Supreme Court came in 2000 in the case Troxel v. Granville: "*It cannot now be doubted that the Due Process Clause of the Fourteenth Amendment protects the fundamental right of parents to make decisions concerning the care, custody, and control of their children.*"[8] (Emphasis mine.)

You may have found reading about all these court cases to be tedious, but they are here for a reason. The government of the United States has been infringing more and more on the rights of parents to raise their children in the way they deem appropriate. Some day you may have to refer to these judicial determinations to protect your own rights.

So how do the schools get away with their offensive questionnaires, immoral teaching, revision of history to fit a political agenda, and standing as the final authority in the instruction of your kids? Because in many cases they can. Without the will, backing, or financial ability to take it to the Supreme Court, parents are left in the cold, subject to the power of unions, politicians, and local judges.

Your rights in public schools

Public education officials, including school boards, local, state, and federal government agencies, along with teachers' unions, have conferred upon themselves the right to design learning programs, and specify the text books, audio/visual materials, outside speakers and other learning resources. School boards are supposed to be the control group, ensuring all materials are vetted for appropriateness and accuracy. Some school boards do an excellent job, but others simply default to "recommendations" from others. Where does your school board fall? Great? Ineffective? Do you know?

This area is closest to your home, your values, and your kids. Get to know the members of the school board personally so you know whether the decisions they make will be aligned with your values and beliefs. This is really where much of who has dibs on your kids is decided. Do they read the textbooks before they approve them? Even if they do, try to find out if they have the knowledge required to know if history revisionism is at work, if history is skewed by placing more emphasis on one aspect than another, or if important knowledge about our founding fathers is left out.

You easily can lose your parents' rights in the education of your kids. If you don't get involved before textbooks and programs are approved, you are essentially giving away your rights. Once you've done that, later on when something unpleasant comes to your attention, it's much harder to fight. They are counting on you surrendering your rights as a parent.

The homeschooling option

Some parents, recognizing the errant path public schools have taken over the last fifty years, decide to homeschool. After all, the government requires you make certain your kids are educated, not that you use the public (government) schools. Still, this option is not without its own set of problems.

Information recently came to light about a girl named Amanda. Amanda's parents divorced in 1999 when she was a newborn; they were given joint decision-making responsibility for her. Although the father disagreed, Amanda was homeschooled by her mother. The disagreement continued over the years and finally went to court. A legal guardian was appointed by the court to represent the best interests of the child. The guardian decided it was in Amanda's best interest to attend a public school, and the court agreed, even though it acknowledged the mother had "*more than kept up with the academic requirements of the Meredith public school system*." (Emphasis mine.)

The Court was "guided by the premises that education is by its nature an exploration and examination of new things, and by the premise that a child requires academic, social, cultural, and physical interaction with a variety of experiences, people, concepts and surroundings in order to grow to an adult who can make intelligent decisions about how to achieve a productive and satisfying life." The Court decided ". . . enrollment in public school will provide Amanda with an increased opportunity for group learning, group interaction, social problem solving, and exposure to a variety of points of view." The "variety of points of view" referred to the court official deciding that Amanda was too "vigorous" in defending her Christian faith. The actual quote says Amanda's "vigorous defense of her religious beliefs to [her] counselor suggests strongly that she has not had the opportunity to seriously consider any other point of view."[9, 10]

The Alliance Defense Fund, working on Amanda's behalf, said while being homeschooled Amanda participated in some public school classes, and was involved in a number of extra-curricular sports activities.

Obviously it made no difference that Amanda was probably ahead of many of the public school students her age. The guardian said Amanda, "would be best served by exposure to a public school setting" and "different points of view at a time when she must begin to critically evaluate multiple systems of belief ... in order to select, as a young adult, which of those systems will best suit her own needs."

The guardian earlier told Amanda's mother, "If I want her in public school, she'll be in public school." She also said she wouldn't even look at her homeschool curriculum. "I don't want to hear it. It's all Christian based."[11]

At least in the United States it is still legal to homeschool. Not so in Germany. Here, in part, is a statement from the German Federal Constitutional Court explaining why they have forbidden homeschooling:

> The general public has a justified interest in counteracting the development of religiously or philosophically motivated "parallel societies" and in integrating minorities in this area. . . . The learning and practicing of this in the sense of experienced tolerance is an important lesson right from the elementary school stage. *The presence of a broad spectrum of convictions in a classroom can sustainably develop the ability of all pupils in being tolerant and exercising the dialogue that is a basic requirement of democratic decision-making process*. (Emphasis mine.)

Apparently the German Court believes the only way for children to learn to be tolerant is for them to attend public school. Parents, in their view, have no ability to teach tolerance at home.

What happens if parents homeschool their kids in Germany? They are taken away from their parents! The Romeike family found out the German government was neither compassionate nor lenient.

The Romeikes wanted to homeschool because they did not approve of some of the teachings in the German public education system, feeling they violated their religious beliefs. When faced with high fines, forcible removal of their children from their care, and possibly being sent to prison, they decided to seek asylum in the United States. The Home School Legal Defense Association (HSLDA) explained: "As with any asylum case, the Romeikes needed to prove two basic propositions to be entitled to asylum. They had to prove they faced either past or future persecution and the persecution was motivated, at least in part, on one of the grounds contained in our asylum statute. Religious persecution is one of these recognized grounds for asylum."

U.S. immigration judge Lawrence Burman granted them asylum based on religious persecution. Attorney General Eric Holder petitioned the Sixth Circuit Court of Appeals for the asylum be overturned. He had his way, but the Romeike's appealed to the Supreme Court. After years of battling, the Supreme Court refused to review the court order directing the Romeikes be deported back to Germany. Thousands of people signed a petition asking President Obama to grant the asylum. The day after the Supreme Court refused to take the case, the Department of Homeland Security told them they could stay here indefinitely as long as they didn't break any laws, and they could continue to homeschool their children.[12]

Opting out of tests

Many people believe the best way to educate their kids is by homeschooling or sending them to a private or religiously affiliated school. But if you don't, if you want to send your kids to public school, do you have any opt out rights? Can you elect not to have your kids participate in specific school studies, reading lists, and tests you don't think are appropriate, or you just strongly disagree with? Most of your opt out opportunities vary from state-to-state, so you will have to check your own state laws.

Opting out of the standardized testing is going to upset some people. You are going to be accused of causing your school district to lose government funding. Part of the incentive to get schools to buy-in to Common Core was to give them waivers to the No Child Left Behind (NCLB) program. NCLB demanded 95% of a state's students take the standardized tests. Also, according to NCLB, schools must demonstrate they are making what is termed as "adequate yearly progress." More than forty states now have those NCLB waivers, so if your school board tries to use pressure on you, check and make certain whether your state has been freed of the sanctions.

Another reason given for participating in the testing is that an abundance of tests are beneficial for your kids. Increasing numbers of parents believe that is a false premise. You will not be alone if you choose to have your kids forego most testing. Assistant Education Secretary Deborah Delisle admitted the federal government has no plans to take funding away from programs that serve children. However, your school district may require students to take certain tests to be promoted.[13]

The California Assessment of Student Performance and Progress (CAASPP) Results were posted September 9, 2015. About 96% of the students in third- through eighth-grades and eleventh-grade were tested. In English Language Arts/Literacy 56% "did not meet" or "nearly met" the standard required. Only 28% met the standard and 16% exceeded it. A similar result was attained in writing. Math achievements overall showed 67% "did not meet" or "nearly met" the standard, with 19% meeting it, and 14% exceeding it.[14]

These tests were aligned to the Common Core State Standards and said to "emphasize reasoning and deep understanding of topics." A state Department of Education official said they have "moved beyond 'proficiency' and on to being college and career-ready." However, only those who *exceed* the standard are considered ready for college. The Department said it would be impossible to compare the scores with those of other years because these new tests are radically different.[15] Check the Internet to see results in your state.

The links to a couple of states' opt-out forms are included in the Chapter Challenge section. As I caution there, what is legal and binding in one state may not be in another. Don't use a form that isn't going to do the job for you, and find out too late you haven't opted out at all.

Opting out of classes

You may be able to opt out of specific classes, or all education based on the Common Core material. The form provided by Arizonans Against Common Core in the Chapter Challenge opts out of all Common Core-based education. This may or may not be a viable option. Even opting out of one or two classes you object to may cause problems. We'll get to those problems in a bit.

Perhaps a better way to eliminate Common Core from your kids' education can be found in Massachusetts. Common Core opponents there are collecting signatures to put the measure End Common Core Massachusetts on the ballot in November 2016. Eliminating Common Core altogether in your state may be a lot easier than doing it year by year, and class by class.

If you want to be on a firm footing, the best place to start is finding out what the laws are in your state regarding a parent's right to opt out or opt in. This will definitely vary from state to state, but it may also include a wide range of possibilities within your state.

One parent signed an opt-out form for all sex education that included homosexuality, and was outraged when this lifestyle was promoted in another class *in the regular curriculum* the student attended. She was told this was not sex education, but a civil rights issue, and so was appropriate for the class.

Carefully read the opt-out form you use before you take it to the school, and evaluate what unintended consequences might ride along with it. One form states you want your child to be placed in a separate classroom, with a different curriculum. Is that possible in your school? What would that education look like? Imagine if your kids were to sit alone in a classroom with a book, an assignment, and no teacher. What "different" curriculum would be used? Would the alternate curricula be any better than the one you are opting out of?

Another form requests permission to opt out of the CCSS-based assessments, and from using computers for testing. All the common standardized tests are either working toward or are already in compliance with CCSS in computerized versions.

How will your student get into a college if they don't take the tests? The latest news is encouraging. In October 2014 *Bloomberg Business* reported since 2012 at least twenty schools have decided to no longer consider standardized tests in their admission requirements. They say high school transcripts are more helpful in deciding which students have the ability to stand up to the rigors of college curricula. In 2013 about 22% of the four-year colleges didn't require an entrance exam.[16]

You might check to see if your school offers authorized paper tests as substitutes; some do. But in reality the people behind the data mining are not dumb. They slide in queries about your kids' attitudes, home life, voting practices, and a multitude of other issues at random. Unless you forbid all use of computers in the school (which I believe would be unreasonable) you cannot keep data mining from happening in today's government schools.

There is a form requesting you be advised about what data is collected concerning your kids and your family, as well as with whom it will be shared. My guess is your school, or school district, won't know the answers. I think the decisions come from much higher up the food chain. Whether your opposition to CCSS, in whole or in part, will become a part of your kids' permanent digital record is not clear.

Don't interpret these cautionary remarks as my telling you using the opt-out form is a bad idea. I just want you to go into the effort with your eyes wide open. Be sure to read the second page of the forms I provide links to. They offer some valuable information.

When the government steps in

The number of students opting out of the Common Core aligned tests is growing steadily. This trend has U.S. Education Secretary Arne Duncan worried. He said in April 2015 the federal government would have to step in if the states can't turn it around. I wonder how many government officials read and understand the Constitution. The federal government has no constitutional authority, as far as I can tell, to get involved in education. That is supposed to be one of the matters left to the states.

An "opt out" advocacy group in New York, United to Counter the Core, reports more than 184,000 students statewide, out of approximately 1.1 million who were eligible, skipped their English exams. Percentage-wise it's not a huge number but it is evidence of growing opposition.[17] The state of New York said so many are opposed to the tests they are changing them. In the spring of 2015, 20% of the students in grades three through eight didn't participate.[18]

The responsibility is yours

When your kids head back to school each year, you are deluged with forms to fill out, and decisions to make. When I had my kids in school, I hardly gave a thought to signing permission slips. Today it would be a dangerous mistake.

Most, if not all, major departures from the basic "three Rs" require notification to parents—or so we believe. The form that gives permission to opt in to certain elements of instruction, including outside speakers, is seldom used today, giving way to the opt-out form; it varies from state to state. It puts the burden completely on the parent to monitor exactly what the school is planning for your child.

Let's look at just one course of what might be optional instruction: sex education. You have to determine if your state says the sex education programs are opt *in*, opt *out*, or required. The website of the National Council of State Legislatures provides the following information:[19] (Following emphases mine.)

- Twenty-two states and the District of Columbia *require* public schools to teach sex education.
- Twenty of those twenty-two states *mandate* sex education *and* HIV education.
- Thirty-three states and the District of Columbia *require* students receive instruction about HIV/AIDS.
- Nineteen states *require* sex education to be medically, factually or technically accurate. (This really caught my attention. Is it a fair assumption that thirty-one states and the District of Columbia do not require sex education to be medically, factually or technically accurate? Scary!)
- Thirty-seven states and the District of Columbia *require* school districts to allow parental involvement in sex education programs.
- *Only three states require* parental consent (opt *in*) before a child can receive sex instruction.
- Thirty-five states and the District of Columbia allow parents to opt out on behalf of their children.

If you scroll down below the statistics on that website, you will find a breakdown by state of the most recent sex education laws. Read a few of these, even if they are not applicable to your state, and you will see some states do not require any sex education courses.

You must check the material to be presented in class. Decide whether it's something you want someone other than yourself teaching your kids, or if it is appropriate at the age or grade level it will be introduced.

If the curriculum says abstinence is included, check exactly what that means. You might discover a statement in the text similar to "Abstinence is the only certain way to avoid STDs, but since we know you will have sex anyway, use protection. Here's how." That may be the only reference to abstinence in the entire sex education program.

If you check who is providing the material, be sure to not only look at that provider's name, but read the material. The book *From Crayons to Condoms* cautions parents to be aware material produced by the Red Cross is not harmless. The Red Cross manual describes *how to more safely engage in high risk sex.*[20]

Be certain to obtain detailed information on any outside speakers. A student complained about having to attend "lectures" by gays advocating the homosexual life-style.

Some things cannot be anticipated or avoided. An openly lesbian physical education teacher handed out a paper to her students titled, "101 Ways to Do It Without Going All the Way." I doubt there was any opt-out form for this.

If you don't want your kids exposed to these kinds of presentations, you will have to ask questions as the school year is beginning. Some districts have parent meetings before school actually starts. If yours does, this would be a good place and time to ask questions, and get answers. Awkward? Yes. Important? It's your call.

Abortion consent and notification rights

If you have a daughter, you may believe you have cautioned her enough. You may be confident she would not have sex before she gets married. However, she might have a friend who follows the promiscuity Pied Piper presented in the sex education classes, and finds herself pregnant. What are the laws in your state concerning the right of the school to take a girl to have an abortion? Do they have to notify the parents? Do the parents have to agree to the abortion?

According to the Guttmacher Institute, thirty-eight states require some kind of involvement by the parent(s), and twenty-five states have mandated either one or both parents have to sign off for their juvenile daughter to have an abortion. Thirteen of those thirty-eight states require one or both of the parents to be notified. The laws of five states, California, Michigan, Nevada, New Jersey, and New Mexico, have been permanently enjoined, and are not in effect. You can find out what parents' rights are in your state at the Guttmacher website provided in the Chapter Challenge.

Read the forms provided regarding health care very carefully. You don't want to think you are giving the school nurse permission to provide an aspirin for a headache when you are in fact giving the school carte blanche discretion regarding any health matters.

Extracurricular activities

If your kids enjoy participating in plays, you have another possible area of concern. The Pioneer Valley Performing Arts (PVPA) School in South Hadley, Massachusetts was deluged with complaints when parents and others in the community-at-large learned the play *The Most Fabulous Story Ever Told* would not be a take-off of *The Greatest Story Ever Told*, but rather a lampoon of *Genesis*—the story of Adam and Steve. (An article in the *Huffington Post* said the school is in a community nicknamed Lesbianville, USA. According to the 2000 census it has more lesbians per capita than anywhere else in the United States.)

Although this was a "performing arts" school, it was a government public school. The theater department director said, "In my opinion, those who find offense with this play will do so because they believe homosexuality is a sin. At PVPA, we do not believe that to be the case." The head of the school entered the fray with the question, "Is it the role of public school to facilitate an exchange of ideas on the themes explored in this particular play?" He declared it was an excellent question deserving debate in a "climate of civility, and a desire to understand others' viewpoints."

Considering the city's "reputation," perhaps questioning in advance of participation would have made sense. But who knew? After the fact, there's not a lot a parent can do other than carefully monitor all other productions or pull the kids out. There is most likely no way to object to extra-curricular activities, as participation is probably viewed as implied consent. This was a charter school with an emphasis on the performing arts, so the play may have been part of regular class assignments. In that case, parents should have the right to opt out of productions they deem unsuitable. Moving to a more faith-friendly area would not be possible for most people.[21]

Shorewood High School, identified as being located "in a liberal suburb of Milwaukee," chose a play based on one from 1890s Germany titled *Spring Awakening*. They billed it as being "updated and rockified." The Kennedy Center website stated this play "puts controversial issues front and center: teen sexuality, domestic and sexual violence, and suicide." The head of the high school's drama department said ". . . students love performing these titles. . . . the excitement level of students can't be underestimated . . . the social themes in these musicals are perfectly relevant to teenagers—homelessness, homophobia, child abuse, physical abuse, etc." Other Shorewood High productions have included *Urinetown* (people pay for the privilege to urinate), *Avenue Q: School Edition* (revised to be more acceptable for high school productions), *The Laramie Project* (based on a true story about the murder of a gay college student), and *Rent: School Edition* (deals with love, loss, AIDS, and modern day life.) Shorewood was a pilot school for the latter. These are all highly acclaimed plays, and you may have no concerns about your kids participating in them. Decide what is right for your family values, and then make sure the productions in which your kids will participate match those values.[22]

Your rights as parents also include the responsibility to exercise caution. The more information you have about the multitude of ways your kids can be affected, the more aware you will become. Using Shorewood as an example, you should be notified when questionable productions will be performed. Make certain you will receive advance notification, and you have the opportunity to opt out. Find out if you can opt out for all such productions with one form, or if each one requires a separate opt out notification. There will be a very upset kid in your house if he or she gets a lead part and *then* you say "no can do."

Be sure you take good care of your kids' health

Unfortunately, some parents don't have their kids' best interests at heart. There are many cases of child neglect and abuse, and sometimes authorities find out about it too late. As you are taking the time to read this book, it is safe to assume you don't fall into that category. However, you have to be aware of the variety of ways laws may take away from you your right to decide about your kids' physical and mental health care.

Did you read how 15-year-old Justina Pelletier was taken from her family? She had a few medical problems, but she was being treated successfully by a highly credentialed doctor at Tufts Medical Center in Boston, Massachusetts. She was a competitive figure skater. Then one day in January 2013 she got a bad case of the flu, and her parents were told to take her to Boston Children's Hospital (BCH). The doctor at BCH was only out of medical school for seven months, and had no medical history on Justina other than what her parents provided when they checked her in. He decided she didn't really have the medical problem Tufts was (successfully) treating her for—she had a mental condition. It was sixteen months before the hospital and the courts, through the efforts of the Liberty Counsel, permitted Justina to return home. By that time, lacking the needed treatment she previously received at Tufts, Justina could barely sit up in a wheelchair. Figure skating was only a memory.[23]

It's encouraging to find that not all courts act in the above manner. It will come as no surprise that kids don't always agree with the decisions of their parents. The Georgia District Court also recognized that possibility and said that you are the parent—unless you are a truly bad parent, parents rule!

> Simply because the decision of a parent is not agreeable to a child, or because it involves risks does not automatically transfer power to make that decision from the parents to some agency or officer of the state. The same characterizations can be made for a tonsillectomy, appendectomy, or other medical procedure. Most children, even in adolescence, simply are not able to make sound judgements concerning many decisions, including their need for medical care or treatment. Parents can and must make those judgements . . . we cannot assume that the result [in another case] would have been different if the children there had announced a preference to learn only English or preference to go to a public, rather than a church school. The fact that a child may balk at hospitalization or complain about a parental refusal to provide cosmetic surgery does not diminish the parent's authority to decide what is best for the child.[24]

Who's intruding in privacy rights—you or the doctor?

Have you ever taken your kids to the doctor, and the nurse told you to stay where you were while they talked privately with them? It happens more often than you think. I can understand the reason. Some children are abused by their parents, and if one is present they won't talk about it to anyone else.

In June 2014 one Michigan mother was told in the doctor's office that seeing the child without the parents was law, and there was no opt out available. There was also a provision in that law permitting kids to access their own medical records, but the kids could block their parents from seeing any of it. At the time this incident happened the mother was told her physician's office "jumped the gun" and the law had not yet been implemented. There is little-to-no chance you can refuse to obey a law. This is where you need to have your antennae up and stop a law before it's passed, or worst case, do what you can to get the law repealed.[25]

A super-charged high-level opt out

Some parents have considered opting out of a whole school. In July 2015 *The Report Card* told of parents being denied their right under the California trigger law to open a new charter school. The law states if a school is underperforming, parents can petition to get the school converted to a charter school. In this case the school had been on the Department of Education list of underperforming schools since 2003. That makes the condition clear. However, the teachers' union was upset about the proliferation and success of charter schools.

Opposition came with both barrels. Claims were made of paperwork errors in a petition. More than 60% of the school's parents signed the petition, but the school district threw out many signatures they said they couldn't verify. Of course, they tried to verify the signatures with the parents between the hours of 8:30 a.m. and 4:30 p.m.—*when the parents were mostly at work*. The petition was rejected.

Hooray for the parents who took this to court and won. The judge called the school district's conduct "unreasonable, arbitrary, capricious and unfair." Sometimes you just can't take no for an answer. Be prepared to press on.[26]

Should you opt out of history or social studies classes?

World history classes continue requiring students to learn the five pillars of Islam. Parents are calling it "indoctrination" and others say it is a legitimate part of world history. Tennessee experienced that as the school year began in the fall of 2015. Requiring students to write out the Shahada (one of the pillars, known as the "conversion creed") went too far. Snopes, the website that verifies or debunks rumors and urban legends, investigated the reporting to verify its accuracy and determined it was true.[27] The articles covering this news referred to the "new standards" which, while unidentified, undoubtedly meant the Common Core State Standards.[28]

On September 3, 2015, Maury County Director of Schools Chris Marczak put a statement on Facebook which read in part, "For this last section on the Islamic World this past week, our educators had students complete an assignment that had an emphasis on Islamic Faith. The assignment covered some sensitive topics that are of importance to Islamic religion and caused some confusion around whether we are asking students to believe in or simply understand the religion." He later continued with counsel for parents: "I encourage all Maury County parents to be their child's first and main teacher. It is our job as parents of our own children to instill in them the beliefs of our individual households."[29] That's good advice, bearing in mind it's what God has told us as well. However, as all tests are being aligned to Common Core, if your kids are not taught this material, ask whether it will affect their test scores if you opt out of certain lessons.

To read or not to read, that is the question

English classes are another area of instruction to be examined carefully. Some of the books on required, as well as recommended, reading lists are delightful. Others are so vulgar I'd put them down if I started to read them myself. These may be discussed in class as part of the reading assignment. If that's not what you want filling your kid's mind, see if you can opt out of the English class for specific assignments only. You may also be able to opt your kids out of just the class hour(s) when the material is discussed. It should be obvious if you didn't want your kids to read it, you would not want them discussing it in class.

Opting out of data mining

Your kids are encountering data mining on a frequent and consistent basis. If you don't want their record to be available to whatever entity the government thinks has a need or use for it, it is probably going to be an uphill climb to opt out.

In, with, and through the *Google* Apps for Education, which many schools use, *Google* admits to scanning your kids' emails. They swore to this in a federal court. They don't run ads in Apps for Education, but behind the scenes a Pied Piper is compiling keywords to use for advertising on other *Google* sites. You can't blame *Google* too much; they got permission to do that from the U.S. Department of Education. The Family Educational Rights and Privacy Act, which is supposed to protect student privacy, was revised downward in 2011. The result left openings for data mining companies such as *Google* to step in. Some think what *Google* does still goes too far based on the Department's "best practices" for online educational service providers.

Because of the watering-down of the Privacy Act, many companies other than *Google* now can probe your kids' records without asking for your permission. A student's privacy rights organization, Education New York, is mobilizing parents to opt out of the use of education records for marketing purposes. They claim the data usually includes name, address, telephone number, and birth date, along with other personal information. On page four of the Document 10-7 in the Federal Register, (2) Conditions for Disclosing Directory Information, it states, ". . . an educational agency or institution must continue to honor a valid request to opt out of directory information disclosures even after the student no longer attends the institution."

If you are sincerely concerned about your parental rights and the privacy rights of your kids, you are going to have to find a way to keep up with legislation and regulations affecting you."[30]

Louisiana Senator Vitter introduced a bill in May 2015 named "The Student Privacy Protection Act." If passed, it would establish new guidelines for any entity connected with the release of student education records to third parties. Senator Vitter seemed to be reading some minds, because he also included privacy protection for homeschooled kids. As of December 2015, the bill was referred to the Committee on Health, Education, Labor, and Pensions.

Vitter's bill would restore the rights that were originally a part of the Family Educational Rights and Privacy Act. It states unequivocally who can have access to your kids' data, and what portions they have a right to get their hands on. It would require your granting permission before they can access the data, so you have some protection.[31,32]

This is the time for another word of caution. Read the forms the school sends home carefully before you sign them. If any entity, educational agency, school, or a third party, doesn't get your consent first, they will have to pay a fine. This may be a weakness in the Act, because this doesn't, and can't, restore the privacy of what's already been accessed. Pandora's box has been opened. For some it may be worthwhile to get the information and pay the fine.

Considering the consequences

Once you've decided what you want and don't want your kids taught, you must find out what the alternatives are when not attending those classes. Some schools move your kids' desks into the hall, and they sit there until the class is over. (Other kids may see this as punishment, and an opportunity to poke fun at them and their beliefs.) They may be sent to a different location, such as the library, and use it as study time. If either is the case, be sure to ask if your kids will lose credit for the class. Some have had to make it up in summer school. You will have to make the effort to find out, because most likely the school will not provide the information without being asked. They may not plan in advance what they will do if someone opts out of a class, a portion of the curriculum, or the entire course.

Make certain:

- Your child brings all permission slips home and gives them to you.
- You read them carefully.
- You return them promptly.

The school will say you have no one to blame but yourself if you don't get the form back to them. Attach a letter explaining your absolute position if you think it is necessary, or schedule a visit with the principal to make sure your wishes are understood.

It's so easy to fall into the trap of believing none of this could happen to your kids, in your schools, in your town. That's probably what the parents of the kids involved in the things described above thought too.

✝

"But be sure to fear the Lord and serve him faithfully with all your heart; consider what great things he has done for you" (1 Samuel 12:24).

Chapter Challenge

Where do you go from here? You have some decisions to make. As you read in this chapter, some opt out options are available to you, and some are not. A better way to handle not having your kids participate in undesirable lessons and activities at school is to lobby for opt-in forms to replace opt-out forms. That will give you a great deal more control.

Read more about opting out of standardized tests at "Why You Can Boycott Standardized Tests Without Fear of Federal Penalties to Your School" at fairtest.org/why-you-can-boycott-testing-without-fear.

You can find a general opt-out form for standardized testing (provided by Kansans Against Common Core) at usd378.org/DocumentCenter/View/4187. The one provided by Arizonans Against Common Core is more thorough, and also can be used to opt out of Common Core State Standards educational materials, and any kind of computerized assessments. There are more requests below the items to be checked, including disclosure about the state longitudinal data system (data mining) that may be of interest to you. You can find the Arizona form at arizonansagainstcommoncore.com/CCSS_Parent_Opt_Out.pdf. What is legal and binding in one state may not be in another. Check your own state to determine what is applicable.

You can find out what parents' rights in your state are regarding your minor daughter's ability to have an abortion on the Guttmacher website at guttmacher.org/statecenter/spibs/spib_OAL.pdf.

If you haven't done so already, this is a good time to start forming a group to help with all the work.

Books

The Test: Why Our Schools are Obsessed with Standardized Testing–But You Don't Have to Be by Anya Kamenetz (January 6, 2015).

Who's Got Dibs on Your Kids? YOU HAVE!

"Blessed is the one who does not walk in step with the wicked or stand in the way that sinners take or sit in the company of mockers" (Psalm 1:1).

Who's got dibs on your kids? *You* have! By your relationship, by confirmation of the Supreme Court of the United States, by the Word of the Almighty God, *you have first dibs on your kids*. The question is, are you ready for that?

You have just read about a few of the many Pied Pipers who are dedicated to leading your kids on a path away from God. If you're all right with that happening, or don't see it as a serious concern, you can close this book and go on your way. Not taking God seriously goes back a long way, as we learn in Jeremiah 7:24: "But they did not listen. They refused to pay any attention to me."

However, if what you read here sends shivers through you, and you worry about how you are going to keep your kids on a godly path through their life, it is going to be up to you to take action. If a waiter in a restaurant spills a plate of food on you, do you patiently wait and hope someone will bring something to clean it up, or do you grab a napkin and start wiping? That's what you have to do now. Don't wait for someone else to magically appear, and tell you, "Don't worry. I've got everything in hand. I'll take care of it, and all will be back to normal." That's living in a dream world. If you have to do it alone, then do it alone. Remember Kim Davis in Kentucky, and the national ruckus she started when as county clerk she refused to issue marriage licenses to same-sex couples? Whether you agree with her stand or not, you have to admit she proved one person can make a big difference.

Decisions, decisions, decisions

There are three obvious ways to approach the problem of keeping your kids on the right path. No one should tell you one is the right way and one is wrong. Each family must consider all of the positive and negative aspects, and decide what is best for their kids, in their personal circumstances.

The first option is keeping them in the government school, and fighting the errant education they will receive. If your kids are in public school now, they can stay in the same school, with their same friends, and you will have the opportunity to use your district's school buses to get them there and home again. You may look at this as the easiest at first, but the effort required to push against the Pied Pipers will be daunting, and it will last throughout their school life. I'll give you some ways to fight these battles later in this chapter.

In addition, consider what your kids will think if you keep telling them what they are learning at school is wrong, less than truthful, and often in opposition to God's laws. Will they wonder why you send them to a school you know will teach them those things?

The second option is sending your kids to a private or religiously-affiliated school. If you choose a private school with no religious affiliation, you will have to check to make certain they are not teaching the same views a public school teaches. If you decide to switch to a religiously-affiliated school, will it be your own faith? To some it will not matter, as long as it has a Bible-based philosophy. However, if you are Catholic, you may want a Catholic school; if you are Lutheran, staying with Lutheran teachings may be very important to you. Nevertheless, all may have some challenges. There will be a financial cost. Some charge more than others, some have adjusted rates for the number of kids in a family attending, but there will be a cost that you do not have with public schooling. Then there is the matter of transportation. Does the school have its own buses to take your kids to and from school? If so, what is the cost? If there is no bus service, will you be able to get them to school on time and pick them up again? If not, is there an accommodation where your kids can stay at school for a short time both before and after classes end? What is the cost for textbooks and other associated fees?

If you are considering going this route, make a spreadsheet with *all* the variables listed in the first column. Have a column following for each school you want to evaluate, so you know you are asking for the same information from each school you contact, and you can easily compare them side-by-side.

The third option is for you to homeschool. Some of you are mentally putting up a roadblock right now. "No way. That's not for me." At least put your doubts temporarily aside, and give it careful consideration. Then, if you still don't think it's the right course for you and your kids, at least you will reject it for good reasons. There is a lot of help available for homeschooling today, from structured textbook courses to online learning. In fact, there is so much out there for homeschoolers you might be overwhelmed by it. I suggest you do a fast overview by visiting the website of the Home School Legal Defense Association (HSLDA) at www.hslda.org. They have a page for Homeschooling Thru High School loaded with links and information that will guide you.

One of the benefits of homeschooling is the kids usually get a better education than at a government school, and they are welcomed with open arms at colleges and universities because they have demonstrated a willingness to put in real effort to learn. The social side is easily taken care of by participation in community sports teams, or by joining groups with similar interests such as art, animals, reading—whatever activities fascinate your kid, there is probably a group in your community for it. HSLDA says "on average, these children engaged in 5.2 activities outside the home, with 98% involved in two or more." Homeschooled kids usually advance faster, too.

There are downsides. If you and your husband both work, or if you are a single parent, you will have to arrange your work schedule to be the teacher. If there are two of you, and you are sufficiently committed, one of you might quit your job, or find a way to work at home. That creates another problem: money. Can your family get by with the loss of an income? And on the emotional side, can you see yourself being with your kids almost all day, every day? Most homeschooling parents find a way to be off on their own regularly just to keep a fresh mind and attitude.

The positive side of homeschooling is expressed often and enthusiastically by those who are using it, or have in the past. HSLDA estimates about two million children are homeschooled in the United States. Achievement test scores are usually well above those of public as well as Catholic and private school students. Kids in grades one through four often do work one grade up from where they would be in public school. Check out the HSLDA page Homeschooled Students Excel in College. A Harvard University admissions officer said most of their home-educated students "have done very well.

They usually are very motivated in what they do."

The important thing is for you to prayerfully determine what is best for your family, and follow that path. Do whatever you can to ensure your kids' education, and the culture of your home, are established not by default, but by design.

Don't forget to include your kids in the decision-making

You are going to have to tell your kids what you are embarking on. The younger they are, the less they need to know, of course. However, even in the lower grades they are going to notice a difference, and you had better prepare them for it before it hits.

The ages of tweens and teens bring with them explosive emotions and a need for evaluating everything—bungee-cord-jumps between love and hate, admiration and jealousy, a need to obey rules and a need to rebel. If you start laying down rules, expectations, and life-altering attitudes during this time, prepare yourself for a very bumpy ride. The best time to start anything with your kids is now, regardless of the age, but the earlier you start preparing them, the easier it will be for both you and them.

Don't wear your religion on your shirtsleeve

There is an old expression, "Don't wear your religion on your shirtsleeve." In other words: don't pray conspicuously in a restaurant; don't object to dirty jokes; don't worry about the impression you give by the way you dress; don't refuse to relinquish your beliefs in the face of retribution from homosexuals. Just—*don't*! It makes other people uncomfortable. But is that the way God taught us to behave?

> "Our lives begin to end the day we become silent about things that matter."
> Martin Luther King, Jr.

His Word says, in Deuteronomy 11:18–19, "You shall therefore lay up these words of mine in your heart and in your soul, and you shall bind them as a sign on your hand, and they shall be as frontlets between your eyes. You shall teach them to your children, talking of them when you are sitting in your house, and when you are walking by the way, and when you lie down, and when you rise." What God was telling us in that passage was not that we should hide His place in our lives, but we should show it conspicuously and proudly.

I recently was a constant visitor in a hospital's Intensive Care Unit. Not one, but two signs at the doorway reminded both hospital personnel and visitors "Gel In—Gel Out." In other words, go into the room clean, and cleanse your hands as you leave. The analogy is a good one for you and your kids. Pray with them before they go to school, asking the Lord to be with them through the day. Then, after school, ask for help in keeping straight the lessons they have learned in light of God's law.

Get your kids in the habit of praying wherever they are, by themselves or with friends, for strength to resist, for direction, and to give thanks. (Let them learn to do this by example. Let them see and hear you praying.) Sometimes a silent five or ten word prayer is all it takes to get the needed reinforcement to stand tall in a godly life in a world that is increasingly more godless. Word of caution: check with your school first for regulations concerning praying—out loud—with others—and silently.

Base your case on facts and know your opponents

The atheist Marquis de Sade (1740–1814) put his finger on what was a godless world-view even then. He said, "If there is no God then all things are permissible." Atheists and evolutionists, humanist promoters of homosexuality and promiscuity, and others like them don't believe there is any foundational need for what we deem a "moral" standpoint. If you hear them using a "moral" argument, be alert; it's not one they believe in, it's one they think they can use to manipulate others. By the same token, it is useless to use a moral-based argument against their beliefs. It won't register.

As I was close to finishing this book, I ran across one by Marybeth Hicks titled *Teachable Moments: Using Everyday Encounters with Media and Culture to Instill Conscience, Character, and Faith*. Hicks covers much of what I have here, but from more of a practical "how to deal with it all" approach rather than an exposé (as I have done) of the garbage that is confronting your kids. I highly recommend you read *Teachable Moments*. Published in 2014, it is current and highly relevant.

Teachable Moments is designed to help with problems with your kids as they arise. It is wonderfully helpful; however, those moments can be reduced in number and intensity by explaining your beliefs, your values, your morals, your patriotism, and your faith, over and over again to your children, starting almost at birth. Dealing with the problem when it arises is necessary, but every time you prepare in advance with your kids for when those moments occur you have, to some extent, already given a fizzle to the fuse. Singing hymns as lullabies, saying prayers even when a baby doesn't quite get "praying" yet, putting up an American flag, going to parades for our military that celebrate their service, and going to church regularly, are all easy ways to demonstrate what you believe is important in life.

It's a battlefield—be prepared for the fight

None of the problems you and your kids face are insurmountable. God has told us He is always with us. We have His armor to wear to protect us from all of the assaults of the Evil One. Put them on daily, and consciously. Just as you dress yourself for a day in the workplace, or at home, or enjoying the beauty of God's creation, one garment at a time, dress yourself to face whatever comes into your life. Consciously welcome the presence of the Holy Spirit in your life—you will be filled with an inexplicable joy. Then teach your kids how to do this. "Now I lay me down to sleep" is a good start, but teach your kids how they can call on God to be with them as they face bullies who ridicule their faith, as they resist the teachings of an anti-God school, and as they consider what is the best course for their professional lives.

What is the greatest threat?

What do you see as the greatest threat to your kids' futures? Is it ISIS with its terrorism and brutality? Is it Iran's getting closer and closer to having nuclear weapons? Or is it China, who by raising interest rates or calling our loans due can destroy America financially?

Let me suggest a worse threat than any of those. It is the subtle, incremental slide away from the Word of God. It is the ridicule your kids will face from evolutionists. It is being called a hater or homophobe by those pushing gay rights. It's being refused a job, or losing a job if they will not yield to beliefs they know are wrong. It is the temptation to "go along to get along" and slowly but surely forgetting the most important future is eternal life in heaven. God is a God of love, but He is also a God of justice. Jesus tells us in Matthew 10:32–33 "Whoever acknowledges me before others, I will also acknowledge before my Father in heaven. But whoever disowns me before others, I will disown before my Father in heaven." Our actions have consequences. You, as the parent of your kids, the gifts from God, have an obligation to, as much as is possible, keep your kids' footsteps on God's path, rather than following the Pied Pipers of this world. Don't be like those parents in Robert Browning's poem who watched their children being enticed away from them, believing with all their heart:

> "He never can cross that mighty top!
> He's forced to let the piping drop,
> And we shall see our children stop!"

Don't live in such a state of delusion that you cannot recognize the truth. The pipers will not stop piping until your kids are firmly in their control.

"And when all were in to the very last,
The door in the mountain-side shut fast."

As you strive to keep or get your kids back on the right track, you will set an example for others through your actions, in the attitude of your kids in school, and among their friends. Even questions about why you do what you do may provide a perfect opportunity to tell others about the love of God. Tell them He loved us all so much that Christ died for our salvation. How can we not want to do what pleases God rather than what offends Him?

When the opportunity arises, show them the Bible passages you rely on when you make decisions. Tell them God's love extends to them and to their children also, and it is not too late to take the path that leads to eternity in heaven.

God promises that even though the road will be difficult at times, He will bless those who follow Him. "But even if you should suffer for what is right, you are blessed. 'Do not fear their threats; do not be frightened.' But in your hearts revere Christ as Lord. Always be prepared to give an answer to everyone who asks you to give the reason for the hope that you have. But do this with gentleness and respect, keeping a clear conscience, so that those who speak maliciously against your good behavior in Christ may be ashamed of their slander" (1 Peter 3:14–16).

Directions help no matter where you are going

Once you decide if you are going to place your kids in a private or religious school, homeschool, or use the public school system, you'll need to find your way around the system. It's a little like planning a vacation: once you know your destination, you want to have good directions to get there, and plan what you're going to do. That trip requires a map, programming the GPS, or asking friends who have been there. Providing the best schooling for your kids is much the same. You need guidance.

So, what are the most important factors to consider when getting directions to the best schooling for your kids? They are important for you to know, because Christian parents are given the responsibility by God to teach their children the way to eternal life.

First, and foremost, know where you want to go. Have a definite destination in mind. No map or other device will get you there if you don't know where you're going.

What is the final destination you want for your children? Eternal life with God?

"Do not let your hearts be troubled. You believe in God; believe also in me. My Father's house has many rooms; if that were not so, would I have told you that I am going there to prepare a place for you?" (John 14:1–2).

Or will that final destination be an eternal life separated from God?

"There will be weeping there, and gnashing of teeth, when you see Abraham, Isaac and Jacob and all the prophets in the kingdom of God, but you yourselves thrown out" (Luke 13:28).

Have an absolute trustworthy source for your directions.

"Jesus answered, 'I am the way and the truth and the life. No one comes to the Father except through me'" (John 14:6).

Pay no attention to the Pied Pipers pointing to this attraction or that amusement; stay on the right path.

"Those who guide this people mislead them, and those who are guided are led astray" (Isaiah 9:16).

How to get started if your kids will be in a government school

You can get started now. You don't have to wait for anyone. One person, one dedicated person, can do remarkable things.

It's better, though, if you can get a group of like-minded people together. Pass this book to them to read, or better yet, have them get their own copy so it doesn't take so long to get everyone up to speed. Decide what you want to tackle first. Don't try to do everything at once. That will only result in everyone burning out before your task is finished.

When at least three people join together to accomplish something they are more effective than individual efforts are. However, groups can also get too big. There is a natural tendency for some to get lazy if there are enough others to pick up the slack. Make every member of the group feel needed, and expected to do the job assigned. This might mean keeping group size to eight to twelve people, and if you are fortunate enough to have more interested in being involved, start another group.

While cohesiveness in a group can influence members to work together, behave in a similar manner, and feel close ties to the group, that very cohesiveness can also cause problems. When there is close to absoluteness in the conformity of the members of the group, there is little or no opportunity for anyone to have nonconforming opinions and viewpoints. Let everyone participate in the discussions.

Good news and bad news. Isn't that always the way?

The good news is there have been many successful efforts to turn the problems with public schools around. Laws have been passed protecting your kids' rights: Common Core has been defeated in some states, reading list complaints have been acknowledged and adjustments made, and history texts are being rewritten to relate the truth more accurately.

The bad news is none of this has come without a lot of hard work, time, and expense, by some very dedicated people. Nothing will happen without action on someone's part—on *your* part. And, as with any task, it will be easier if you have others to share the work and give

> Failing to plan is planning to fail.
>
> Benjamin Franklin

ideas of how to go forward.

Let's say you decide to tackle evolution first. Make a list of what you would like to do, and the steps it will take to get there. Depending on how many are in the group, you may be able to assign one task to each. Have one look into current law regarding teaching of creation or intelligent design in public schools. Have another read the science text books for a particular school district, or for a particular grade in all districts in your county. Have another sit in classes when evolution is taught. Meet regularly to compare notes, and decide on the next steps. Do you want to get a law passed requiring intelligent design be taught as a viable alternative to the theory of evolution? Do you want to be able to opt out of the classes where evolution is taught, without any negative results for your kids? Make a plan.

Starting the journey

Let's get down to business. If you decide to send your kids to a public school, here is a list of things you can think about doing. Not all will apply to everyone, but some will strike you as being important to you and your specific needs. This is only a partial list, but even then it can be intimidating. Don't be discouraged. God will be with you: "But as for you, be strong and do not give up, for your work will be rewarded" (2 Chronicles 15:7).

Here's your map. You may want to add a few extra stops, or take a detour here and there, but the important thing is to get on the road. These are things you can do at the school and community level:

- Educate yourself about the issues – this book is only your starting point
    - Check out what is happening in your own school district
    - Talk to other parents for their viewpoints
    - Talk to your kids
- Investigate the schools your kids attend
    - Check out the textbooks—you may want to enlist help

with this.
  * Investigate content of non-textbook information such as reading lists and outside speakers.
  * Ask to see ancillary learning material.
  * Ask about special "awareness" days such as pink shirt day, earth day, etc.
  * Get a written statement of opt out and opt in policies.
  * If your school says it is dedicated to developing critical thinking skills, find out how this is applied in teaching evolution, climate science, etc.
  * Decide if you want your kids to participate in computerized testing and data mining. Find out if paper tests are an option.
  * Find out where your kids will go on field trips. Some go to mosques where students are required to bow before Allah. Be aware, and take appropriate action.
  * Attend school board meetings.
  * Get to know the members of your school board—know their viewpoints.
  * Try to get on the textbook adoption or review committee.
- When you know where the weaknesses are, ask for changes.
  * Recommend change from an objectionable program or curriculum to a specific one that you prefer. (Don't just complain without a solution.)
  * Advocate for a global change from opt out to opt in for anything not expressly and thoroughly identified as mandatory class work.
  * Read every form carefully before you sign it. Keep a copy in your files. If you have any question about what it means, ask before signing.
  * Write letters to the members of the district school board expressing your displeasure, and suggesting alternatives.

* Circulate a petition to send to the district, demonstrating you are not the only one objecting.
* Run for a position on the school board.
* If you aren't running, endorse others you think are good candidates.

You might find it's important to ramp it up: start to learn about state laws, determine how they personally affect you and your kids, and see if they need changing:

- Learn about the educational directives for your state. Most of you will find this involves some level of Common Core.
  * Find out what your state standards are, and what they are based on.
  * Learn what tests will be given to your kids, if they are aligned with Common Core, and if they are stated as "mandatory."
- Look up laws for your state concerning parental notification and/or permission regarding abortion.

There are more things to tackle as soon as you think you have a good sense of what is happening, and what needs to be done:

- Get interested, concerned parents and grandparents to form a group with you to share the tasks.
- Write a letter to the editor of your local newspaper about matters that concern you.
- Try to get on a local radio talk show to get your views more widely known.
- If you don't have success getting changes made, campaign against any more tax increases in any form for your school district.

At home, you can and should talk constantly to your kids about what they are learning in school, and if it is consistent with God's Word. Also:

- Teach your kids there is a difference between sharing with others out of love for them, as God directs us to do, and having mandatory "sharing" imposed by the government (as in socialism.)
- Teach your kids to love their country. They are American citizens, not global citizens. The laws we live under are set up under our Constitution, not a global set of laws.
- Teach your kids to do math in a logical process if they are being taught otherwise at school.
- Teach your kids the truth about promiscuity, homosexuality, and God's view on those matters.
- Teach your kids cursive writing if it is not taught at school. Organize an after-school club for learning cursive.
- Start your kids reading early. Teach them using phonics. This sounds like a huge task, but it's really easy and logical. Start when they are very young with colorful letters on a magnetic board at their level on the wall. They first use the letters to learn the ABCs, and then hear how they sound and see how you move them to make words.
- Take your kids to the library. There's plenty there for every age.
- Take your kids on little "field trips" to expand their interests and imagination.
- Tell your kids to refuse to answer certain questions, or entire surveys and tests, if they have any sort of uneasy feeling about them. Let them know they may "get into trouble" with their teacher or principal for standing their ground, but tell them to say that is what their parents instructed them to do. Sometimes they may not even be sure why they feel uncomfortable with the questions, but that's all right. They shouldn't be forced into anything that troubles them.
- Set a time for regular study of God's Word at home. A good

time is right before bed. Give every child a chance to read a portion of the story, lesson, or Scripture as soon as they are able to. Leave time for questions and discussion.

Do you feel a bit daunted? I don't blame you. This is not a decision to make without a firm resolve to face up to every enemy, endure taunts, and possibly take a lot of flak from your kids, depending on their ages.

Then there is the final evaluation when considering what's best for your kids. Is it "WINNING!" by the standards of this world, or is it the salvation won through Jesus Christ, and spending an unfathomably wonderful life with Him for eternity? As a parent, you have the responsibility to make the right decisions for your kids. Consider all alternatives carefully.

Remember, Christians have been bearing these types of crosses since Jesus' time. Some became martyrs. Martyrdom is probably not in your future, but you may feel this to be one of the most painful roads you ever choose to travel.

Words of caution I read recently come to mind: "There are many things God will put up with—second place is not one of them."

✝

You are assured in Micah 5:9 "Your hand will be lifted up in triumph over your enemies, and all your foes will be destroyed," and again in Matthew 10:22, "All men will hate you because of me, but he who stands firm to the end will be saved."

END NOTES

INTRODUCTION

1. "The Pied Piper of Hameln and related legends from other towns." Retrieved Dec, 2015, from http://www.pitt.edu/~dash/hameln.html#browning.
2. "The Pied Piper of Hamelin." Retrieved Dec, 2015, from http://www.public-domain-poetry.com/robert-browning/pied-piper-of-hamelin-6725.

CHAPTER 2: WHO'S GOT DIBS ON YOUR KIDS' ORIGINS?

3. "General Theory of Relativity." http://www.physicsoftheuniverse.com/topics_relativity_general.html.14 Dec,2015,
4. "*The Big Bang - NASA Science*." http://science.nasa.gov/astrophysics/focus-areas/what-powered-the-big-bang/.23 May, 2015.
5. Behe, Michael J. *Darwin's Black Box: The Biochemical Challenge to Evolution*. Second ed. New York: Free Press, 2006. 1996.
6. Myers, P. Z. "Behe's Edge of Evolution, Part I." http://scienceblogs.com/pharyngula/2007/06/05/behes-edge-of-evolution-part-i/.24 Apr,2015.
7. Grigg, Russell. "Fraud Rediscovered." *Creation*, Mar 1998, 49-51.
8. Stewart, David J. Compiler. http://www.jesus-is-savior.com/Evolution%20 Ho"'Lucy' Is Not the Missing Link! " ax/lucy.htm.23 May,2015.
9. Lieberman, Daniel E. "Another Face in Our Family Tree." *Nature* 410, no. 6827 22 Mar 2001: 419-20.
10. Mervis, Jeffrey. "Why Many U.S. Biology Teachers Are 'Wishy-Washy'." *Science*, 06 Mar 2015.
11. Yates, Tony B., and Edmund A. Marek. "Teachers Teaching Misconceptions: A Study of Factors Contributing to High School Biology Students' Acquisition of

Biological Evolution-Related Misconceptions." [In en]. *Evolution: Education and Outreach* 7 28 Mar 2014.

12. Uzoma, Kay. "How Much TV Does the Average Child Watch Each Day?" livestrong.com, http://www.livestrong.com/article/222032-how-much-tv-does-the-average-child-watch-each-day/.22 Mar,2015.
13. "Anti-NGSS Bill in Iowa | NCSE." National Center for Science Education, http://ncse.com/news/2015/03/anti-ngss-bill-iowa-0016212.3 Mar,2015.
14. "Antiscience Bill Dies in Oklahoma | NCSE." National Center for Science Education, http://ncse.com/news/2015/02/antiscience-bill-dies-oklahoma-0016209.27 Feb,2015.

Chapter 3: Who's Got Dibs on Your Kids' ENVIRONMENT?

1. "ESRL Global Monitoring Division - Global Greenhouse Gas Reference Network." US Department of Commerce, NOAA, Earth System Research Laboratory, http://www.esrl.noaa.gov/gmd/ccgg/trends/.
2. Matthews Jr, Merrill. "Who's Afraid of Co2?" National Center for Policy Analysis (NCPA), http://www.ncpa.org/pub/ba256.
3. United Nations, Department of Economic and Social Affairs, Population Division. "World Population Prospects: 2012 Revision, Dvd Edition." 2013.
4. "All Standards, All Students - Appendix D." In *Making the Next Generation Science Standards Accessible to All Students*: Next Generation Science Standards, 2013.
5. Bohannon, John. "Balmy Arctic Stymies Climate Modelers." *Science*, 2006.
6. NSTA, National Science Teachers Association -. "NSTA Pressroom "NSTA Statement on the Distribution of "an Inconvenient Truth"." National Science Teachers Association, http://www.nsta.org/about/pressroom.aspx?id=52977.
7. Daly, John L. "The Hockey Stick: A New Low in Climate Science." http://www.john-daly.com/hockey/hockey.htm.
8. Tyson, P.D., *et al*. "The Little Ice Age and Medieval Warming in South Africa." *South African Journal of Science*, no. 96 (2000): 121-26.
9. Monckton of Brenchley, Christopher, *35 Inconvenient Truths: The Errors in Al Gore's Movie*, 18 October 2007, http://scienceandpublicpolicy.org/images/

stories/press_releases/monckton-response-to-gore-errors.pdf.

10. "Latest Global Warming Report: No Man Made Global Warming." *Federalist Press* (2 Apr 2015). 2 Apr 2015. http://federalistpress.com/latest-global-warming-report-no-man-made-global-warming.php.
11. Simmons, Randy T. "What Do We Have to Show for Governments Subsidies of Wind Power?" *The Hill*. Online, 2015. http://thehill.com/blogs/pundits-blog/energy-environment/233562-what-do-we-have-to-show-for-government-subsidies-of.
12. Hollingsworth, Barbara. "Despite $39b in Annual Gov't. Subsidies, Solar Produced 0.5% of Electricity in US." *CNSNews.com* (2015). 17 February 2015. http://cnsnews.com/news/article/barbara-hollingsworth/despite-39b-annual-govt-subsidies-solar-produced-05-electricity.5 May 2015.
13. Duhamel, Jonathan. "Ivanpah Solar Plant Wants to Burn More Natural Gas." Arizona Daily Independent, https://arizonadailyindependent.com/2014/08/22/ivanpah-solar-plant-wants-to-burn-more-natural-gas/.23 Dec,2015,
14. Hollingsworth, Barbara.17 February 2015.
15. Chamberlain, Andrew, *Who Benefits from Free Emission Allowances? An Economic Analysis of the Waxman-Market Cap-and-Trade Program*, Sep 2009, http://instituteforenergyresearch.org/media/pdf/FINAL%20Waxman-Markey%20Study%2009-28-2009.pdf.
16. Beisner, PhD E. Calvin. "Environmentalists Claim "Just Solution" to Climate Change Is Wealth Redistribution | Cornwall Alliance." *Cornwall Alliance* (2015). 6 Apr 2015. http://www.cornwallalliance.org/2015/04/06/environmentalists-claim-just-solution-to-climate-change-is-wealth-redistribution/.
17. "'Fair Shares' and Intended Nationally Determined Contributions: What Can We Learn from an Equity Review?". Stockholm Environment Institute, https://www.sei-international.org/mediamanager/documents/Publications/Climate/SEI-DB-2014-INDCs-equity-analysis.pdf.9 Sep, 2015
18. Unruh, Bob. "Scientists Eviscerate Feds' 'Hottest Year' Claim." *WND*. 16 Jan 2015. http://www.wnd.com/2015/01/scientists-undermine-hottest-year-claim-by-feds/.5 May 2015.
19. Matthews Jr, Merrill. "Who's Afraid of Co2?" National Center for Policy

Analysis (NCPA), http://www.ncpa.org/pub/ba256.

Chapter 4: Who's Got Dibs on Your Kids' MORALITY?

1. CNN Wire Staff. "Montana City's Sex Ed Plans Draw Fire." *CNN.com*. 16 Jul 2010. http://www.cnn.com/2010/US/07/15/montana.sex.education/.
2. National Guidelines Task Force, *Guidelines for Comprehensive Sexuality Education: Kindergarten-12th Grade - 3rd Edition*, 2004, Sexuality Information and Education Council of the United States, http://www2.gsu.edu/~wwwche/Sex%20ed%20class/guidelines.pdf.
3. Ye Hee Lee, Michelle. "For Planned Parenthood Abortion Stats, '3 Percent' and '94 Percent' Are Both Misleading." *Washington Post*, 12 August 2015.
4. Tillotson, Mary C. "Obamacare to Fund Planned Parenthood Sex Ed." *Heartlander Magazine*. 9 Nov 2012. http://news.heartland.org/newspaper-article/2012/11/09/obamacare-fund-planned-parenthood-sex-ed.6 May 2015.
5. "If Children Can't Consent to Sex, Why Are We Teaching Them About It in Kindergarten??". SodaHead, http://www.sodahead.com/united-states/if-children-cant-consent-to-sex-why-are-we-teaching-them-about-it-in-kindergarten/question-3626039/.17 Dec,2015,
6. Unruh, Bob. "'Is It Ok If I Take Off My Pants?'." *WND* (14 Jan 2015). 14 Jan 2015. http://www.wnd.com/2015/01/is-it-ok-if-i-take-off-my-pants/.5 May 2015.
7. Hallowell, Billy. "Another Planned Parenthood Counselor Caught on Hidden Cam Giving Shocking Advice to 'Teen' About Porn, BDSM and Sex Shops." *The Blaze* (15 Jul 2014). http://www.theblaze.com/stories/2014/07/15/new-shocking-hidden-cam-footage-shows-planned-parenthood-counselors-advice-to-teen-about-porn-bdsm-and-sex-shops/.15 Jul 2014.
8. Klimas, Liz. "'Oh My Gosh': Mom Looking at High School's Sex Education Book Expressed Shock When Seeing Its 'Pornographic' Content." *The Blaze* (8 Aug 2014). 8 Aug 2014. http://www.theblaze.com/stories/2014/08/08/oh-my-gosh-mom-looking-at-high-schools-sex-education-book-expressed-shock-when-seeing-its-pornographic-content/.2014-08-08T08:09:55+00:00.
9. Collins, Chris, *et al.*, *Abstinence Only vs. Comprehensive Sex Education*, http://

www2.gsu.edu/~wwwche/Sex%20ed%20class/abstinence.pdf, 4 May 2015.

10. "Number of Abortions in US & Worldwide - Number of Abortions since 1973." http://www.numberofabortions.com/.
11. Michelle, Susan. "Proposed SIECUS Sex Education Curriculum for Grades K-12 under Fire | Live Action News." *Live Action News*. 30 Sep 2014. https://liveactionnews.org/proposed-siecus-sex-education-curriculum-for-grades-k-12-under-fire/.2 May 2015.
12. Coleman, Priscilla K. "Abortion and Mental Health: Quantitative Synthesis and Analysis of Research Published 1995–2009." [In en]. *British Journal of Psychiatry* 199, no. 3 (September 2011: 180-86.
13. "Adverse Psychological Reactions: A Fact Sheet." http://hopeafterabortion.com/?page_id=213.2 May 2015.
14. "Abortion's Physical Complications Factsheet Citations." National Right to Life Educational Trust Fund, http://www.nrlc.org/uploads/factsheets/FS06References.pdf.3 May 2015.
15. "State Policies in Brief: Parental Involvement in Minors' Abortions." Guttmacher Institute, http://www.guttmacher.org/statecenter/spibs/spib_PIMA.pdf. 4 May 2015.
16. "Laws Restricting Teenagers' Access to Abortion." American Civil Liberties Union (ACLU), https://www.aclu.org/laws-restricting-teenagers-access-abortion.4 May,2015.
17. Reagan, Ronald. "I've Noticed That Everyone Who Is for Abortion Is Already Born." studentsforlife.org, http://studentsforlife.org/here-we-go-again-high-school-censors-students-for-life/.5 May,2015.
18. Staff, LifeSiteNews. "Minnesota School Says It Has 'Every Right to Prohibit' 6th Graders' Pro-Life Speech." *LifeSiteNews* (2013). 29 Apr 2013. https://www.lifesitenews.com/news/minnesota-school-says-it-has-every-right-to-prohibit-6th-graders-pro-life-s.6 May 2015.
19. "A.Z. v. Nova Classical Academy - Alliance Defending Freedom." (2013). 10 Jul 2013. http://www.alliancedefendingfreedom.org/News/PRDetail/8310.6 May 2015.
20. Zagorski, Sarah. "Activists Destroy Pro-Life Sign at University of Oregon,

Tell Pro-Lifers "Get Off Our Campus." LifeNews.com.21 Aug,2015.

21. "World Association of Girl Guides and Girl Scouts (WAGGGS)." My Girl Scout Council, http://mygirlscoutcouncil.com/uploads/3/2/6/7/3267198/wagggs.pdf.7 May,2015.
22. *Abstinence Works 2013*, 2013, National Abstinence Education Foundation, http://www.thenaea.org/docs/Abstinence-Works.pdf, 9 May 2015.

CHAPTER 5: WHO'S GOT DIBS ON YOUR KIDS' GENDER?

1. Yourish, Karen, et al. "Recent Attacks Demonstrate Islamic State's Ability to Both Inspire and Coordinate Terror." The New York Times, 7 Dec 2015.
2. Scheiner, Eric. "Arne Duncan: Gov't-Funded Preschool a 'Social Movement' Like Civil Rights, Gay Marriage." *cnsnews.com*. 6 Nov 2014. http://www.cnsnews.com/news/article/eric-scheiner/arne-duncan-govt-funded-preschool-social-movement-civil-rights-gay.25 May 2015,
3. Starr, Penny. "Education Secretary Backs Public Boarding Schools: 'Certain Kids We Should Have 24/7'." *cnsnews.com*. 12 May 2015. http://www.cnsnews.com/news/article/penny-starr/education-secretary-backs-public-boarding-schools-certain-kids-we-should.25 May 2015,
4. Lott, Maxim. "Critics Assail Obama's 'Safe Schools' Czar, Say He's Wrong Man for the Job." *Fox News*. Published electronically 23 Sep 2009. http://www.foxnews.com/politics/2009/09/23/critics-assail-obamas-safe-schools-czar-say-hes-wrong-man-job/.27 May 2015,
5. "An Outline History of Religion in American Schools (No Bible/Prayer in Public Schools? Show Me)." http://www.freerepublic.com/focus/religion/2201818/posts.25 May,2015.
6. "Early Learning." U.S. Office of the President, https://www.whitehouse.gov/issues/education/early-childhood.24 May,2015.
7. "Arne Duncan Speaks at Federal LGBT Youth Summit." http://cnsnews.com/video/obama-administration-instructs-schools-forming-gay-student-clubs.25 May,2015,
8. "Secular Humanists Give Dunphy Another Platform." Eagle Forum, http://www.eagleforum.org/educate/1995/nov95/dunphy.html.25 May,2015.

9. Unruh, Bob. "Judge Rules on Student Punished for Criticizing Lesbians." *WND*. 20 Oct 2014. http://mobile.wnd.com/2014/10/judge-rules-on-student-punished-for-criticizing-lesbians/.25 May 2015.
10. Graff, Amy. "Jazz Jenning's New Children's Book Tells Transgender Story." *SFGATE* (22 Sep 2014). 22 Sep 2014.
11. Lukoff, Kyle. "Evaluating Transgender Picture Books; Calling for Better Ones." *School Library Journal* no. 12 May. http://www.slj.com/2015/05/diversity/evaluating-transgender-picture-books-requesting-better-ones/.12 May 2015.
12. Starnes, Todd. "Students Who Refuse to Affirm Transgender Classmates Face Punishment." Fox News Radio, http://radio.foxnews.com/toddstarnes/top-stories/students-who-refuse-to-affirm-transgender-classmates-face-punishment.html2015,
13. Leopold, Todd. "Boy Scouts Change Policy on Gay Leaders." CNN, http://www.cnn.com/2015/07/27/us/boy-scouts-gay-leaders-feat/.22 Aug,2015.
14. Boesveld, Sarah. "The End of Gender? North American Society May Be Ready for More Shades in between Male and Female." *National Post*. 30 May 2014. http://news.nationalpost.com/news/canada/the-end-of-gender-north-american-socicty-may-be-ready-for-more-shades-in-between-male-and-female.20 May 2015.
15. "Homosexuality in Schools - Conservapedia." 6 Jul 2013. http://www.conservapedia.com/Homosexuality_in_Schools.21 May 2015.
16. Macedo, Diane. "Gay Reversal Advocates Say School Libraries Banning Their 'Ex-Gay' Books." T, *FoxNews.com*. 22 Oct 2009. doi:8d51bc95-2f00-4519-86c8-6120fb5cee11, http://www.foxnews.com/story/2009/10/22/gay-reversal-advocates-say-school-libraries-banning-their-ex-gay-books.html.19 May 2015.
17. "Library Bill of Rights." American Library Association, http://www.ala.org/advocacy/intfreedom/librarybill.25 May, 2015.
18. Chapman, Michael W. "Johns Hopkins Psychiatrist: Transgender Is 'Mental Disorder;' Sex Change 'Biologically Impossible'." *cnsnews.com*. 20 Aug 2014. http://cnsnews.com/news/article/michael-w-chapman/johns-hopkins-psychiatrist-transgender-mental-disorder-sex-change.19 May 2015.

19. Dhejne, Cecilia, *et al*. "Long-Term Follow-up of Transsexual Persons Undergoing Sex Reassignment Surgery: Cohort Study in Sweden." Research Article, *PLOS ONE*. 22 Feb 2011. doi:10.1371/journal.pone.0016885, http://journals.plos.org/plosone/article?id=10.1371/journal.pone.0016885.19 May 2015.
20. Servick, Kelly. "Study of Gay Brothers May Confirm X Chromosome Link to Homosexuality." *American Association for the Advancement of Science*. 17 Nov 2014. http://news.sciencemag.org/biology/2014/11/study-gay-brothers-may-confirm-x-chromosome-link-homosexuality.20 May 2015.
21. "Marxism and Religion." Ask, http://www.ask.com/wiki/Marxism_and_religion.25 May,2015.
22. "Socialism,Atheism or Religion? | the Socialist Party of Great Britain." http://www.worldsocialism.org/spgb/socialist-standard/1960s/1969/no-773-january-1969/socialism-atheism-or-religion.25 May,2015.
23. "Homeschooling: The Alternative for Caring Christian Families-Chapter 114." American Life League - Eternal Word Television Network (EWTN), https://www.ewtn.com/library/prolenc/encyc114.htm.26 May,2015.
24. *New Programme and New Constitution of the Revolutionary Communist Party, USA: The Proletariat, Upon Seizing Power, Will Immediately Take up the Transformation of Society*, Revolutionary Communist Party, https://www.marxists.org/history/erol/ncm-5/rcp-new-pro/section13.htm, 22 Aug 2015.

Chapter 6: Who's Got Dibs on Your Kids' MEDIA?

1. Rideout, Victoria J., *et al*., *Generation M2: Media in the Lives of 8- to 18-Year-Olds*, Jan 2010, https://kaiserfamilyfoundation.files.wordpress.com/2013/04/8010.pdf, 30 May 2015.
2. Rideout, Victoria, *Learning at Home: Families' Educational Media Use in America*, Jan 2014, http://www.joanganzcooneycenter.org/wp-content/uploads/2014/01/jgcc_learningathome.pdf, 30 May 2015.
3. Lenhart, Amanda, *Teens, Social Media & Technology Overview 2015: Mobile Access Shifts Social Media Use and Other Online Activities*, 09 Apr 2015,

Pew Research Center, http://www.pewinternet.org/2015/04/09/mobile-access-shifts-social-media-use-and-other-online-activities/, 30 May 2015.

4. "Daily Media Use among Children and Teens up Dramatically from Five Years Ago." The Henry J. Kaiser Family Foundation, http://kff.org/disparities-policy/press-release/daily-media-use-among-children-and-teens-up-dramatically-from-five-years-ago/.17 Dec,2015,
5. O'Keeffe, Gwenn Schurgin, *et al.*, *Clinical Report - the Impact of Social Media on Children, Adolescents, and Families*, 4 Apr 2011, American Academy of Pediatrics, http://pediatrics.aappublications.org/content/early/2011/03/28/peds.2011-0054.full.pdf, 01 Jun 2015.
6. "Cell Phone Use: General Statistics." The Children's Hospital of Philadelphia | Research Institute, http://www.teendriversource.org/stats/support_teens/detail/64.1 Jun,2015.
7. "Distracted Driving." U. S. Centers for Disease Control and Prevention, http://www.cdc.gov/Motorvehiclesafety/Distracted_Driving/index.html.1 Jun,2015.
8. Strasburger, Victor C. "Media and Children: What Needs to Happen Now?". *Journal of the American Medical Association* 301. 03 Jun 2009: 2265-66.
9. *Media Use by Children Younger Than 2 Years*, 17 Oct 2011, American Academy of Pediatrics, http://pediatrics.aappublications.org/content/128/5/1040.full.pdf+html?sid=71cb491b-910a-469f-9f8a-9d5e4d65c1d3, 2 Jun 2015.
10. "Kids Wireless Use Facts." Growing Wireless, http://www.growingwireless.com/get-the-facts/quick-facts#privacy.3 Jun,2015.
11. Hohmann, Leo. "Media Blitz to 'Normalize' Transgenderism." *WND*. 24 Apr 2015. http://www.wnd.com/2015/04/media-blitz-to-normalize-transgenderism/.4 Jun 2015.
12. Gilmore, Natasha. "Transgender Titles for Young Readers: Titles Aimed at Young Readers Address the Transgender Experience." *Publishers Weekly*. Published electronically 22 May 2015. http://www.publishersweekly.com/pw/by-topic/childrens/childrens-book-news/article/66750-lgbtq-publishing-books-for-every-body.html.12 Jun 2015.

Chapter 7: Who's Got Dibs on Your Kids' RELIGIOUS BELIEFS?

1. "An Outline History of Religion in American Schools (No Bible/Prayer in Public Schools? Show Me)." http://www.freerepublic.com/focus/religion/2201818/posts.25 May, 2015.
2. "The House of Representatives Rules We Are a Christian Nation." Reclaiming America For Christ, http://www.reclaimamericaforchrist.org/thehouseofrepresentativesrulesweareachristiannation.htm.12 Jun,2015.
3. "Time Line of Christian Religion in American Schools." Voter Voice, https://votervoice.net/AFAKY/newsletters/13423.12 Jun, 2015.
4. Griffing, John. "Students Made to Wear Burqas – in Texas." WND, http://www.wnd.com/2013/02/students-made-to-wear-burqas-in-u-s-state/.8 Jun, 2015.
5. Ssenyonjo, Manisuli. "The Islamic Veil and Freedom of Religion, the Rights to Education and Work: A Survey of Recent International and National Cases." [In en]. *Chinese Journal of International Law* 6, no. 3 (01 Nov 2007 2007): 653-710.
6. Starnes, Todd. "Students Told to Call 9-11 Hijackers 'Freedom Fighters'." http://radio.foxnews.com/toddstarnes/top-stories/students-told-to-call-9-11-hijackers-freedom-fighters.html.8 Jun, 2015.
7. Hohmann, Leo. "School Snubs Christianity in 'Be Muslim' Assignment." WND, http://www.wnd.com/2015/04/pretend-to-be-muslim-assignment-had-no-christian-equivalent/.8 Jun, 2015.
8. "Marine Dad Banned from School Property; Daughter Gets Failing Grade for Refusing Islamic Indoctrination – the Thomas More Law Center Steps In." Thomas More Law Center, https://www.thomasmore.org/news/marine-dad-banned-school-property-daughter-gets-failing-grade-refusing-islamic-indoctrination-thomas-law-center-steps/.22 Jun, 2015.
9. Cox, Carrie. "Common Core Funds the Muslim Brotherhood." American New Media, http://anmnews.com/common-core-funds-the-muslim-brotherhood/.12 Jun, 2015.
10. *Education or Indoctrination? The Treatment of Islam in 6th through 12th Grade American Textbooks - Executive Summary*, 2011, Inc. ACT! for America Education, http://www.actforamerica.org/downloads/Executive_Summary.pdf, 22 June 2015.

11. Blankley, Bethany. "Common Core Ties to Libya, Qatar, Saudi Arabia." Washington Times, http://www.washingtontimes.com/news/2015/apr/7/bethany-blankley-parents-must-reject-common-core-i/?page=all.
12. Jackson, Victoria. "Why Are U.S. Textbooks Suddenly Pushing Islam? - Victoria Jackson." http://victoriajackson.com/9997/u-s-textbooks-suddenly-pushing-islam.22 Jun, 2015.
13. Starnes, Todd. "Does This HS History Textbook Have a Pro-Islam Bias?" Fox News, http://insider.foxnews.com/2013/07/29/prentice-history-textbook-criticized-pro-islam-bias.12 Jun, 2015.
14. "Islam Studies Required in California District." WND, http://www.wnd.com/2002/01/12325/.12 Jun, 2015.
15. "Yoga Goes to Court!". The National Center for Law & Policy, http://www.nclplaw.org/wp-content/uploads/2011/12/Sedlock-Yoga-Oral-Argument-Press-Release-2-13-15-FINAL.pdf.29 Jun, 2015.
16. Unruh, Bob. "Christians Ordered to Teach Wiccan, Pagan Rites." WND, http://www.wnd.com/2014/03/christians-ordered-to-teach-wiccan-pagan-rites/.15 Jun, 2015.
17. Kidd, Thomas S. "Watch Your Religious Language, Mr. President - Usatoday.Com." USA Today, http://usatoday30.usatoday.com/news/opinion/forum/2010-12-09-kidd10_ST_N.htm.25 Jun, 2015.

Chapter 8: Who's Got Dibs on Your Kids' FUTURE?

1. Burke, Lindsey. "States Must Reject National Education Standards While There Is Still Time." The Heritage Foundation, http://www.heritage.org/research/reports/2012/04/states-must-reject-national-education-standards-while-there-is-still-time.24 Jul, 2015.
2. Gallagher, Maggie. "Two Moms Vs. Common Core." National Review, http://www.nationalreview.com/article/347973/two-moms-vs-common-core-maggie-gallagher.24 Jul, 2015.
3. Kittle, M.D. "How Much Will Common Core Cost You?" Watchdog, http://watchdog.org/104325/how-much-will-common-core-cost-you/.25 Jul, 2015.
4. "Common Core: 3 * 4 = 11 Is Okay - Longer ". https://www.youtube.com/

watch?v=DW0VxxoCrNo

5. Brean, Joseph. "Math Wars: Rote Memorization Plays Crucial Role in Teaching Students How to Solve Complex Calculations, Study Says " National Post, http://www.nationalpost.com/m/wp/blog.html?b=news.nationalpost.com/2014/08/21/math-wars-rote-memorization-plays-crucial-role-in-teaching-students-how-to-solve-complex-calculations-study-says.25 Jul, 2015.
6. Milgram, R. James, and Sandra Stotsky. "Can This Country Survive Common Core's College Readiness Level?" ftp://math.stanford.edu/pub/papers/milgram/ZimbaMilgramStotskyFinal.pdf.13 Jul, 2015.
7. Stotsky, Sandra. "Common Core's Invalid Validation Committee." http://www.uaedreform.org/downloads/2013/11/common-cores-invalid-validation-committee.pdf.14 Jul, 2015.
8. Stotsky, Sandra. "Common Core Standards' Devastating Impact on Literary Study and Analytical Thinking." The Heritage Foundation, http://www.heritage.org/research/reports/2012/12/questionable-quality-of-the-common-core-english-language-arts-standards.25 Jul, 2015.
9. Konnikova, Maria. "What's Lost as Handwriting Fades." The New York Times, http://www.nytimes.com/2014/06/03/science/whats-lost-as-handwriting-fades.html?_r=0.27 Jul, 2015.
10. "Statewide Longitudinal Data Systems Grant Program." National Center for Education Statistics. Online: Institute of Education Sciences.
11. Robbins, Jane. "Common Core & Data Collection." Truth in American Education, http://truthinamericaneducation.com/privacy-issues-state-longitudinal-data-systems/common-core-data-collection/.29 Jul, 2015.
12. "InBloom and the Need to Protect Student Privacy." Class Size Matters, http://www.classsizematters.org/inbloom_student_data_privacy/.1 Aug, 2015.
13. "Does the Common Core Include a National Database?". HSLDA, https://www.hslda.org/commoncore/topic10.aspx.30 Jul, 2015.
14. Tillotson, Mary C. "Parents' Concerns About Unsecured Student Data Grow." Heartland, http://news.heartland.org/newspaper-article/2014/08/04/parents-concerns-about-unsecured-student-data-grow.29 Jul, 2015.
15. Shechtman, Nicole, *et al.*, *Promoting Grit, Tenacity, and Perseverance: Critical*

Factors for Success in the 21st Century, 14 Feb 2013, U.S. Department of Education, http://tech.ed.gov/files/2013/10/OET-Draft-Grit-Report-2-17-13.pdf, 30 Jul 2015.

16. Berry, Dr. Susan. "Student Data Tied to Common Core Off-Limits to Parents." Breitbart, http://www.breitbart.com/big-government/2014/07/12/student-data-tied-to-common-core-off-limits-to-parents/.7 Aug, 2015.
17. Simon, Stephanie. "Data Mining Your Children." Politico, http://www.politico.com/story/2014/05/data-mining-your-children-106676.html.7 Aug, 2015.
18. Haimson, Leonie. "Blumenthal/Daines Student Privacy Bill; Good Start but Needs Improvement." Student Privacy Matters, http://www.studentprivacy-matters.org/.30 Jul, 2015.
19. Daines, Steve, and Richard Blumenthal. ""Safeguarding American Families from Exposure by Keeping Information and Data Secure Act" ("Safe Kids Act") 7 Sec.", United States Senate. Online, 2015.
20. Hohmann, Leo. "Education? No, It's About Data-Mining:'Opt out' Movement Surges in Response to Common Core." WND, http://www.wnd.com/2014/05/education-no-its-about-data-mining/.30 Jul, 2015.
21. *An Overview of NEDM: The National Education Data Model*. National Center for Education Statistics, 17 Jul 2010.
22. "National Education Data Model: National Center for Education Statistics." Online: Institute of Education Sciences.
23. Tienken, Christopher H. "Common Core State Standards: An Example of Data-Less Decision Making." *AASA Journal of Scholarship & Practice* 7, no. 4 (Winter 2011: 12.
24. Weingarten, Benjamin. "A Scathing Interview with a 5th Grade Teacher Who Was in the Room When Common Core Was Being Created." The Blaze, http://www.theblaze.com/blog/2014/05/22/a-scathing-interview-with-a-5th-grade-teacher-who-was-in-the-room-when-common-core-was-being-created/.16 Jul, 2015.
25. *San Antonio Independent School Dis. V. Rodriguez*, (1973).
26. Layton, Lyndsey. "How Bill Gates Pulled Off the Swift Common Core Revolution." The Washington Post, http://www.washingtonpost.com/politics/

how-bill-gates-pulled-off-the-swift-common-core-revolution/2014/06/07/a830e32e-ec34-11e3-9f5c-9075d5508f0a_story.html.17 Jul, 2015.

27. Ibid.
28. "Common Core State Standards Initiative: Myths Vs. Facts." http://www.corestandards.org/about-the-standards/myths-vs-facts/.21 Jul, 2015.
29. Gabbay, Tiffany. "CSCOPE: Exposing the Nation's Most Controversial Public School Curriculum System." The Blaze, http://www.theblaze.com/stories/2013/03/07/cscope-exposing-the-nations-most-controversial-public-school-curriculum-system/.3 Aug, 2015.
30. Griffing, John. "Parents Told to Pay to See School Curriculum." WND, http://www.wnd.com/2013/05/parents-told-to-pay-to-see-school-curriculum/.21 Jul, 2015.

Chapter 9: Who's Got Dibs on Your Kids' MINDS?

1. Gutzman, Kevin. "US History Rewritten or Ignored." The Report Card, http://education-curriculum-reform-government-schools.org/w/2015/06/us-history-rewritten-or-ignored/.24 Aug, 2015.
2. Thornton, Bruce. "Is Leftist School Indoctrination Unstoppable?" Frontpage, http://www.frontpagemag.com/fpm/179180/leftist-school-indoctrination-unstoppable-bruce-thornton.11 Sep, 2015.
3. Aman, John. "U.S. History Takes Drastic Left Turn This Fall." WND, http://www.wnd.com/2014/08/u-s-history-takes-drastic-left-turn-this-fall/.31 Aug, 2015.
4. Carey, Brycchan. "Slavery, Abolition, and Emancipation." http://www.brycchancarey.com/slavery/index.htm.03 Sep, 2015.
5. Cardinale, Alexandra. "Bluest Eye Banned: Why Parents Want Toni Morrison's Book out of Schools." Arts.Mic, http://mic.com/articles/60609/bluest-eye-banned-why-parents-want-toni-morrison-s-book-out-of-schools.03 Sep, 2015.
6. Clark, Danette. "American Library Association to Children: 'Your Parents Have No Say in What You Read, Listen to, or Watch… and We Won't Tell Them'." Danette Clark, https://danetteclark.wordpress.com/2013/07/25/american-library-association-to-children-your-parents-have-no-say-in-what-you-

read-listen-to-or-watch-and-we-wont-tell-them/.04 Sep, 2015.

7. Buchanan, Wyatt. "New State Law Requires LGBT History in Textbooks." SFGate, http://www.sfgate.com/news/article/New-state-law-requires-LGBT-history-in-textbooks-2354578.php.03 Sep, 2015.
8. Lakhani, Dave. *Subliminal Persuasion: Influence & Marketing Secrets They Don't Want You to Know*. Hoboken: John Wiley & Sons, 2008.
9. Brodie, Richard. *Virus of the Mind: The New Science of the Meme*. New York: Hay House, 1996.
10. Kupelian, David. *The Marketing of Evil: How Radicals, Elitists, and Pseudo-Experts Sell Us Corruption Disguised as Freedom*. Nashville: Cumberland House, 2005.

Chapter 10: Who's Got Dibs on Your PARENTAL RIGHTS?

1. "Ninth Circuit Decision Denies Parents' Rights." *Education Reporter*, December 2006.
2. Rep. Murphy, Tim [R-PA-18]. "H.Res.547 - Expressing the Sense of the House of Representatives That the United States Court of Appeals for the Ninth Circuit Deplorably Infringed on Parental Rights in Fields V. Palmdale School District". Congressional Record: United States Congress, 2005.
3. *Pierce V. Society of Sisters, 268 U.S. 510 (1925)*, (1925).
4. *Wisconsin V. Yoder, 406 U.S. 205 (1972)*, 406 (1972).
5. *Meyer V. Nebraska, 262 U.S. 390 (1923)*, 262 (1923).
6. *Pierce V. Society of Sisters, 268 U.S. 510 (1925)*, (1925).
7. Klicka Esq., Christopher J. "Decisions of the United States Supreme Court Upholding Parental Rights as "Fundamental"." Home School Legal Defense Association, http://www.hslda.org/docs/nche/000000/00000075.asp#.24 Sep, 2015.
8. "U.S. Supreme Court: Parents' Rights Are Fundamental." Home School Legal Defense Association, http://www.hslda.org/docs/nche/000010/20011210.asp.24 Sep, 2015.
9. Crusco, Kysa. "New Hampshire Court's Decision Regarding Home Schooling Grabs National Attention " New Hampshire Family Law, http://

www.nhfamilylawblog.com/2009/09/articles/parenting-rights-responsibilit/new-hampshire-courts-decision-regarding-home-schooling-grabs-national-attention/2015.

10. "Court Orders Christian Child into Government Education." WND, http://www.wnd.com/2009/08/108084. 24 Sep, 2015.
11. Ibid.
12. Smith, J. Michael. "Romeike Family Can Stay in U.S." Home School Legal Defense Association, 2 March 2015, http://www.hslda.org/legal/cases/romeike.asp.24 Sep,2015,
13. Strauss, Valerie, and Monty Neill. "Will Schools Lose Federal Funds If Kids Don't Take Mandated Tests? Fact Vs. Threat." *The Washington Post*, 2 April 2015.
14. "Test Results for English Language Arts/Literacy and Mathematics." California Assessment of Student Performance and Progress (CAASPP), http://caaspp.cde.ca.gov/sb2015/iewReport?ps=true&lstTestYear=2015&lstTestType=B&lstCounty=&lstDistrict=&lstSchool. 24 Sep, 2015.
15. Yarbrough, Beau. "Less Than Half of California Students Pass New Common Core-Aligned Statewide Tests." *Los Angeles Daily News*, 09 Sep 2015.
16. Lorin, Janet. "Wesleyan, Temple among Colleges Scrapping Admission Tests "Bloomberg, http://www.bloomberg.com/news/articles/2014-10-03/wesleyan-temple-among-colleges-scrapping-admission-tests. 25 Sep, 2015.
17. Wall, Patrick. "As Opt-out Numbers Grow, Arne Duncan Says Feds May Have to Step In." http://ny.chalkbeat.org/2015/04/21/as-opt-out-numbers-grow-arne-duncan-says-feds-may-have-to-step-in/#.VgV0Ym-raUm. 25 Sep, 2015.
18. Harris, Elizabeth A. "New York Will Trim Common Core Exams after Many Students Skipped Them." *The New York Times*, 16 Sep 2015 2015.
19. "State Policies on Sex Education in Schools ". National Conference of State Legislatures, http://www.ncsl.org/research/health/state-policies-on-sex-education-in-schools.aspx. 25 Sep, 2015.
20. *From Crayons to Condoms: The Ugly Truth About America's Public Schools.* edited by Steve Baldwin and Karen Holgate Los Angeles: WND Books, 2008.

21. McGuinness, William. "'The Most Fabulous Story Ever Told' at Pioneer Valley Performing Arts School Draws Complaints." Huffingtonpost, http://www.huffingtonpost.com/2013/03/07/the-most-fabulous-story-ever-told-protest_n_2829599.html. 25 Sep, 2015.
22. McCollum, Sean. *Dealing with Sensitive Themes Onstage: Navigating the Risks and Rewards of Controversial Themes in School Theaters*. Online: The Kennedy Center.
23. Wen, Patricia, and Neil Swidey. "A Difficult Return to Hospital for Justina Pelletier." *Boston Globe*, 07 Dec 2014 2014.
24. *Parham V. J.R., 442 U.S. 584 (1979)*, (1979).
25. Howerton, Jason. "'I. Am. The. Mom.': It Didn't Go over Well When a Hospital Allegedly Told a Mother They'd Need to Have a 'Private' Conversation with Her Teenage Daughter." The Blaze, http://www.theblaze.com/stories/2014/06/03/i-am-the-mom-it-didnt-go-over-well-when-a-hospital-allegedly-told-a-mother-theyd-need-to-have-a-private-conversation-with-her-teenage-daughter/. 25 Sep, 2015.
26. Korach, W. "Cal Judge Rules against Union for New Charter School." The Report Carc, http://cducation-curriculum-reform-government-schools.org/w/2015/07/cal-judge-rules-against-union-for-new-charter-school/. 25 Sep, 2015.
27. Boucher, Dave. "Lawmakers Fear Islamic 'Indoctrination' in Tn Classes." The Tennessean, http://www.tennessean.com/story/news/politics/2015/09/10/blackburn-alludes—islamic-indoctrination—tn-classes/72015122/. 25 Sep, 2015.
28. "The Five Pillars of Curriculum." Snopes, http://m.snopes.com/islam-tennessee-school/#Jr7weZII4gMvI9mQ.99.25 Sep, 2015.
29. Ibid.
30. *Case 1:12-Cv-00327-Abj*, 73.
31. Vitter, David. "Vitter Introduces Student Privacy Protection Act." U. S. Senator David Vitter, http://www.vitter.senate.gov/newsroom/press/vitter-introduces-student-privacy-protection-act.25 Sep, 2015.
32. "Student Privacy Bill of Rights." epic.org, https://epic.org/privacy/student/bill-of-rights.html.25 Sep, 2015.

Acknowledgments

All our paths in life are affected by those with whom we surround ourselves. Those in my American Christian Writers Group not only provided excellent critiquing as I worked on this book, but kept me walking forward on the path to write and publish it. Thank you all for your perceptive insights and reassurance when doubts assailed me.

I also thank my husband Rich who took over the laundry when I buried my head in the computer, not hearing the ding of the dryer when it needed to be unloaded. He never questioned my desire to write, nor asked me to leave it. His patience and support have been a great blessing throughout this project. Without him I would be . . . this sentence can't be finished. I can't imagine life without him.

In Memoriam

This book is dedicated to my son, Geoffrey, who lost his battle with cancer in October 2015. His constant love, support, and encouragement for my writing efforts will remain in my heart, even as he is now in his home in heaven.

Betty Pfeiffer writes for both adults and children. She has three feature articles in *Odyssey Magazine*, four English as a Foreign Language (EFL) books, a feature article in *Forward in Christ*, and an article about the challenges facing the Navajo people that appeared in the Navajo Nation annual magazine.

Following a trip to Thailand to help with a vacation Bible school for Hmong children, Betty wrote *Driven*. It is a tale of escape from Laos following the Vietnamese War—an escape from extermination of the Hmong by the Pathet Lao, the new communist government—only to find death a constant companion as they wandered for months in the jungle. Their day-to-day survival continued in refugee camps when they finally reached Thailand.

After coming to the United States, and learning to live as Americans, they returned to that land of their nightmares to spread the good news of salvation through Jesus Christ . . . to that same land where discovery and apprehension by the Pathet Lao could still mean a slave camp, or possible death.

Driven is a stunning story of survival as told to Betty by those who lived it. Purchase your copy of *Driven* at www.amazon.com or contact Betty at betty@bettypfeiffer.com. All profit from the sale of *Driven* is directed to bringing the knowledge of salvation through Jesus Christ to the Hmong in Thailand.

Betty Pfeiffer is available to speak on her books *Driven* and *Who's Got Dibs on Your Kids*? She has twice been the keynote speaker at conferences, but she also gives presentations to small groups.

CPSIA information can be obtained
at www.ICGtesting.com
Printed in the USA
FSOW04n0428250316
18423FS

9 781498 462549